Medical Tourism

Medical and health tourism is a significant area of growth in the export of medical, health and tourism services. Although spas and improved well-being have long been part of the tourist experience, health tourism now includes travel for medical purposes ranging from cosmetic and dental surgery through to transplants and infertility treatment. Many countries including China, Cuba, Hungary, India, Thailand, Malaysia and Singapore actively promote and compete for the medical tourist dollar, while many developed countries also provide niche private services. However, the field of medical tourism is increasingly being subject to scrutiny and debate, particularly as a result of concerns over regulatory, ethical and wider health issues.

Drawing on a range of theoretical and methodological perspectives, this book is one of the first to critically address the substantial political, philosophical and ethical issues that arise out of the transnational practices of medical tourism. Through a series of chapters, this book engages with key issues such as the role of regulatory and policy structures in influencing medical and health tourism-related mobilities. These issues are investigated by considering a range of developing and developed countries, medical systems and health economic perspectives.

This book adopts a multi-layered perspective to not only investigate the business and marketing practices of medical and health tourism but places these within a broader framework of contemporary globalisation, policy and practice. By doing so, it opens up debate of the ethical space in which medical and health tourism operates as well as reinforces the wide-ranging perspectives that exist on the subject in both the public and academic imagination. This significant contribution will be of interest to students, academics in tourism and medical policy, trade and economic development fields.

C. Michael Hall is a Professor in the Department of Management, University of Canterbury, New Zealand; Docent in the Department of Geography, University of Oulu and a Visiting Professor at Sheffield Hallam University, UK, and Linneaus University, Sweden.

Contemporary geographies of leisure, tourism and mobility

Series Editor: C. Michael Hall

Professor at the Department of Management, College of Business and Economics, University of Canterbury, Christchurch, New Zealand

The aim of this series is to explore and communicate the intersections and relationships between leisure, tourism and human mobility within the social sciences. It will incorporate both traditional and new perspectives on leisure and tourism from contemporary geography, e.g. notions of identity, representation and culture, while also providing for perspectives from cognate areas such as anthropology, cultural studies, gastronomy and food studies, marketing, policy studies and political economy, regional and urban planning and sociology, within the development of an integrated field of leisure and tourism studies.

Also, increasingly, tourism and leisure are regarded as steps in a continuum of human mobility. Inclusion of mobility in the series offers the prospect to examine the relationship between tourism and migration, the sojourner, educational travel and second home and retirement travel phenomena.

The series comprises two strands:

Contemporary geographies of leisure, tourism and mobility aims to address the needs of students and academics, and the titles will be published in hardback and paperback. Titles include the following:

1. **The Moralisation of Tourism**
   Sun, sand . . . and saving the world?
   Jim Butcher

2. **The Ethics of Tourism Development**
   Mick Smith and Rosaleen Duffy

3. **Tourism in the Caribbean**
   Trends, development, prospects
   Edited by David Timothy Duval

4. **Qualitative Research in Tourism**
   Ontologies, epistemologies and methodologies
   Edited by Jenny Phillimore and Lisa Goodson

5. **The Media and the Tourist Imagination**
   Converging cultures
   Edited by David Crouch, Rhona Jackson and Felix Thompson

6. **Tourism and Global Environmental Change**
   Ecological, social, economic and political interrelationships
   Edited by Stefan Gössling and C. Michael Hall

7. **Cultural Heritage of Tourism in the Developing World**
   Edited by Dallen J. Timothy and Gyan Nyaupane

8. **Understanding and Managing Tourism Impacts**
   An integrated approach
   C. Michael Hall and Alan Lew

9. **An Introduction to Visual Research Methods in Tourism**
   Edited by Tijana Rakic and Donna Chambers

10. **Tourism and Climate Change**
    Impacts, adaptation and mitigation
    C. Michael Hall, Stefan Gössling and Daniel Scott

Routledge studies in contemporary geographies of leisure, tourism and mobility is a forum for innovative new research intended for research students and academics, and the titles will be available in hardback only. Titles include the following:

1. **Living with Tourism**
   Negotiating identities in a Turkish village
   Hazel Tucker

2. **Tourism, Diasporas and Space**
   Edited by Tim Coles and Dallen J. Timothy

3. **Tourism and Postcolonialism**
   Contested discourses, identities and representations
   Edited by C. Michael Hall and Hazel Tucker

4. **Tourism, Religion and Spiritual Journeys**
   Edited by Dallen J. Timothy and Daniel H. Olsen

5. **China's Outbound Tourism**
   Wolfgang Georg Arlt

6. **Tourism, Power and Space**
   Edited by Andrew Church and Tim Coles

7. **Tourism, Ethnic Diversity and the City**
   Edited by Jan Rath

8. **Ecotourism, NGOs and Development**
   A critical analysis
   Jim Butcher

9. **Tourism and the Consumption of Wildlife**
   Hunting, shooting and sport fishing
   Edited by Brent Lovelock

10. **Tourism, Creativity and Development**
    Edited by Greg Richards and Julie Wilson

11. **Tourism at the Grassroots**
Villagers and visitors in the Asia-Pacific
Edited by John Connell and Barbara Rugendyke

12. **Tourism and Innovation**
C. Michael Hall and Allan Williams

13. **World Tourism Cities**
Developing tourism off the beaten track
Edited by Robert Maitland and Peter Newman

14. **Tourism and National Parks**
International perspectives on development, histories and change
Edited by Warwick Frost and C. Michael Hall

15. **Tourism, Performance and the Everyday**
Consuming the Orient
Michael Haldrup and Jonas Larsen

16. **Tourism and Change in Polar Regions**
Climate, environments and experiences
Edited by C. Michael Hall and Jarkko Saarinen

17. **Fieldwork in Tourism**
Methods, issues and reflections
Edited by C. Michael Hall

18. **Tourism and India**
A critical introduction
Kevin Hannam and Anya Diekmann

19. **Political Economy of Tourism**
A critical perspective
Edited by Jan Mosedale

20. **Volunteer Tourism**
Theoretical frameworks and practical applications
Edited by Angela Benson

21. **The Study of Tourism**
Past trends and future directions
Richard Sharpley

22. **Children's and Families' Holiday Experience**
Neil Carr

23. **Tourism and National Identity**
An international perspective
Edited by Elspeth Frew and Leanne White

24. **Tourism and Agriculture**
New geographies of consumption, production and rural restructuring
Edited by Rebecca Torres and Janet Momsen

25. **Tourism in China**
Policy and development since 1949
David Airey and King Chong

26. **Real Tourism**
Practice, care, and politics in contemporary travel culture
Edited by Claudio Minca and Tim Oakes

27. **Last Chance Tourism**
Adapting tourism opportunities in a changing world
Edited by Raynald Harvey Lemelin, Jackie Dawson and Emma Stewart

28. **Tourism and Animal Ethics**
David A. Fennell

29. Actor Network Theory and Tourism
Ontologies, methodologies and performances
Edited by René van der Duim, Gunnar Thór Jóhannesson and Carina Ren

30. Liminal Landscapes
Travel, experience and spaces in-between
Edited by Hazel Andrews and Les Roberts

31. Tourism in Brazil
Environment, management and segments
Edited by Gui Lohmann and Dianne Dredge

32. Slum Tourism
Edited by Fabian Frenzel, Malte Steinbrink and Ko Koens

33. Medical Tourism
Edited by Michael Hall

34. Tourism and War
Edited by Richard Butler and Wantanee Suntikul

Forthcoming:

Sexuality, Women and Tourism
Susan Frohlick

Gender and Tourism
Social, cultural and spatial perspectives
Cara Atchinson

Backpacker Tourism and Economic Development in the Less Developed World
Mark Hampton

Adventure Tourism
Steve Taylor, Peter Varley and Tony Johnson

Dark Tourism and Place Identity
Elspeth Frew and Leanne White

Scuba Diving Tourism
Kay Dimmcock and Ghazali Musa

Travel, Tourism and Green Growth
Min Jiang, Terry DeLacy and Geoffrey Lipman

Medical Tourism

The ethics, regulation, and marketing of health mobility

Edited by
C. Michael Hall

Routledge
Taylor & Francis Group
LONDON AND NEW YORK

First published 2013
by Routledge
2 Park Square, Milton Park, Abingdon, Oxon OX14 4RN

Simultaneously published in the USA and Canada
by Routledge
711 Third Avenue, New York, NY 10017

Routledge is an imprint of the Taylor & Francis Group, an informa business

British Library Cataloguing in Publication Data
A catalogue record for this book is available from the British Library

Library of Congress Cataloging in Publication Data
Medical tourism: the ethics, regulation, and marketing of health mobility / edited by Michael Hall.—1st ed.
p. cm.
Includes bibliographical references and index.
1. Medical tourism. 2. Medical care—Quality control. I. Hall, Colin Michael, 1961–
RA793.5.M43 2012
362.1—dc23
2012003039

ISBN: 978-0-415-66575-9 (hbk)
ISBN: 978-0-203-10945-8 (ebk)

Typeset in Times New Roman
by Book Now Ltd, London

Contents

Illustrations

Figures

Tables

Boxes

Contributors

Tanja C. Boga, Institute of Strategic Management, Marketing and Tourism, Innsbruck University School of Management, Innsbruck, Austria.

Changsan Boo, Jeju Sea Grant, Jeju National University, 1, Ara 1-dong, 102 Jejudaehakno, Jeju-si, Jeju Special Self-Governing Province 690-756 Republic of Korea.

Nik Brown, Department of Sociology, University of York, Heslington, York, UK.

Peta S. Cook, Faculty of Arts, School of Sociology and Social Work, University of Tasmania, Launceston, Tasmania, Australia.

Hilary du Cros, Hong Kong Institute of Education, 10 Lo Ping Road, Tai Po, Hong Kong, China S.A.R.

Lydia L. Gan, Department of Economics, Finance, and Decision Sciences, University of North Carolina at Pembroke, Box 1510, Pembroke, NC 28372, USA.

Stephen T. Green, Sheffield Teaching Hospitals Foundation NHS Trust, Sheffield, UK.

C. Michael Hall, Department of Management, University of Canterbury, Christchurch, New Zealand; Department of Geography, University of Oulu, Oulu, Finland; Centre for Tourism Studies, University of Eastern Finland, Savonlinna, Finland; Freiburg Institute of Advanced Studies, University of Freiburg, Freiburg, Germany.

Daniel Horsfall, Social Policy and Social Work, University of York, Heslington, York, UK.

Gavin Kendall, Queensland University of Technology, Kelvin Grove, Queensland, Australia.

Mincheol Kim, Department of Management Information Systems, Jeju National University, 1, Ara 1-dong, 102 Jejudaehakno, Jeju-si, Jeju Special Self-Governing Province 690-756, Republic of Korea.

Young Hoon Kim, Department of Hospitality and Tourism Management, University of North Texas, 1155 Union Circle, #311100, Denton, TX 76203-5017, USA.

Halina Kotikova, Department of Recreology, Palacky University, Olomouc, Czech Republic.

Cindia Ching-Chi Lam, Institute for Tourism Studies, Macao, Colina de Mong-Ha Macao, China S.A.R.

Cornelia Locher, School of Biomedical, Biomolecular and Chemical Sciences, University of Western Australia, Crawley, Western Australia, Australia.

Neil Lunt, Social Policy and Social Work, University of York, Heslington, York, UK.

Russell Mannion, School of Social Policy, University of Birmingham, Edgbaston, UK.

Mike Michael, Department of Sociology, Centre for the Study of Invention and Social Process, Goldsmiths College, University of London, London, UK.

Wong Kee Mun, Faculty of Business and Accountancy, University of Malaya, Kuala Lumpur, Malaysia.

Ghazali Musa, Faculty of Business and Accountancy, University of Malaya, Kuala Lumpur, Malaysia.

Meghann Ormond, Socio-Spatial Analysis Group, Wageningen University, Gaia, Building number 101, Droevedaalsesteeg 3, 6708 PB Wageningen, The Netherlands.

Christof Pforr, School of Management & CBS Tourism Research Cluster, Curtin University, Western Australia, Australia.

László Puczkó, Xellum Ltd, Oktober 6 Utca 14, 1051, Budapest, Hungary.

Eva Schwartzhoffova, Department of Recreology, Palacky University, Olomouc, Czech Republic.

Melanie Smith, Budapest Business School, College of Commerce, Catering and Tourism, Department of Tourism, 9–11 Alkotmany Street, H-1054, Budapest, Hungary.

Ivett Sziva, Tourism Competence Centre, Department of Economic Geography, Faculty of Business, Corvinus University, Fővám Tér 8, 1093 Budapest, Hungary.

Louis Vong, Institute for Tourism Studies, Macao, Colina de Mong-Ha Macao, China S.A.R.

Klaus Weiermair, Institute of Strategic Management, Marketing and Tourism, Innsbruck University School of Management, Innsbruck, Austria.

Acknowledgements

The relationship between health, tourism and personal mobility, from both the perspective of the traveller as well as that of the destination has been a long-standing personal research interest. In part because of my own health travails as a tourist but also because of a geographer's interest in mobility and the spatial aspects of relationships between health and the environment. However, in recent years, it has also included work on issues related to biosecurity, governance and regulation and social marketing. Some of these themes emerge in the present volume. However, this is a collection of papers that is not designed to reflect my voice on medical and health tourism. Rather, it presents a range of chapters from different authors who are themselves established researchers in the field to highlight the different – and often competing – perspectives that exist on medical and health tourism in a single volume. Significantly, the chapters are not just from researchers whose primary academic specialisation is tourism but are also from authors with backgrounds in medicine and health studies as well as in business studies and the broader social sciences. Although the chapters in this book have been organised thematically, the range of perspectives and papers on medical tourism is clearly not concordant throughout. But as stressed in both the introduction and the conclusion to this book, this situation is reflective of the field itself and of the public and personal controversies, debates and ethical issues that surrounds work in the field.

I would like to gratefully acknowledge the patience and support of the contributors to this book, the preparation and publication of which was delayed because of the effects of the Christchurch earthquakes of 2010–11, in which both my home and work offices were severely damaged and became unusable. Becoming an environmental refugee is certainly one way to gain new insights into relationships between natural disasters, health and mobility, although not one I would recommend! I would also like to offer thanks to Peter and Jane Finch and Jim and Nita Cowper for helping with work and personal accommodation over this period without which the book would have been delayed much further. I would also like to acknowledge the support of numerous colleagues, both in New Zealand and overseas, for offers of assistance. The help and support of Tim Baird, Melissa Su, Paul Ballantine and Tony Garry at Canterbury, as well as the magnificent office staff, Donna, Irene and Irene, and Angela in the faculty office who sorts out my financials, must also be noted.

A number of colleagues with whom I have undertaken research with or discussed health, tourism and mobility issues over the years have also contributed to this volume – even if unwittingly. In particular, thanks to Tim Coles, Jo Connell, David Duval, Ghaz Musa, Dieter Müller, Stephen Page, Jarkko Saarinen and Anna Dóra Sæþórsdóttir, for their thoughts, as well as for the stimulation of Tori Amos, Nick Cave, Bruce Cockburn, Zach Condon, Stephen Cummings, Chris Difford and Glenn Tilbrook, Ebba Fosberg, P.J. Harvey, Frida Hyvönen, Ed Kuepper, Morphine, Vinnie Reilly, David Sylvian, Twinemen, Jennifer Warnes, Chris Wilson and *The Guardian*, KCRW and BBC – without whom the four walls of many a hotel room would be much more confining, and my mental health when travelling much worse.

I would also like to extend my thanks to my editor Emma Travis at Routledge as well as to the rest of the team who have continued to support the project through trying circumstances and particularly Carol Barber who was never quite sure when the manuscript would appear on her computer screen! Finally, Michael would like to thank the many people who have supported his work over the years, and especially the Js and the Cs who stay at home, or whatever or wherever home now is.

Riverstones
January 2012

Part I

Introductory context

1 Medical and health tourism

The development and implications of medical mobility

C. Michael Hall

Introduction

Medical and health tourism is one of the fastest growing areas of academic research interest this century in both tourism and health and medical studies (De Arellano 2007; Reed 2008; Leahy 2008; Whittaker 2008; Economic and Social Commission for Asia and the Pacific (ESCAP) 2009; Balaban and Marano 2010; Crooks *et al.* 2010; Hopkins *et al.* 2010; Kangas 2010; Karuppan and Karuppan 2010; Morgan 2010; Underwood and Makadon 2010; Reisman 2010; Connell 2011; Hall 2011a). The emergence of the subject is arguably a reflection of its reported economic significance, for example, Evans (2008) reported that the estimated value of the international medical tourism market was about US$ 60 billion in 2006 and projected it to reach US$ 100 billion by 2012; as well as a growing recognition of the consequences of increased human mobility, including the rapid spread of pandemics (Hall 2005; Hall and James 2011). Indeed, a significant dimension of medical tourism is the extent to which it serves as an example of the way in which globalisation is more than an abstract idea but it is something that has real effects on people and places (Woodward *et al.* 2002).

However, travel for health and medical reasons is nothing new and has long been recognised as a driver of visitors to destinations such as thermal springs and coastal locations as well as other areas with favourable climates (Walton 1983, 2005; Becheri 1989; Lanquar 1989; Hembry 1990; Mesplier-Pinet 1990; Niv 1989; Hall 1992, 2003; Towner 1996; Chambers 1999). In the nineteenth century, wealthy tuberculosis sufferers in northern Europe, including authors such as D.H. Lawrence and Robert Louis Stevenson, travelled to and lived in the Mediterranean, south-west United States or even in the South Pacific on advices as to the health-giving benefits of the climate in order to improve their health (Hall 2003), arguably predating modern-day lifestyle retirement and second home migration to some of the same locations for similar reasons of extending quality of life.

Historical dimensions and developments

The taking of waters at mineral spas and hot springs has occurred since Roman times and the 'taking to the waters' of the elites of seventeenth century Europe provided one of the foundations for the modern pleasure resort concept (Lowenthal

1962; Mackaman 1993; Towner 1996). In the United Kingdom, the development of seaside resorts, such as Blackpool or Margate, had its genesis in the belief of the British elite in the curative powers of sea air (the 'ozone' as it was described) and bathing in sea waters, though not initially directly in the sea itself. In the mid-nineteenth century the combination of improved transport accessibility to leisure because of the growth of the railways and economic accessibility because of rapidly increasing per capita incomes for the new middle classes led to the massification of what was previously available only to the wealthy. However, the middle and, later, working class access to the seaside resorts was built upon not only the desire for the health benefits of recreation away from urban industrial centres but also continued belief in the curative value of the seaside (Pimlott 1947; Walvin 1978; Walton 1983, 2005; Towner 1996; Hall 2003; Hall and Page 2006).

In mainland Europe, many cities and towns have grown up around mineral springs and health spas include Baden, Lausanne, St. Moritz, and Interlaken in Switzerland; Baden-Baden and Wiesbaden in Germany; Vienna, Austria and Budapest, Hungary (Goodrich and Goodrich 1987; Towner 1996). There is also a long history of people using spas and mineral water since ancient times to cure such ailments as rheumatism, skin infections and poor digestion (Becheri 1989; Carone 1989; Erfurt-Cooper and Cooper 2009; Smith and Puczkó 2009). Some spring waters are exported internationally, including Apolinaris from Germany, Hunyadi-Janos from Hungary and Vichy from France. Indeed, the sale of bottled water, including the export of brands such as Perrier from France, is perhaps testimony to the continued belief in the healthy characteristics of mineral water, although research suggests that there is considerable variability in the mineral content of commercial bottled water with subsequent implications for their actual health effects (Garzon and Eisenberg 1998).

In the United States and Canada, mineral springs even provided opportunities for the development of spa tourism around which were created some of the first national parks (Runte 1979; Buchholtz 1983; Frost and Hall 2009). Indeed, Hall (2003) even suggests that the growth of public interest in adventure, health and wellness in tourism and leisure in the late twentieth and early twenty-first centuries parallels the attention given to the physical, moral and spiritual 'damage' of urban living at the turn of the nineteenth century in North America, Europe and Australia, and the resultant growth in national parks, sport and physical education as formal recreational activities and spaces (Altmeyer 1976; Nash 1982; Hall 1985). In the contemporary travel setting, the escape or 'push' from mundane or alienating urban environment and lifestyles has been long recognised as a major motivating force in tourism (Hall 2005). In addition, the desire for a perceived healthy lifestyle is a major component of leisure behaviour and products related to spas and wellness that have become increasingly important in tourism since the early 1990s (Erfurt-Cooper and Cooper 2009; Smith and Puczkó 2009). Finally, one can note the role of fashion and the significance of body image as major influence on individual motivations not only to attend beauty clinics and spas but, in more extreme expressions of concern over body image, to engage in cosmetic surgery as part of so-called 'surgery tourism' (Grossbart and Sarwer 2003; Birch *et al.* 2010; Edmonds 2011; Jeevan *et al.* 2011).

Recent rapid growth in the field

The relationship between tourism and health and medicine is therefore clearly not new. However, even though it is hard to quantify exactly, it is clear that there has been a massive shift in the amount of medical-related mobility. Allied with the growth in the numbers of people travelling for medical and health reasons has been an increasing embrace by governments of market solutions to the problems of providing medical and health services to populations that are not only increasing but are also aging. This has also meant that since the late 1990s there has been a significant qualitative and quantitative change in how health and medical tourism is reported and understood (Hall 2011a; Mainil *et al.* 2011). One way of illustrating this is shown in Table 1.1 which details the number of articles on medical and health tourism and cognate terms recorded in the Scopus database. Even disregarding issues of definition, which is discussed in greater detail below, it is apparent that there has been a massive shift of awareness in medical and health studies, and to a lesser extent, the tourism literature, on the significance of voluntary international mobility for health- and medical-related reasons (the 'working definition' used here) (Hall 2011a). Also of significance though is the realisation that approximately 60 per cent of all journal articles on medical tourism had been written in the two years (2010–2011) prior to the publication of this chapter, while other subjects that seemingly have some profile in the media such as 'dental tourism', 'surgery tourism', 'fertility tourism' or 'transplant tourism' have only recently become subject to substantial academic reporting and scrutiny.

What the expansion of writing on medical and health tourism does not immediately reveal is the wide range of perspectives and philosophies that surround the subject and the controversy and debates that have arisen (Hall 2011a). Indeed, the field is one that arguably provides a mirror for some of the wider debates in society as to the limits of the market, the role of regulation and the rights of individuals. It is also one in which academic writing, opinion and influence has perhaps not been subject to the same degree of ethical scrutiny and reflexion as some of the topics under review.

This first chapter aims to provide a brief overview of the academic study of medical and health tourism in order to provide a context for the following chapters and builds on a recent review by the author (Hall 2011a) as well as other recent studies of the subject (Connell 2011). If first discusses some of the issues surrounding definitions of health and medical tourism and proposes a framework to indicate their interrelationships. It then goes on to identify some of the key issues and debates in medical tourism before providing an outline of the book.

Defining health and medical tourism

Health tourism was defined by the International Union of Tourist Organizations (IUTO), the forerunner to the United Nations World Tourism Organization (UNWTO), as 'the provision of health facilities utilizing the natural resources of the country, in particular mineral water and climate' (IUTO 1973: 7). Goeldner (1989: 7) in reviewing the international health-tourism literature, defined health

Table 1.1 Articles on medical and health tourism and cognate terms in Scopus database 1963–2011

Year	*Total article*	*Medical*	*Type of tourism*									
			Health	*Spa*	*Wellness*	*Transplant*	*Reproductive/ fertility*	*Dental*	*Stem cell*	*Surgery*	*Abortion*	*Xeno-*
2011	212	148	11	6	3	15	16	3	7	4	1	1
2010	191	126	13	2	5	21	7	4	16	2		
2009	118	60	16	5	4	21	5	6	5			
2008	70	34	7		1	18	2	8		1		
2007	48	28	5	2	1	6	3	3		1		
2006	24	12	6		1	2	4					
2005	24	5	6	1	1	2	10					
2004	5	1	1	1			1					1
2003	12	4	7				1					
2002	7	2	2	1	1		1					1
2001	2	2										
2000	3	1	1	1								
1999	3	1	1	1								
1998	2		2									
1997	3	2	1									
1996	2			1							1	
1995	2		2									
1994	0											
1993	3	1	1							1		
1992	1										1	
1991	1		1									
1990	6	1	4	1								
1989	1		1									
1988	1		1									
1987	0											
1986	1	1										
1985	1		1									
1984	2			2								
1973	1									1		
1963	1	1										
Total	764	430	90	24	17	85	50	24	28	10	3	3

Accessed January 2012.

tourism as '(1) staying away from home, (2) health [as the] most important motive, and (3) done in a leisure setting'. Goodrich and Goodrich (1987: 217) and Goodrich (1993, 1994) defined health tourism in terms of the narrower concept of health-care tourism as 'the attempt on the part of a tourist facility (e.g. hotel) or destination (e.g. Baden, Switzerland) to attract tourists by deliberately promoting its health-care services and facilities, in addition to its regular tourist amenities.' More recently, Laesser (2011) suggested that health travel is among the fastest growing tourism market segments and is being driven by five main changes in society:

- shifts in demographic structures as well as lifestyles and an active aging population;
- the need for stress reduction among the working population;
- a shift in the medical paradigm towards prevention and alternative practices;
- increased interaction between public health and health psychology;
- the shift from mass tourism towards customised forms of travel.

Nevertheless, even given its economic and social significance, Laesser (2011) did stress that health tourism 'is (still) a niche and special interest market' although it did appear to be increasing, noting that in 2004 5.8 per cent of all domestic and international tourism trips of Swiss residents could be considered health oriented, up from 3.3 per cent in 2001 and 1.9 per cent in 1998. Unfortunately, readily comparable statistics are not readily available from other jurisdictions.

Goeldner (1989) suggested that there are five components of the health-tourism market, each relating to a more specific market segment which can have categories of health-related tourism attached to it:

1 sun and fun activities (leisure tourism);
2 engaging in healthy activities, but health is not the central motive (outdoor recreation, adventure tourism, sports tourism, wellness tourism);
3 principle motive for travel is health (e.g. a sea cruise or travel to a different climate) (health tourism, wellness tourism);
4 travel for sauna, massage and other health activities (spa tourism, wellness tourism);
5 medical treatment (medical tourism, dental tourism).

Such continuums of classification are extremely useful in reflecting some of the realities of defining the subject from the perspective of consumption (Hall 2003, 2011a). However, while the above classification is helpful for identifying elements of the demand for health and spa tourism, it fails to acknowledge the importance that health products play in destination and attraction marketing and promotion or as a component of tourism-development strategies (McNeil and Ragins 2005). Furthermore, it also reflects the situation that the vast majority of tourism is likely to have some health component at some stage of the trip (Hall 2005). Indeed, as Voigt *et al.* (2011: 17) notes with respect to wellness-related travel, 'as most tourism activities promote health and well-being in some way, a pure demand-based definition of wellness tourism seems to be of little practical value'. Therefore, Hall (2003), in seeking to provide a definition, consistent with official definitions of tourism, suggested that health tourism be defined as 'a commercial phenomena of industrial society which involves a person travelling overnight away from the normal home environment for the express benefit of maintaining or improving health, and the supply and promotion of facilities and destinations which seek to provide such benefits' (Hall 2003: 274).

On this basis, spa tourism, which is a major tourism sector in its own right (Smith and Puczkó 2009), is a component of health tourism that relates to the provision of specific health facilities and destinations that traditionally include the provision of mineral and thermal waters but which may also be used to refer to tourist resorts which integrate health facilities with accommodation (Hall 2011a). Spas are therefore not only used by those who are looking for a cure from diseases such as arthritis, back pain syndrome, obesity, trauma, asthma and medical concerns relating to sterility and post-surgical rehabilitation, but also by guests who are seeking relaxation and 'pampering' as well as beauty and longevity treatments (Marvel 2002; Puczkó and Bacharov 2006; Smith and Puczkó 2009). Indeed, in the German literature on wellness tourism, which is closely related to spa product offerings, it is possible to distinguish between those who seek a 'cure' (*kur* in German) and those who seek wellness (Smith and Puczkó 2009). Pollmann (2005) in reviewing the activities of the International Spa Association identified seven different types of spas:

1 club spa: Primary purpose is fitness, spa services on a day-use basis;
2 cruise ship spa: Fitness, wellness, spa cuisine menu choices and other spa services aboard a cruise ship;
3 day spa: Spa services offered on a day-use basis;
4 destination spa: On-site accommodation, spa cuisine, spa services, educational programming and physical fitness offered to improve lifestyle and health enhancement of guests;
5 medical spa: Integrated spa services as well as conventional and complementary therapies and treatments in order to provide wellness and medical care, e.g. hospitals that offer spa treatments;
6 mineral spring spa: Traditional spa with an on-site source of mineral, thermal or seawater used for hydrotherapy treatments;
7 resort/hotel spa: Fitness, wellness, spa cuisine menu choices and other spa services offered by and located within a resort or hotel.

One of the difficulties in defining health tourism is that it has historically been a term more associated with Europe than the Americas (Goodrich 1994; Hall 2003). Nevertheless, the term has come to be more widely used internationally along with the notion of medical tourism as the business of health tourism and its promotion have expanded.

An important driver for health tourism is a change in the understanding of health and tourism that focuses on wellness and prevention as well as curing illness (Smith 2003; Nahrstedt 2004; Smith and Kelly 2006; Steiner and Reisinger 2006). Although, as Laesser (2011: 83) comments, 'Actually, personal health influences all patterns of consumer behavior – including travel'. According to Messerli and Oyama (2004: 9), 'wellness can be defined as the balanced state of body, spirit and mind, including such holistic aspects as self-responsibility, physical fitness/beauty care, healthy nutrition, relaxation, mental activity and environmental sensitivity as fundamental elements'. Similarly, Müller and Kaufmann (in Smith and Puczkó 2009: 5) define wellness tourism as

> The sum of all the relationships and phenomena resulting from a journey and residence by people whose main motive is to preserve or promote their health. They stay in a specialised hotel which provides the appropriate professional know-how and individual care. They require a comprehensive service package comprising physical fitness/beauty care, healthy nutrition/diet, relaxation/meditation and mental activity/education.

Nevertheless, difficulties of definition are also evidenced by the manner in which the different types of spas, and spa tourism (González and Brea 2005; Mak *et al.* 2009), noted above, clearly overlaps substantially with wellbeing, wellness and other health-tourism concepts (Ivanisevic 1999; Kušen 2002; Mair 2005; Chen *et al.* 2008; Erfurt-Cooper and Cooper 2009; Magdalini and Paris 2009; Smith and Puczkó 2009; Konu *et al.* 2010; Rodrigues *et al.* 2010). For example, Voigt *et al.* (2011) suggested a typology of wellness tourists consisting of three groups: beauty spa visitors; lifestyle resort visitors; and spiritual retreat visitors and utilised a narrow definition of wellness tourism in their study of motivations to engage in wellness tourism by focussing in use of specifically designed wellness tourism infrastructure:

> …the sum of all the relationships resulting from a journey by people whose motive, in whole or in part, is to maintain or promote their health and well-being, and who stay at least one night at a facility that is specifically designed to enable and enhance people's physical, psychological, spiritual and/or social well-being.
>
> (Voigt *et al.* 2011: 17)

One of the main reasons for this situation is the extent to which terms such as 'wellness tourism', 'health tourism' and 'medical tourism' means different things in different countries and cultures (Wolsko *et al.* 2006; Konu 2010; Voigt *et al.* 2011) as well as in different fields of study. For example, the notion of wellness tourism is utilised in the business and tourism literature rather than in medical research. In addition, in Western countries the wellness dimension of health tourism has also increasingly come to include activities and topics such as massage (Lea 2006), new age tourism (Pernecky and Johnston 2006), yoga (Lehto *et al.* 2006; Smith 2007; Ali-Knight 2009) and spirituality (Smith 2003; Smith and Kelly 2006), while some authors even include activities such as hiking and other outdoor adventure activities (Kulczycki and Lück 2009) and volunteering (Brown and Lehto 2005). As Smith and Puczkó (2009: 7) observe, 'there is an increasing globalisation and hybridisation of wellness products, whereby eastern philosophies and traditions infiltrate western contexts; traditional spas expand to include emotional and spiritual activities as well as physical ones; and pop psychology blends with more esoteric practices to enhance mental wellness'. Interestingly, with respect to the relationship between wellness tourism and more conventional medical treatment, Voigt *et al.* (2011: 16) suggest that in addition to rising health costs, 'growing scepticism of orthodox Western medicine, and rising consumer-centeredness in Western health-care systems have stimulated a desire to live healthier lives, and to experiment with more holistic, alternative healing therapies' that are exemplified by the wellness industry. Of course, given the increased marketisation of health services, and the industrialisation of wellness, the enthusiasm of many writers for spas and wellness also assumes that people can afford such services and there appears little consideration of the implications for those who cannot and who are therefore ignored in much of the writing on tourism (see Hall and Brown (1996, 2006) as notable exceptions).

Medical tourism is also a contested term (Hall 2011a) and the range of different approaches to its definition consequently affects estimates of how substantial the field is in terms of human mobility. For example, Lunt and Carrera (2011) note that estimates of international medical tourism ranged from a McKinsey report that estimated the number of medical tourists at 60,000–80,000 (Ehrbeck *et al.* 2008), to a response to the report by Youngman (2009) who took a far more expansive definition, including day-surgery and cross-border exchanges, and suggested a figure of five million globally.

According to Connell (2006), medical tourism is a niche that emerged from the rapid growth of people travelling often long distances internationally to obtain medical, dental and surgical care while simultaneously being holidaymakers, in a more conventional sense. ESCAP (2009: 1), in a report on medical tourism in the Asia-Pacific region defines 'Medical travel' as 'the international phenomenon of individuals travelling, often great distances, to access health-care services that are otherwise not available due to high costs, long waiting lists or limited health-care capacity in the country of origin' and medical tourism referring 'specifically to the increasing tendency among people from developed countries to undertake medical travel in combination with visiting tourist attractions. Medical tourism is often seen as adding medical services to common tourism'.

In contrast, in the medical and health studies literature, medical tourism is usually understood as a more generic term that simply refers to 'foreign travel for the purpose of seeking medical treatment' (Balaban and Marano 2010: e135), with or without a holiday or the consumption of tourism services (Connell 2006; Turner 2007a). Such an approach is consistent with technical definitions of tourism (a point often missed by many medical-tourism researchers). In order to try and clarify the increasingly complex series of categories of travel and tourism, the United Nations and United Nations World Tourism Organization (UN and UNWTO) (2007) have recommended use of the term visitor rather than tourist per se, with a number of criteria needing to be satisfied for an international traveller to qualify as an international visitor, although the terms international visitor and international tourist tend to be used interchangeably in everyday usage:

- the place of destination within the country visited is outside the traveller's usual environment;
- the stay, or intention of stay, in the country visited should last no more than 12 months, beyond which this place in the country visited would become part of his/her usual environment. At which point this would lead to a classification as a migrant or permanent resident. Significantly, for the present discussion the UN and UNWTO recommend that this criterion should be applied to also cover long-term patients, even though their stay might be interrupted by short stays in their country of origin or elsewhere;
- the main purpose of the trip is other than being employed by an organisation or person in the country visited. Therefore health and medical purposes satisfy the technical definition of being an international visitor;
- the traveller is not engaged in travel for military service or is a member of the diplomatic services;
- the traveller is not a nomad or refugee.

Domestic visitors are similarly classified. Therefore, rather than using the lay interpretation of tourism as being a form of leisure or pleasure travel (Hall 2005), a technical definition of tourism clearly encompasses all short-term (i.e. less than 12 months) travel for medical and health-related purposes. Therefore, using this approach we can state that medical tourism occurs when individuals volunteer to travel outside of their home environment with the primary intention of receiving medical treatments with a visit that lasts no more than 12 months.

Arguably such a definition may go some way to responding to Connell's (2011) question as to whether medical and health tourism really is tourism? Indeed, it supports to a great extent his conclusion:

> So it is tourism: a rather unusual but increasingly valuable niche in the ever more competitive travel industry. While many painful activities, such as transplant surgery, have no relationship to the pleasure and even frivolity usually associated with tourism, and 'suicide tourism' can be excluded, despite its termination of pain and suffering, most components of medical tourism have parallels in other forms of tourism, and obvious impacts on the tourism industry.
>
> (Connell 2011: 171)

Medical tourism can therefore be either international or domestic in scope and it is also undertaken voluntarily. Though this does not preclude cross-border treatment under the aegis of public or private health services as is increasingly the case within the EU for example (see Chapter 2). The types of medical procedures engaged in are therefore usually, but not exclusively, elective. It does not refer to

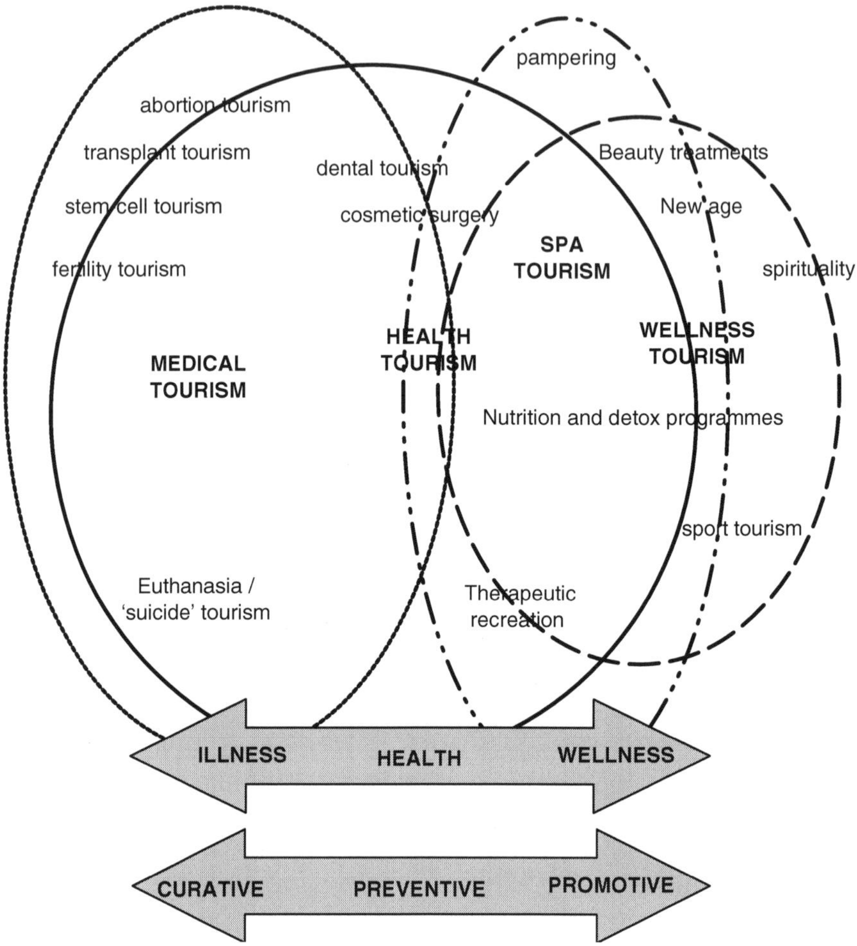

Figure 1.1 Interrelatedness of health and medical tourism domains and product niches.

Sources: After Hall 1992, 2003, 2011a.

situations in which tourists become sick or injured while travelling and have to receive treatment, as widespread as this might be (Hall 2005). Instead, the decision to receive medical treatment prior to travel to a destination is a determining factor in identifying medical tourism activities from the reception of medical treatment when travelling per se.

Some of these issues are illustrated in Figure 1.1, which provides a representation of the medical, health, spa and wellness tourism and shows them in relation as to whether they are focussed on continuums of wellness to illness, and promotion of health to preventive and curative health approaches. It should be stressed that these continuum are ideal relationships and that some categories of medical tourism, such as fertility and abortion tourism as well as emerging medical practices such as stem cell and xenotransplantation, are closely connected to issues surrounding the regulation and commodification of the body and access to health and medical services and perhaps highlight the ethical and political complexities that phrases such as wellness and health tourism can easily hide.

Medical tourism is usually curative in focus as opposed to the more preventative scope of health and wellness tourism. In medical tourism, health services are usually being consumed for at least one of seven reasons (Hall 2011a) discussed below.

Financial cost

Cross-border and foreign medical services can be cheaper than those available in the medical tourist generating country or region (economic cost dimension) (Milstein and Smith 2006). According to Bookman and Bookman (2007) in their study of the flows of medical tourists from the developed to the less developed countries, 'Everyone, coming from everywhere, is shopping for a doctor in the international health services market, and as a result, enjoys a cost savings over the alternative at home' (Bookman and Bookman 2007: 2). Nevertheless, flows may also occur within jurisdictions – as in the case of the EU – as well as domestically as in the case of medical-related mobility in federal systems where there may be different public and private medical services, as well as different funding and insurance mechanisms, between states and provinces.

Time cost

Related to the above in terms of time cost is that medical services may be available elsewhere in a more timely manner (Eggertson 2006; MacReady 2007). This has certainly been a major factor behind the growth of 'dental tourism', for example, (Turner 2008; Sterle *et al.* 2009) as well as for transplant tourism where patients may otherwise be on lengthy waiting lists for an available donor organ to become available (Schiano and Rhodes 2010), and may even be considered a factor for international travel for abortions where the regulatory measures covering abortion practices in the home location may be regarded as too lengthy or too restrictive (Daly 2011; Gilmartin and White 2011). However, while international travel for treatment for serious medical problems often gets considerable publicity – including with respect to public fundraising efforts for specialist treatment in some cases – the reality is that the majority of time-related decisions to travel for medical services are connected with waiting times for elective surgery in government funded health services.

Holidays and the consumption of tourism and hospitality services

Medical services will tend to be consumed in conjunction with a holiday (for those who are employed) and tourism and hospitality services (commercial behavioural dimension) (Henderson 2004; Connell 2006, 2011; De Arellano 2007; Alleman *et al.* 2011). This is sometimes portrayed as occurring in a relatively exotic location (Connell 2006). However, the reality is that many destinations are already likely to be relatively familiar to the medical tourist as a result of previous visits, media information and word of mouth.

Cultural proximity: language, culture and diaspora

As a result of migration and the demands of a global labour market, expatriates and migrants may return to their country of origin for medical treatment for cultural, family and language reasons (a non-commercial behavioural dimension) (Lee *et al.* 2010). Indeed, the increased mobility of people around the world as witnessed in the presence of large migrant, expatriate and sojourner populations in many countries means that the diasporic dimensions of medical tourism are becoming increasingly important (Inhorn 2011). Indeed, the role of diasporas in flows of medical tourists has even led to calls for the establishment of new bilateral governance and regulatory structures (Martinas Álvarez *et al.* 2011).

Regulatory structures and governance

The absence of regulatory structures in the destination jurisdiction that restrict the availability of a medical service in the generating country (regulatory cost dimension) can be a significant incentive for engaging in medical tourism in some circumstances. Hall (2011a) argued that this dimension can be further broken down by differentiating between regulation that makes some services completely unavailable even though the medical technology exists, that is, abortion whereby a woman has to travel internationally so as to have an abortion procedure that would not be legal in their country of origin – what is sometimes termed 'abortion tourism' (Serrano Gil and García Casado 1992; Nowicka 1996; Daly 2011; Gilmartin and White 2011), and where procedures are regulated because they are regarded as highly experimental or even unethical in the country of origin, as in the case of stem cell medicine ('stem cell tourism') (MacReady 2009; Mitka 2010; Miller 2011; Sipp 2011) and some fertility and reproductive procedures ('fertility', 'procreation' and 'reproductive tourism') (Pennings 2002; Spar 2005; Storrow 2005; Matorras and Pennings 2005; Cohen 2006; Inhorn and Patrizio 2009; McKelvey *et al.* 2009; Shenfield *et al.* 2010; Voigt and Laing 2010; Bergmann 2011). It should also be noted that some forms of government-funded assistance with reproduction is illegal or restricted in some countries, for example, to gay or unmarried couples, so that some forms of fertility and reproduction tourism are regulated on the basis of who is requesting the treatment rather than the nature of the treatment per se.

Non-availability of organs in home jurisdiction

A sixth reason for medical tourism may lie in the non-availability of an organ for transplant in the country of origin of the medical tourist (Bramstedt and Xu 2007; Cohen 2009; Schiano and Rhodes 2010). This area is particularly controversial because of concerns over organ trafficking (Scheper-Hughes 2003), and the ethics surrounding the availability of organs for purchase (Concejero and Chen 2009) and is therefore also linked to issues of medical regulation (Reed 2008).

Quality

The final reason why someone may choose to engage in medical tourism is because the standard of medical services, including patient care may be of a better quality than in the tourists home environment or at least be of an acceptable quality. Although issues of quality of medical tourism services have long been significant in the literature (see Chapter 2 for a further discussion), it is only recently that consumer/patient perceptions and the role that quality plays in their decision to purchase medical services has been discussed (Guiry and Vequist 2011; Lertwannawit and Guild 2011).

The different dimensions of medical tourism are clearly not mutually exclusive, particularly as the regulation of medical and health services also has implication for costs and waiting times for treatments. Indeed, the regulative and policy dimension of international trade in health services is arguably fundamental to the development of the various forms of health and medical tourism. Indeed, the policy drivers for medical tourism are often derived not so much from health and welfare policy but from international trade and economic development.

Major themes and issues

A number of major themes can be identified in health and medical tourism and are echoed by the various chapters in this book. In part, themes and issues depend on the disciplinary and cultural context within which the research has taken place. For example, much of the research within tourism and business studies has focussed on ways within which the medical tourism market can be identified, branded, marketed to and the tourism product developed (García-Altés 2005; Spiegel *et al.* 2008; Cormany and Baloglu 2011; Michalkó and Rátz 2010; Reddy *et al.* 2010; Boga and Weiermair 2011; Martin *et al.* 2011; Laesser 2011), often for the reason of improved firm or destination positioning (Lam *et al.* 2011), although a number of more critical reflections on the topic also exist (Mair 2005; Connell 2006, 2011). Much of the research that occurs within tourism studies therefore often does not question the underlying reasons or societal conditions that encourage people to travel internationally to seek medical assistance and health improvements (this criticism can arguably also be made of some of the medical literature as well). Instead, the focus is generally on improving the conditions by which products can be developed, commodified and sold to consumers who need them.

Nevertheless, as Hall (2011a) argued, critical to understanding the academic context in which research on medical and health tourism occur are the different ideologies and philosophies that surround the provision of health care in different countries and the design of health-care systems. This is especially the case with respect to the extent to which national, and in some cases, regional governments believe that health provision should be marketised and promoted as with any other kind of service export and, related to this, the extent to which the decision to engage in medical tourism becomes one of personal choice and the use of market solutions to health provision (Blumenthal 2006; United States Senate Special Committee on Aging 2006; Milstein and Smith 2007; Reddy *et al.* 2010; Vijaya 2010; Meghani 2011; Ormond 2011).

However, if the commoditisation and marketisation of individual health is acceptable in some jurisdictions then new questions arise as to where the limits of commercialisation should lie, and the ethical (and medical) demands of the individual versus the ethical demands of other individual and organisational stakeholders. Ethical issues remain one of the most significant areas of medical tourism, given not only the strong ethical tradition in medical research and its application but also because of its broader implications (Crozier and Baylis 2010; Hunter and Oultram 2010; Lunt and Carrera 2010; Shetty 2010; Meghani 2011; Widdows 2011). Issues raised in this context include the extent to which medical services should be exported while local populations suffer ill-health and/or poor or no medical services (De Arellano 2011; Sengupta 2011); the purchase of human body parts for transplant tourism and the potential for organ trafficking (Luscombe 2010; Schiano and Rhodes 2010; Biller-Andorno and Capron 2011; Caplan *et al.* 2011); travel for reasons of assisted suicide in the case of terminal illnesses (Huxtable 2009; Shaw 2009; Mullock 2010; Ost 2010; Higginbotham 2011); and stem cell tourism (Chandler 2010; Devereaux and Loring 2010; Murdoch and Scott 2010; Sipp 2010; Zarzecnzy and Caulfield 2010).

An important issue with respect to medical and health tourism that is gaining growing recognition is its potential biosecurity risks with respect to humans acting as vectors for disease and drug-resistant bacteria (Hall 2010; Fernando *et al.* 2010; Kumarasamy *et al.* 2010; Wilson 2010; Hall and James 2011). As Hall (2011a: 9) notes,

> … medical tourism is intrinsically different from general tourism activities with respect to increasing biosecurity risks because individuals who engage in medical tourism are deliberately travelling to a medical environment and engaging in medical practices that potentially exposes them to new pathogens and microbiologic fauna and flora.

Hall and James (2011; see also Chapter 13) identified several examples of tourism-related nosocomial infections including

- the role of travel in the spread of noroviruses (gastric flu);
- complications following arthroplasty (joint replacement) (Cheung and Wilson 2007) and aesthetic/cosmetic/plastic surgery (Centers for Disease Control 2004; Newman *et al.* 2005a, 2005b; Furuya *et al.* 2008; Handschin *et al.* 2007; Jeevan *et al.* 2011);
- hepatitis B as a result of unhygienic hospital conditions, and hepatitis C virus infections as a result of holiday haemodialysis (Bhattacharya *et al.* 2009);
- a higher incidence of post-operative tissue rejection and severe infectious complications among transplant tourists compared to other transplant patients (Balaban and Marano 2010).

Substantial concerns have also been raised about the health risks associated with xenotransplantation and 'stem cell tourism' (Kiatpongsan and Sipp 2008; Nelson 2008; Kimball and Hodges 2010; see Chapter 4). The risks inherent in medical tourism are also leading to new ethical questions for health and medical professionals. Hall (2011a) noted that in the same way that concerns are raised about treating illnesses and health complications that are clearly linked to risky behaviours such as smoking, alcohol and drug abuse, to what extent are health professionals then obliged to treat patients whose problems have arisen from participating in medical tourism (Asai and Jones 2007). Furthermore, such ethical concerns are even more pronounced in the case of medical tourism because it is substantially at odds with a health service model that encourages the creation and maintenance of long-term relationships between practitioners and patients.

Given concerns over public and individual health risk increasing attention is therefore being given as to how medical and health tourism should or can be regulated (Reed 2008; Hanna *et al.* 2009; Turner 2011) as well as the broader regulation of health dimensions of international mobility (Hall 2011b). Yet, as Hall (2011a) notes, the regulation of medical tourism faces the same issues as the regulation of other goods and services that carry potential health or environmental risks in that the primary regulatory structures are economic, and the World Trade Organisation regime in particular, rather than risk oriented (Hall 2011b).

Structure of the book

The chapters in this volume are broadly organised into three main sections. The first section examines issues of regulation and meta-ethical issues. In the second chapter, Lunt *et al.* focus on issues of quality and risk in international trade in medical services. Their observations on regulatory needs, which come from a European context, provide a significant contrast to the US grounded chapter of Gan (Chapter 3) that discusses different impediments to the development of medical tourism for American consumers. Chapter 4 by Cook *et al.* examines the ethical issues associated with xenotourism but places them in a broader context by noting the influence of marketisation on medical tourism.

The second major section consists of four chapters that illustrate different policy settings in medical tourism. Chapter 5 by Pforr and Locher discusses the way in which changes in domestic health policies in Germany have affected medical tourism. Chapter 6 by Smith *et al.* looks at the way that medical tourism has developed in Hungary, a country with a long history of health-spa tourism, and notes the difficulties in reconciling public and private health and spa sector needs, especially when medical tourism is of considerable importance for economic development in a number of regional destinations. The central European focus continues in Chapter 7 by Kotikova and Schwartzhoffova who examine health-spa tourism in the Czech and Slovak Republics. The chapter presents a unique perspective on policy differences that have emerged post the split of Czechoslovakia and while being neighbours and having a common history different policy approaches for developing the health-spa sector have been adopted. The final chapter in the section is that of Lam *et al.*, which focuses on the competiveness of Macao as a medical tourism destination with respect to other Asian destinations and the potential positioning of government policy.

The third section focuses on different business and marketing dimensions of medical tourism. Chapter 9 by Boga and Weiermair focuses on branding issues for medical and health tourism and is based on empirical research of German consumers. Chapter 10 by Kim *et al.* also looks at branding issues, but in a Korean context. Chapter 11 by Wong and Musa provides a comparison of medical tourism in four countries in south and south-east Asia: Thailand, Singapore, Malaysia and India and notes their different approaches and positioning in the international medical tourism market. The final chapter in the section by Ormond (Chapter 12) analyses the way in which the cultural attributes of Malaysia have been harnessed in the promotion of Malaysia as an international medical tourism destination. The book is then concluded by a brief chapter by Hall that outlines significant future research issues in medical tourism as well as major policy debates.

Conclusion

Health and medical tourism is a complex and contested area of study. Many governments, international agencies and the medical industries see it as a means of economic development, that may cross-subsidise domestic health access where that is a government objective, as in the case of Singapore (Economic and Social Commission for Asia and the Pacific 2009; Vijaya 2010), and provide a competitive cure for the problems facing the global health system and the delivery of health services (Horowitz and Rosensweig 2007; Underwood and Makadon 2010). However, such perspectives are increasingly problematic and debatable as, in contrast, others see medical tourism as symptomatic of a process of marketisation of public health services already under pressure from neoliberal political agendas that only serves to reinforce gaps between have and have-nots both within and between societies (Turner 2007a, 2007b; Vijaya 2010; Sengupta 2011). Such criticisms are also notable given that the media discourse on medical tourism itself is regarded as having shifted from one that included significant criticism and ethical debate to a discourse that focuses on the benefits of the market (Mainil *et al.* 2011).

Undoubtedly the benefits, costs and risks attached to medical tourism both for individual and collective public health are a vital area for future research (Crooks *et al.* 2010; Fernando *et al.* 2010; Talbot *et al.* 2010; Turner 2011). As Hall (2011a) suggested, such research must include contributions not only from medical and health research but also from tourism studies and the wider social sciences. It is hoped that this volume will therefore make at least one small contribution to a better understanding and awareness of the field and improved engagement between different approaches to the subject.

References

Ali-Knight, J. (2009) 'Yoga tourism', in R. Bushell and P.J. Sheldon (eds) *Wellness and Tourism: Mind, Body, Spirit, Place*, New York: Cognizant Communication Corporation.

Alleman, B.W., Luger, T., Reisinger, H.S., Martin, R., Horowitz, M.D. and Cram, P. (2011) 'Medical tourism services available to residents of the United States', *Journal of General Internal Medicine*, 26(5): 492–97.

Altmeyer, G. (1976) 'Three ideas of nature in Canada, 1893–1914', *Journal of Canadian Studies*, 11(3): 21–36.

Asai, R. and Jones Jr., K. (2007) 'Ethical moment: am I obligated to treat a patient whose need for emergency care stems from dental tourism?, *Journal of the American Dental Association*, 138: 1018–19.

Balaban, V. and Marano, C. (2010) 'Medical tourism research: a systematic review', *International Journal of Infectious Diseases*, 14(Supp.) (14th International Congress on Infectious Diseases (ICID) Abstracts): e135.

Becheri, E. (1989) 'From thermalism to health tourism', *Revue de Tourisme*, 44(4): 15–19.

Bergmann, S. (2011) 'Fertility tourism: circumventive routes that enable access to reproductive technologies and substances', *Signs*, 36(2): 280–89.

Bhattacharya, S., Price, N., Boxall, E., Adu, D., Lipkin, G., Smith, S. and Osman, H. (2009) 'Holiday haemodialysis and imported hepatitis C virus infection: a series of sixteen cases in two large haemodialysis units', *Journal of Clinical Virology*, 4(4): 296–99.

Biller-Andorno, N. and Capron, A.M. (2011) '"Gratuities" for donated organs: ethically indefensible', *The Lancet*, 377(9775): 1390–91.

Birch, D.W., Vu, L., Karmali, S., Stoklossa, C.J. and Sharma, A.M. (2010) 'Medical tourism in bariatric surgery', *The American Journal of Surgery*, 199: 604–08.

Blumenthal, D. (2006) 'Employer-sponsored health insurance in the United States – origins and implications', *New England Journal of Medicine*, 355(1): 82–88.

Boga, T.C. and Weiermair, K. (2011) 'Branding new services in health tourism', *Tourism Review*, 66(1/2): 90–106.

Bookman, M.Z., and Bookman, K.R. (2007) *Medical Tourism in Developing Countries*. New York: Palgrave MacMillan.

Bramstedt, K.A. and Xu, J. (2007) 'Checklist: passport, plane ticket, organ transplant', *American Journal of Transplantation*, 7(7): 1698–1701.

Brown, S. and Lehto, X.Y. (2005) 'Travelling with a purpose: understanding the motives and benefits of volunteer vacationers', *Current Issues in Tourism*, 8(6): 479–96.

Buchholtz, C.W. (1983) *Rocky Mountain National Park: A History*. Boulder, CO: Colorado Associated University Press.

Caplan, A., Danovitch, G., Shapiro, M., Lavee, J. and Epstein, M. (2011) 'Time for a boycott of Chinese science and medicine pertaining to organ transplantation', *The Lancet*, 378(9798): 1218.

Carone, G. (1989) 'Pour un thermalisme différent – considérations sur le cas de l'Italie', *Revue de Tourisme*, 44(3): 23–26.

Centers for Disease Control (2004) 'Brief report: nontuberculous mycobacterial infections after cosmetic surgery – Santo Domingo, Dominican Republic, 2003–2004', *Morbidity and Mortality Weekly Report*, 53(23): 509.

Chambers, T.A. (1999) 'Fashionable disease: promoting health and leisure at Saratoga Springs, New York and the Virginia Springs, 1790–1860', unpublished Ph.D. dissertation, Department of History, College of William and Mary, Williamsburg, VA.

Chandler, J. (2010) 'Stem cell tourism: doctors' duties to minors and other incompetent patients', *American Journal of Bioethics*, 10(5): 27–28.

Chen, J.S., Prebensen, N. and Huan, T.C. (2008) 'Determining the motivation of wellness travellers', *Anatolia*, 19(1): 103–15.

Cheung, I.K. and Wilson, A. (2007) 'Arthroplasty tourism', *Medical Journal of Australia*, 187(11–12): 666–67.

Cohen, D.J. (2009) 'Transplant tourism: a growing phenomenon', *Nature Clinical Practice Nephrology*, 5(3): 128–29.

Cohen, J. (2006) 'Procreative tourism as a last resort', *Gynecologie Obstetrique Fertilite*, 34(10): 881–82.

Concejero, A.M. and Chen, C.-L. (2009) 'Ethical perspectives on living donor organ transplantation in Asia', *Liver Transplantation*, 15(2): 1658–61.

Connell, J. (2006) 'Medical tourism: Sea, sun, sand and…surgery', *Tourism Management*, 27: 1093–100.

Connell, J. (2011) *Medical Tourism*. Wallingford: CABI.

Cormany, D. and Baloglu, S. (2011) 'Medical travel facilitator websites: an exploratory study of web page contents and services offered to the prospective medical tourist', *Tourism Management*, 32(4): 709–716.

Crooks, V.A., Kingsbury, P., Snyder, J. and Johnston, R. (2010) 'What is known about the patient's experience of medical tourism? A scoping review', *BMC Health Services Research*, 10,266 DOI: 10.1186/1472-6963-10-266/j.tourman.2010.02.008.

Crozier, G.K.D. and Baylis, F. (2010) 'The ethical physician encounters international medical travel', *Journal of Medical Ethics*, 36(5): 297–301.

Daly, B. (2011) 'Access to abortion services: the impact of the European convention on human rights in Ireland', *Medicine and Law*, 30(2): 267–78.

De Arellano, A.B.R. (2007) 'Patients without borders: the emergence of medical tourism', *International Journal of Health Services*, 37(1): 193–98.

De Arellano, A.B.R. (2011) 'Medical tourism in the Caribbean', *Signs*, 36(2): 289–97.

Devereaux, M. and Loring, J.F. (2010) 'Growth of an industry: How U.S. scientists and clinicians have enabled stem cell tourism', *American Journal of Bioethics*, 10(5): 45–46.

Economic and Social Commission for Asia and the Pacific (2009) *Medical Travel in Asia and the Pacific. Challenges and Opportunities*, Bangkok: United Nations Economic and Social Commission for Asia and the Pacific.

Edmonds, A. (2011) 'Almost invisible scars': medical tourism to Brazil. *Signs: Journal of Women in Culture and Society*, 36: 297–302.

Eggertson, L. (2006) 'Wait-list weary Canadians seek treatment abroad', *CMAJ: Canadian Medical Association Journal = journal de l'Association medicale canadienne*, 174(9): 1247.

Ehrbeck, T., Guevara, C. and Mango, P.D. (2008) 'Mapping the market for medical tourism', *The McKinsey Quarterly*, May: 1–11.

Erfurt-Cooper, P. and Cooper, M. (2009) *Health and Wellness Tourism: Spas and Hot Springs*. Bristol: Channel View.

Evans, R.W. (2008) 'Ethnocentrism is an unacceptable rationale for health care policy: a critique of transplant tourism position statements', *American Journal of Transplantation*, 8: 1089–95.

Fernando, G.A.T.P., Collignon, P.J. and Bell, J.M. (2010) 'A risk for returned travellers: the "post-antibiotic era"', *Medical Journal of Australia*, 193(1): 59.

Frost, W. and Hall, C.M. (eds) (2009) *Tourism and National Parks*. London: Routledge.

Furuya, E.Y., Paez, A., Srinivasan, A., Cooksey, R., Augenbraun, M., Baron, M., Brudney, K., Della-Latta, P., Estivariz, C., Fischer, S., Flood, M., Kellner, P., Roman, C., Yakrus, M., Weiss, D. and Granowitz, E.V. (2008) 'Outbreak of *Mycobacterium abscessus* wound infections among "lipotourists" from the United States who underwent abdominoplasty in the Dominican Republic', *Clinical Infectious Diseases*, 46(8): 1181–88.

García-Altés, A. (2005) 'The development of health tourism services', *Annals of Tourism Research*, 32(1): 262–66.
Garzon, P. and Eisenberg, M.J. (1998) 'Variation in the mineral content of commercially available bottled waters: implications for health and disease', *The American Journal of Medicine*, 105(2): 125–30.
Gilmartin, M. and White, A. (2011) 'Comparative perspectives symposium: gender and medical tourism interrogating medical tourism: Ireland, abortion, and mobility rights', *Signs*, 36(2): 275–80.
Goeldner, C. (1989) '39th Congress AIEST: English workshop summary', *Revue de Tourisme*, 44(4): 6–7.
González, M.E.A. and Brea, J.A.F. (2005) 'An investigation of the relationship among service quality, customer satisfaction and behavioural intentions in Spanish health spas', *Journal of Hospitality and Leisure Marketing*, 13(2): 67–90.
Goodrich, J.N. (1993) 'Socialist Cuba: a study of health tourism', *Journal of Travel Research*, 32(1): 36–42.
Goodrich, J.N. (1994) 'Health tourism: a new positioning strategy for tourist destinations', *Journal of International Consumer Marketing*, 6(3–4): 227–37.
Goodrich, J.N. and Goodrich, G.E. (1987) 'Health-care tourism – an exploratory study', *Tourism Management*, 8: 217–22.
Grossbart, T.A. and Sarwer, D.B. (2003) 'Psychosocial issues and their relevance to the cosmetic surgery patient', *Seminars in Cutaneous Medicine and Surgery*, 22: 136–47.
Guiry, M. and Vequist, D.G. (2011) 'Travelling abroad for medical care: U.S. medical tourists' expectations and perceptions of service quality', *Health Marketing Quarterly*, 28(3): 253–69.
Hall, C.M. (1985) 'Outdoor recreation and national identity: a comparative analysis of Australia and Canada', *Journal of Canadian Culture*, 2(2): 25–39.
Hall, C.M. (1992) 'Review. Adventure, health and sports tourism', in B. Weiler and C.M. Hall (eds.) *Special Interest Tourism*, London: Belhaven Press.
Hall, C.M. (2003) 'Health and spa tourism', in S. Hudson (eds) *International Sports & Adventure Tourism*, New York: Haworth Press.
Hall, C.M. (2005) *Tourism: Rethinking the Social Science of mobility*, Harlow: Prentice Hall.
Hall, C.M. (2010) 'Crisis events in tourism: subjects of crisis in tourism', *Current Issues in Tourism*, 13(5): 401–07.
Hall, C.M. (2011a) Health and medical tourism: kill or cure for global public health? *Tourism Review*, 66(1/2): 4–15.
Hall, C.M. (2011b) 'Biosecurity, tourism and mobility: institutional arrangements for managing tourism related biological invasions', *Journal of Policy Research in Tourism, Leisure and Events*, 3(3): 256–80.
Hall, C.M. and James, M. (2011) 'Medical tourism: emerging biosecurity and nosocomial issues', *Tourism Review*, 66(1/2): 118–26.
Hall, C.M. and Page, S. (2006) *Geography of Tourism and Recreation*, 3rd ed. London: Routledge.
Hall, D. and Brown, F. (1996) 'Towards a welfare focus for tourism research', *Progress in Tourism and Hospitality Research*, 2: 41–57.
Hall, D. and Brown, F. (2006) *Tourism and Welfare: Ethics, Responsibility and Sustainable Well-being*. Wallingford: CABI.
Handschin, A.E., Banic, A. and Constantinescu, M.A. (2007) 'Pulmonary embolism after plastic surgery tourism', *Clinical and Applied Thrombosis/Hemostasis*, 13(3): 340.

Hanna, S.A., Saksena, J., Legge, S. and Ware, H.E. (2009) 'Sending NHS patients for operations abroad: is the holiday over?' *Annals of the Royal College of Surgeons of England*, 91(2): 128–30.

Hembry, P.M. (1990) *The English Spa, 1560–1815: A Social History*, London: Athlone Press.

Henderson, J.C. (2004) 'Healthcare in Southeast Asia', *Tourism Review International*, 7: 111–22.

Higginbotham, G. (2011) 'Assisted-suicide tourism: is it tourism?' *Tourismos*, 6(2): 177–85.

Hopkins, L., Labonté, R., Runnels, V. and Packer, C. (2010) 'Medical tourism today: what is the state of existing knowledge', *Journal of Public Health Policy*, 31(2): 185–98.

Horowitz, M.D. and Rosensweig, J.A. (2007) 'Medical tourism – health care in the global economy', *Physician Executive*, 33(6): 24–26, 28–30.

Hunter, D., Oultram, S. (2010) 'The ethical and policy implications of rogue medical tourism', *Global Social Policy*, 10(3): 297–99.

Huxtable, R. (2009) 'The suicide tourist trap: compromise across boundaries', *Journal of Bioethical Inquiry*, 6(3): 327–36.

Inhorn, M.C. (2011) 'Diasporic dreaming: return reproductive tourism to the Middle East', *Reproductive BioMedicine Online*, 23(5): 582–91.

Inhorn, M.C. and Patrizio, P. (2009) 'Rethinking reproductive "tourism" as reproductive "exile"', *Fertility and Sterility*, 92(3): 904–06.

International Union of Tourism Organisations (IUTO) (1973) *Health Tourism*, Geneva: United Nations.

Ivanisevic, G. (1999) 'Marine remedies of the island of Losinj – the basis for the development of health and spa tourism', *Turizam*, 47(2): 132–49.

Jeevan, R., Birch, J. and Armstrong, A.P. (2011) 'Travelling abroad for aesthetic surgery: informing healthcare practitioners and providers while improving patient safety', *Journal of Plastic Reconstructive and Aesthetic Surgery*, 64(2): 143–47.

Kangas, B. (2010) 'Traveling for medical care in a global world', *Medical Anthropology: Cross Cultural Studies in Health and Illness*, 29(4): 344–62.

Karuppan, C.M. and Karuppan, M. (2010) 'Changing trends in health care tourism', *Health Care Manager*, 29(4): 349–58.

Kiatpongsan, S. and Sipp, D. (2008) 'Offshore stem cell treatments', *Nature Reports Stem Cells*, Published online: 3 December 2008, doi:10.1038/stemcells.2008.151.

Kimball, A.M. and Hodges, J. (2010) 'Risky trade and emerging infections', in *Institute of Medicine, Infectious Disease Movement in a Borderless World*, Washington, DC: The National Academies Press.

Konu, H. (2010) 'Identifying potential wellbeing tourism segments in Finland', *Tourism Review*, 65(2): 41–51.

Konu, H., Tuohino, A., Komppula, R. (2010) 'Lake wellness – a practical example of a new service development (NSD) concept in tourism industries', *Journal of Vacation Marketing*, 16(2): 125–39.

Kulczycki, C. and Lück, M. (2009) 'Outdoor adventure tourism, wellness, and place attachment', in R. Bushell and P.J. Sheldon (eds) *Wellness and Tourism: Mind, Body, Spirit, Place*, New York: Cognizant Communication Corporation.

Kumarasamy, K.K., Toleman, M.A., Walsh, T.R., Bagaria, J., Butt, F., Balakrishnan, R., Chaudhary, U., Doumith, M., Giske, G.C., Irfan, S., Krishnan, P., Kumar, A.V., Maharjan, S., Mushtaq, S., Noorie, T., Paterson, D.L., Pearson, A., Perry, C., Pike, R., Rao, B., Ray, U., Sarma, J.B., Sharma, M., Sheridan, E., Thirunarayan, M.A., Turton, J., Upadhyay, S., Warner, M., Welfare, W., Livermore, D.M. and Woodford, N. (2010) 'Emergence of a new antibiotic resistance mechanism in India, Pakistan, and the UK: a molecular, biological, and epidemiological study', *Lancet Infectious Diseases*, 10(9): 597–602.

Kušen, E. (2002) 'Health tourism', *Tourism*, 50(2): 175–88.

Laesser, C. (2011) 'Health travel motivation and activities: insights from a mature market – Switzerland', *Tourism Review*, 66(1/2): 83–89.

Lam, C., du Cros, H. and Vong, T. (2011) 'Macao's potential for developing regional Chinese medical tourism', *The Tourism Review*, 66(1/2): 68–82.

Lanquar, R. (1989) 'La Filière du Tourisme de Santé', *Revue de Tourisme*, 44(4) 25–30.

Lea, J. (2006) 'Experiencing festival bodies: connecting massage and wellness', *Tourism Recreation Research*, 31(1): 57–66.

Leahy, A.L. (2008) 'Medical tourism: the impact of travel to foreign countries for healthcare', *Surgeon*, 6(5): 260–61.

Lee, J.Y., Kearns, R.A. and Friesen, W. (2010) 'Seeking affective health care: Korean immigrants' use of homeland medical services', *Health and Place*, 16(1): 108–15.

Lehto, X., Brown, S., Chen, Y. and Morrison, A.M. (2006) 'Yoga tourism as a niche within the wellness sector', *Tourism Recreation Research*, 31(1): 25–36.

Lertwannawit, A. and Guild, N. (2011) 'International tourists' service quality perception and behavioral loyalty toward medical tourism in Bangkok Metropolitan area', *Journal of Applied Business Research*, 27(6): 1–11.

Lowenthal, D. (1962) 'Tourists and thermalists', *Geographical Review*, 52(1): 124–27.

Lunt, N. and Carrera, P. (2010) 'Medical tourism: assessing the evidence on treatment abroad', *Maturitas*, 66(1): 27–32.

Lunt, N. and Carrera, P. (2011) 'Systematic review of web sites for prospective medical tourists', *The Tourism Review*, 66(1/2): 57–67.

Luscombe, R. (2010) 'The declaration of Istanbul on organ trafficking and transplant tourism', *CANNT journal = Journal ACITN*, 20(2): 6–7.

Mackaman, D.P. (1993) 'Doctoring on vacation: medicine and culture at the spas of Nineteenth-Century France', unpublished Ph.D. dissertation. Berkeley, CA: University of California.

McKelvey, A., David, A.L., Shenfield, F. and Jauniaux, E.R. (2009) 'The impact of cross-border reproductive care or 'fertility tourism' on NHS maternity services', *BJOG: An International Journal of Obstetrics and Gynaecology*, 116(11): 1520–23.

McNeil, K.R. and Ragins, E.J. (2005) 'Staying in the spa marketing game: trends, challenges, strategies and techniques', *Journal of Vacation Marketing*, 11(1): 31–39.

MacReady, N. (2007) 'Developing countries court medical tourists', *Lancet*, 369(9576): 1849–50.

MacReady, N. (2009) 'The murky ethics of stem-cell tourism', *The Lancet Oncology*, 10(4): 317–18.

Magdalini, V. and Paris, T. (2009) 'The wellness tourism market in Greece – an interdisciplinary methodology approach', *Tourismos*, 4(4): 127–44.

Mainil, T., Platenkamp, V. and Meulemans, H. (2011) 'The discourse of medical tourism in the media', *Tourism Review*, 66(1/2): 31–44.

Mair, H. (2005) 'Tourism, health and the pharmacy: towards a critical understanding of health and wellness tourism', *Tourism*, 53(4): 335–46.

Mak, A.H.N., Wong, K.K.F. and Chang, R.C.Y. (2009) 'Health or self-indulgence? The motivations and characteristics of spa-goers', *International Journal of Tourism Research*, 11(2): 185–99.

Martin, D.S., Ramamonjiarivelo, Z. and Martin, W. (2011) 'MEDTOUR: a scale for measuring medical tourism intentions', *The Tourism Review*, 66(1/2): 45–56.

Martinas Álvarez, M., Chanda, R. and Smith, R.D. (2011) 'The potential for bi-lateral agreements in medical tourism: a qualitative study of stakeholder perspectives from the UK and India', *Globalization and Health*, 7, article no 11.

Marvel, M. (2002) 'Spa tourism in Central & Eastern Europe', *Travel and Tourism Analyst*, December: 1–25.

Matorras, R. and Pennings, G. (2005) 'Reproductive exile versus reproductive tourism', *Human Reproduction*, 20(12): 3571–72.

Meghani, Z. (2011) 'A robust, particularlist ethical assessment of medical tourism', *Developing World Bioethics*, 11(1): 16–29.

Mesplier-Pinet, J. (1990) 'Thermalisme et curistes: les contraintes', *Revue de Tourisme*, 45(2): 10–17.

Messerli H.R. and Oyama Y. (2004) 'Health and wellness tourism – global', *Travel and Tourism Analyst*, August: 1–54.

Michalkó, G. and Rátz, T. (2010) 'Hungarian spa destinations in the tourism-oriented property market', *Foldrajzi Ertesito/Hungarian Geographical Bulletin*, 59(2): 131–46.

Miller, N.R. (2011) 'Stem cell "tourism"', *Ophthalmology*, 118(12): 2530–31.

Milstein, A. and Smith, M. (2006), 'America's new refugees – seeking affordable surgery offshore', *New England Journal of Medicine*, Vol. 355 No. 16, pp. 1637–40.

Milstein, A. and Smith, M. (2007) 'Will the surgical world become flat?' *Health Affairs*, 26(1): 137–41.

Mitka, M. (2010) 'Troubled by "stem cell tourism" claims, group launches web-based guidance', *JAMA – Journal of the American Medical Association*, 304(12): 1315–16.

Morgan, D. (2010) 'The growth of medical tourism', *OECD Observer*, 281: 12–13.

Mullock, A. (2010) 'Overlooking the criminally compassionate: what are the implications of prosecutorial policy on encouraging or assisting suicide?' *Medical Law Review*, 18(4): 442–70.

Murdoch, C.E. and Scott, C.T. (2010) 'Stem cell tourism and the power of hope', *American Journal of Bioethics*, 10(5): 16–23.

Nahrstedt, W. (2004) 'Wellness: a new perspective for leisure centers, health tourism, and spas in Europe on the global health market', in K. Weimermaier and C. Mathies (eds) *The Tourism and Leisure Industry: Shaping the Future*, New York; Haworth Hospitality Press.

Nash, R. (1982) *Wilderness and the American Mind*, 2nd edn. New Haven, CT: Yale University Press.

Nelson, B. (2008) 'Stem cell researchers face down stem cell tourism', *Nature Reports Stem Cells*, Published online: 5 June 2008 | doi:10.1038/stemcells.2008.89.

Newman, M.I., Camberos, A.E., Clynes, N.D. and Ascherman, J.A. (2005a) 'Outbreak of atypical mycobacteria infections in U.S. patients traveling abroad for cosmetic surgery', *Plastic and Reconstructive Surgery*, 115(3): 964–65.

Newman, M.I., Camberos, A.E., Ascherman, J., Zienowicz, R.J. and Vaccaro, J.J. (2005b) '*Mycobacteria abscessus* outbreak in US patients linked to offshore surgicenter', *Annals of Plastic Surgery*, 55(1): 107–10.

Niv, A. (1989) 'Health tourism in Israel: a developing industry', *Revue de Tourisme*, 44(4): 30–32.

Nowicka, W. (1996) 'The effects of the 1993 anti-abortion law in Poland', *Entre nous (Copenhagen, Denmark)*, 34–35: 13–15.

Ormond, M. (2011) 'Shifting subjects of health-care: placing 'medical tourism' in the context of Malaysian domestic health-care reform', *Asia Pacific Viewpoint*, 52(3): 247–59.

Ost, S. (2010) 'The de-medicalisation of assisted dying: is a less medicalised model the way forward?' *Medical Law Review*, 18(4): 497–540.

Pennings, G. (2002) 'Reproductive tourism as moral pluralism in motion', *Journal of Medical Ethics*, 28(6): 337–41.

Pernecky, T. and Johnston, C. (2006) 'Voyage through numinous space: applying the specialization concept to new age tourism', *Tourism Recreation Research*, 31(1): 37–46.

Pimlott, J.A.R. (1947) *The Englishman's Holiday: A Social History*. London: Faber.

Pollmann, S.K. (2005) 'Health tourism in Hungary', unpublished Graduate Diploma, Department of Tourism, University of Otago, Dunedin.

Puczkó, L. and Bacharov, M. (2006) 'Spa, bath, thermae: what's behind the labels?' *Tourism Recreation Research*, 31(3): 83–91.

Reed, C.M. (2008) 'Medical tourism', *Medical Clinics of North America*, 92(6): 1433–46.

Reddy, S.G., York, V.K. and Brannon, L.A. (2010) 'Travel for treatment: students' perspective on medical tourism', *International Journal of Tourism Research*, 12(5): 510–22.

Reisman, D. (2010) *Health Tourism: Social Welfare through International Trade*. Cheltenham: Edward Elgar.

Rodrigues, Á., Kastenholz, E. and Rodrigues, A. (2010) 'Hiking as a relevant wellness activity – an exploratory study of hiking tourists in Portugal', *Journal of Vacation Marketing*, 16(4): 331–43.

Runte, A. (1979) *National Parks: The American Experience*. Lincoln, NE: University of Nebraska Press.

Scheper-Hughes, N. (2003) 'Keeping an eye on the global traffic in human organs', *Lancet*, 361(9369): 1645–48.

Schiano, T.D. and Rhodes, R. (2010) 'Transplant tourism', *Current Opinion in Organ Transplantation*, 15(2): 245–48.

Sengupta, A. (2011) 'Medical tourism: reverse subsidy for the elite', *Signs*, 36(2): 312–19.

Serrano Gil, A. and García Casado, M.L. (1992) 'Conscientious objection in the matter of abortion [La objeción de conciencia en materia de aborto]', *Revista de enfermeria (Barcelona, Spain)*, 15(163): 45–46.

Shaw, J.J.A. (2009) 'Recent developments in the reform of English law on assisted suicide', *European Journal of Health Law*, 16(4): 333–49.

Shenfield, F., De Mouzon, J., Pennings, G., Ferraretti, A.P., Nyboe Andersen, A., De Wert, G. and Goossens, V. (2010) 'Cross border reproductive care in six European countries', *Human Reproduction*, 25(6): 1361–68.

Shetty, P. (2010) 'Medical tourism booms in India, but at what cost?' *The Lancet*, 376(9742): 671–72.

Sipp, D. (2010) 'Hope alone is not an outcome: why regulations make sense for the global stem cell industry', *American Journal of Bioethics*, 10(5): 33–34.

Sipp, D. (2011) 'The unregulated commercialization of stem cell treatments: a global perspective', *Frontiers of Medicine in China*, 5(4): 348–55.

Smith, B.R. (2007) 'Body, mind and spirit? Towards an analysis of the practice of yoga', *Body & Society*, 13(2): 25–46.

Smith, M. (2003) 'Holistic tourism: tourism and the reconciliation of body, mind and spirit', *Tourism Recreation Research*, 28(1): 103–08.

Smith, M. and Kelly, C. (2006) 'Holistic holidays: journeys of the self?' *Tourism Recreation Research*, 31(1): 15–24.

Smith, M. and Puczkó, L. (eds) (2009) *Health and Wellness Tourism*, Oxford: Elsevier.

Spar, D. (2005) 'Business and medicine: reproductive tourism and the regulatory map', *New England Journal of Medicine*, 352(6): 531–33.

Spiegel, J.M., Gonzalez, M., Cabrera, G.J., Catasus, S., Vidal, C. and Yassi, A. (2008) 'Promoting health in response to global tourism expansion in Cuba', *Health Promotion International*, 23(1): 60–69.

Steiner, C. and Reisinger, Y. (2006) 'Ringing the fourfold: a philosophical framework for thinking about wellness tourism', *Tourism Recreation Research*, 31(1): 5–14.

Sterle, A., Balázs, P. and Delgado, J. (2009) 'Travelling for teeth: characteristics and perspectives of dental care tourism in Hungary', *British Dental Journal*, 206(8): 425–28.

Storrow, R.F. (2005) 'Quests for conception: Fertility tourists, globalization and feminist legal theory', *Hastings Law Journal*, 57(2): 295–330.

Talbot, E.A., Chen, L.H., Sanford, C., McCarthy, A. and Leder, K. (2010) 'Travel medicine research priorities: establishing an evidence base', *Journal of Travel Medicine*, 17(6): 410–15.

Towner, J. (1996) *An Historical Geography of Recreation and Tourism in the Western World 1540–1940*, Chichester: Wiley.

Turner, L. (2007a) 'From Durham to Delhi: "medical tourism" and the global economy', in J.C. Cohen-Kohler and M.B. Seaton (eds) *Comparative Program on Health and Society Lupina Foundation Working Papers Series 2006–2007*, Toronto: Munk Centre for International Studies, University of Toronto, Toronto.

Turner, L. (2007b) '"First world health care at third world price": globalization, bioethics and medical tourism', *BioSocieties*, 2: 303–25.

Turner, L. (2008) 'Cross-border dental care: 'dental tourism' and patient mobility', *British Dental Journal*, 204: 553–54.

Turner, L.G. (2011) 'Quality in health care and globalization of health services: accreditation and regulatory oversight of medical tourism companies', *International Journal for Quality in Health Care*, 23(1): 1–7.

Underwood, H.R. and Makadon, H.J. (2010), 'Medical tourism: game-changing innovation or passing fad?' *Healthcare Financial Management: Journal of the Healthcare Financial Management Association*, 64(9): 112–114, 116, 118.

United Nations and United Nations World Tourism Organization (UN and UNWTO) (2007) *International Recommendations on Tourism Statistics (IRTS) Provisional Draft*. New York and Madrid: UN and UNWTO.

United States Senate Special Committee on Aging (2006) *'The Globalization of Health Care: Can Medical Tourism Reduce Health Care costs?' Senate Hearing, June 27, 2006. 109th Congress, Second Session*. Washington, DC: Government Printing Office.

Vijaya, R.M. (2010) 'Medical tourism: revenue generation or international transfer of healthcare problems?' *Journal of Economic Issues*, 44(1): 53–69.

Voigt, C. and Laing, J.H. (2010) 'Journey into parenthood: commodification of reproduction as a new tourism niche market', *Journal of Travel and Tourism Marketing*, 27(3): 252–68.

Voigt, C., Brown, G. and Howat, G. (2011) 'Wellness tourists: in search of transformation', *Tourism Review*, 66(1/2): 16–30.

Walton, J. (1983) *The English Seaside Resort: A Social History 1750–1914*, Leicester: Leicester University Press.

Walton, J.. (2005) *Histories of Tourism: Representation, Identity and Conflict*, Clevedon: Channelview Publications.

Walvin, J. (1978) *Besides the Seaside: A Social History of the Popular Seaside*. London: Allen Lane.

Whittaker, A. (2008) 'Pleasure and pain: medical travel in Asia', *Global Public Health*, 3: 271–90.

Widdows, H. (2011) 'Localized past, globalized future: towards an effective bioethical framework using examples from population genetics and medical tourism', *Bioethics*, 25(2): 83–91.

Wilson, M.E. (2010) 'Global travel and emerging infections', in *Institute of Medicine, Infectious Disease Movement in a Borderless World*, Washington, DC: The National Academies Press.
Wolsko, C., Lardon, C., Hopkins, S. and Ruppert, E. (2006) 'Conceptions of wellness among the Yupík of the Yukon–Kuskokwim delta: the vitality of social and natural connection', *Ethnicity and Health*, 11(4): 345–63.
Woodward, D., Drager, N. and Beaglehole, R. (2002) 'Globalization, global public goods, and health', in N. Drager and C. Vieira (eds) *Trade in Health Services: Global Regional and Country Perspectives*, Washington, DC: Pan American Health Organization.
Youngman, I. (2009) 'Medical tourism statistics: why McKinsey has got it wrong', *International Medical Travel Journal*. [Online]. Available at: www.imtjonline.com/articles/2009/mckinsey-wrong-medical-travel (accessed 1 April 2011).
Zarzeczny, A. and Caulfield, T. (2010) 'Stem cell tourism and doctors' duties to minors – a view from Canada', *American Journal of Bioethics*, 10(5): 3–15.

Part II

Regulation and meta-ethics

2 Quality, safety and risk in medical tourism

Neil Lunt, Stephen T. Green, Russell Mannion and Daniel Horsfall

Introduction

The forces of globalisation have led to a more transnational and international focus for health policy, funding and service delivery (Lunt 2006; Smith *et al.* 2009). On the demand side in the new global market for health care are an increasing number of patients who are willing to travel across international borders to receive health care services. Such movement typically involves individuals from higher income countries paying out of their own pocket and travelling to less developed areas of the world to receive treatment. The distance travelled varies from intercontinental travel (Europe and North America to Asia, for example) and shorter cross-border trips (travel within Europe and the United States to neighbouring countries). On the supply side, new providers are springing up to tap in to this lucrative market (Ehrbeck *et al.* 2008; Cormany and Baloglu 2010; Lunt and Carrera 2010). This internationalisation of health care provision presents new challenges for health policy with potential new threats to the quality and safety of care provided to patients travelling overseas for treatment.

Health trade and patient mobility

Medical tourism may be situated within the wider growth in trade in health services, as well as patient mobility more generally (see Chapter 1; see also Hall 2011). The General Agreement on Trade in Services' Modes of Services Delivery details the range of formats whereby health trade can take place. Patients consuming abroad are one dimension (Mode 2) of health mobility.

- Mode 1: *Cross-border trade*, where the trade takes place from one country into the other and the service itself crosses the border.
- Mode 2: *Consumption abroad*, where the customer travels to the country where the service is supplied.
- Mode 3: *Commercial presence*, where the supplier establishes a commercial presence abroad.
- Mode 4: *Movement of natural persons*, where the provider of the service crosses the border (Sapir and Winter 1994: 27).

Medical tourism and International medical travel are terms that have been used to describe a wide variety of health services ranging across the full range of medical specialities, and typically include services such as cosmetic surgery and dental procedures, orthopaedic surgery, cardiac surgery, assisted reproductive technology and organ and cellular transplantation (see Hall 2011, Chapter 1).

Medical tourism may be set within the wider context of patient mobility, which includes other categories of patients – temporary visitors abroad, long-term residents of other countries and outsourced patients (Bertinato *et al.* 2005; Rosenmöller *et al.* 2006; Glinos *et al.* 2010a, 2010b).

- *Temporary visitors abroad:* low-cost travel (and particularly the expansion of budget airlines) has led to an expansion in the number of people travelling overseas on short-term visits. Although most individuals who travel abroad on holiday will not require the use of domestic health care, a small number of tourists will always need to use health care abroad as a result of an accident or a sudden illness. The cost of such medical treatment is usually covered by travel insurance or cross-national agreements between collaborating countries. For example, citizens of the European Union can use the European Health Insurance Card to fund emergency use of health services in Member States.
- *Long-term residents:* mobility of older people commonly known as "retirement migration" is a growing internationally and an increasing number of Western European citizens are deciding to retire overseas (Rosenmöller *et al.* 2006; Lunt 2008). Depending on circumstances, these residents domiciled overseas may receive health services funded variously by the country of residence, the country of origin, private insurance and private contributions.
- *Outsourced patients:* this refers to those individuals who after discussions with their commissioning authorities opt to go overseas. Commissioning authorities will have sourced a relatively small number of providers – usually to relieve pressures on domestic waiting lists. Typically, patients travel short distances and contracted services (both public and private) are subject to stringent quality and safety regulations. Crucially, such outsourced patients would travel as a national patient referral (see Lowson *et al.* 2002; Burge *et al.* 2004; Glinos *et al.* 2006).
- *Medical tourists:* are the most heterogeneous group of individuals and the subject of this chapter. These patients are mobile through their own volition *and pay out of their own pocket for medical services overseas.*

In a European context, a medical tourist may be seen in one of two ways, either as a citizen or as a consumer. European *citizens* have rights as patients to move across EU borders to other Member States and receive treatment, which is reimbursed by purchasers in their own country (Carrera and Lunt 2010). These rights have been established by successive European Court of Justice Rulings and the Directive on patient mobility. In such cases, patients usually avoid paying for health-care treatment as it is paid on their behalf by the state or a third-party insurer. Here, the patient does not travel as a patient referral (unlike those that

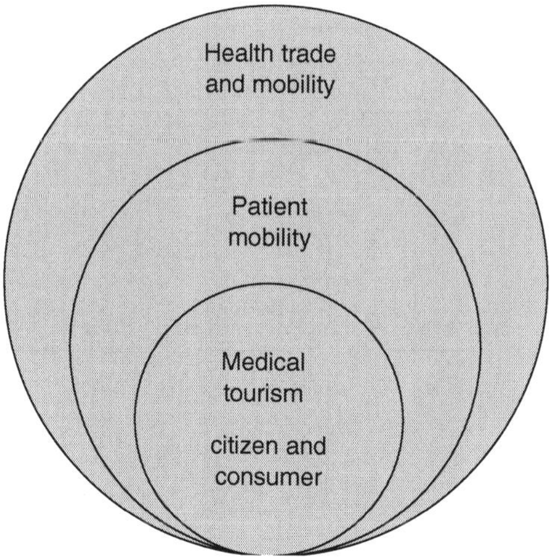

Figure 2.1 Mobility and medical tourism.

Source: Authors.

are outsourced) because EU cross-border reimbursement does not require that clinicians in the country of origin make the referral. Patients electing to avoid waiting lists or preferring to use specialists elsewhere in the EU thus assume the responsibility for making informed choices about the choice of provider.

A second group of medical tourists, *consumers*, are those European medical tourists who pay 'out-of-pocket' to access a range of dental, cosmetic, heart and joint surgery and fertility treatment which is not reimbursed. Such patients may choose to travel outside of the EU. Some of the treatments they receive may be available in their own country but individuals may simply prefer to travel overseas.

Thus, there is a distinct European perspective on the phenomenon of medical tourism. These twin identities of citizen and consumer distinguish Europeans from their American counterparts where medical tourists are more accurately described as active consumers rather than citizens exercising rights to treatment (Figure 2.1).

The rise of medical tourism

The increase in the numbers of medical tourists travelling abroad for medical care is due to the interaction of several supply and demand factors. Probably the most important attraction for individuals seeking health care abroad is the growing availability of low-cost medical care and after-care services, often at a fraction of the cost of those provided by the private providers at home (see Table 2.1 for cost comparisons). Other drivers include eligibility criteria, waiting lists or where the services are outlawed or not yet approved. The growing ease and affordability of international travel and the expansion of internet marketing – the primary source

Table 2.1 Medical tourism advertised prices in selected countries[a,b]

Procedure	*United States*	*United Kingdom*	*Singapore*	*India*	*Poland*	*Thailand*	*Mexico*
Heart bypass (CABG)	113,000	13,921	20,000	10,000	7,140	13,000	3,250
Heart-valve replacement	150,000		13,000	9,500	9,520	11,000	18,000
Angioplasty	47,000	8,000	13,000	11,000	7,300	10,000	15,000
Hip replacement	47,000	12,000	11,000	9,000	6,120	12,000	17,300
Knee replacement	48,000	10,162	13,000	8,500	6,375	10,000	14,650
Gastric bypass	35,000		20,000	11,000	11,069	15,000	8,000
Hip resurfacing	47,000		12,000	8,250	7,905	10,000	12,500
Spinal fusion	43,000		9,000	5,500		7,000	15,000
Mastectomy	17,000		12,400	7,500		9,000	7,500
Rhinoplasty	4,500	3,500	4,375	2,000	1,700	2,500	3,200
Tummy tuck	6,400	4,810	6,250	2,900	3,500	3,500	3,000
Breast reduction	5,200	5,075	8,000	2,500	3,146	3,750	3,000
Breast implants	6,000	4,350	8,000	2,200	5,243	2,600	2,500
Crown	385	330	400	180	246	243	300
Tooth whitening	289	500		100	174	100	350
Dental implants	1,188	1,600	1,500	1,100	953	1,429	950

Source: Authors, July 2011, compiled from medical tourism providers and brokers online.

Notes

a Costs of surgeries around the world. Costs given in US$.

b The price comparisons for surgery take into account hospital and doctor charges, but do not include the costs of flights and hotel bills for the expected length of stay.

of information for individuals seeking treatment abroad – are also factors influencing the decision to seek treatment overseas (Lunt *et al.* 2010). Some medical tourists are also likely to be attracted by the privacy and confidentiality afforded by far away destinations when undergoing medical treatment for sensitive reasons such as cosmetic surgery and gender reassignment. There is also the lure of tourist attractions and places of treatment themselves. While previously, travel for health care (from high-income countries) was limited to particular social groups, this picture is now shifting (Whittaker 2008; Crooks *et al.* 2010).

The commercial sector has responded quickly to the growing global international trade in health-care services. Several governments, most notably India, Singapore and Thailand, are investing heavily in their health-care infrastructure and recruiting and training health-care professionals with the aim of delivering high-quality care, while a developed European market is also in existence (Carrera and Bridges 2006; Chee, 2007; Carrera and Lunt, 2010). State support for Poland and Hungary are outlined in Box 2.1.

Box 2.1 **The rise of European providers**

In Poland, a popular destination for dental tourists and cosmetic tourists, medical tourism is facilitated through private companies, many of the clinics used are state owned, serving Polish citizens alongside medical tourism. This reflects the Polish government's desire to capture the potential of medical tourism and marked by the creation of the Polish Medical Tourism Chamber of Commerce (Reisman 2010: 133) and networking with the Polish Association of Medical Tourism. The Polish government is actively attempting to harness the potential of recent EU ascension to compete with more far-flung destinations for the custom of European medical tourists.

Hungary has also sought to harness the opportunities presented by EU ascension and develop a medical tourism industry. While many of the clinics offering treatment to medical service are undoubtedly private, the role of the Hungarian government should not be overlooked, promoting free spa days to tourists and marking 2003 as the Year of Health Tourism. Terry (2007: 419) refers to Hungary as the "dental capital of the world" and only a cursory glance at medical tourism sites reveals that a wide range of procedures are being actively marketed to tourists.

Commercial agencies have also emerged to service this lucrative market. These provide a 'brokerage' service to prospective medical tourists and offer assistance and advice on travel arrangements, the selection of providers and even individual surgeons (Cormany and Baloglu 2010; Crooks *et al.* 2010). Figure 2.2 outlines the range of services which support the medical-tourist treatment pathway.

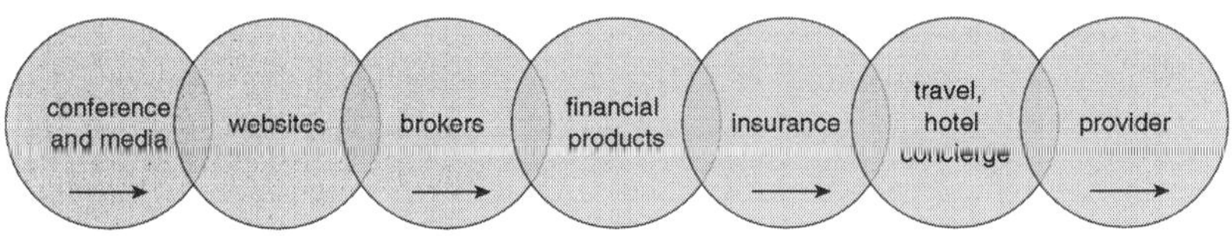

Figure 2.2 The medical tourism industry.

Source: Authors.

The growth of medical tourism presents new opportunities and benefits for individuals, but at the same time presents a number of risks and challenges for the delivery of high-quality and safe care which need to be better understood and resolved as increasing numbers of individuals travel abroad for medical care. We now discuss a number of issues relating to choice and decision making within medical travel; the quality and safety of care provided to nationals abroad, including regulation and accreditation; and regulation and future global development of the medical-tourist industry.

Deciding to travel

Little is known about how medical tourists make decisions regarding treatments and destinations and what forms of hard data (performance measures, quality markers, safety metrics) and soft intelligence (website information, family, friends, internet chat rooms) they access when making such decisions. What is the role of primary-care physicians in encouraging or discouraging residents considering undertaking medical-tourist treatments? Given the prominence of medical-tourist websites, there are important questions about their role and function including: the type, veracity and availability of information provided; confidentiality; and how information provided over the internet shapes choice of treatment, provider and destination. How do individuals assimilate and understand the advertising and information they retrieve? Do they, for example, take into account commercial interests and bias when making decisions over providers and destination country? In brief, what are the triggers and sources of information for becoming a consumer of health treatments abroad (Lunt *et al.* 2010)?

Patients also generally lack the technical knowledge to assess the quality and appropriateness of care and may struggle with language or understanding the health system of the destination country (Legido-Quigley *et al.* 2008). In many cases, the main source of information on quality is provided by a website created by intermediary organisations (Lunt and Carrera 2011). While consumer-friendly websites may well provide reassurance about the quality of treatments and competences of foreign providers, they remain largely unregulated. A systematic review of 50 medical-tourism websites, which market treatments and services in mainland Europe, found that only nine stated explicitly that staff fluent in English were employed. Indeed, on a small number of websites, grammar and spelling of text were both poor, giving little confidence in a clinic's English proficiency and communication ability (Lunt and Carrera 2011). This is particularly significant when considering the importance of good communication within the patient–clinician relationship and for informed consent processes for medical treatment.

Assuring quality and safety

Modern health care is an inherently complex, risky undertaking with the potential for clinical errors and/or slips. Lapses and medical malpractice are ever present, particularly when accessing health care in countries where providers are poorly regulated. Evidence is growing that harm to patients resulting from errors and mistakes by health-care professionals are a significant problem (Hurwitz and Sheikh 2009; Weingart *et al.* 2000). In the NHS and many other highly developed health systems, around 10 per cent of hospital patients experience an adverse event during their stay (Institute of Medicine 2001; Vincent *et al.* 2001; Davis *et al.* 2003; Sari *et al.* 2007). This has given rise to increased regulation, inspection and accreditation of health-care providers to assure high quality and safeguard care in many developed health systems. However, there is little comparable information with regard to the quality and safety of care provided by many of the facilities used by medical tourists.

Evidence of clinical outcomes for medical-tourist treatments is sparse and research reports are difficult to obtain and verify. Little is known about the relative clinical effectiveness and outcomes for particular treatments, institutions, clinicians and organisations. There is scant evidence on long- or short-term follow up of patients returning home following treatment abroad. That positive treatment outcomes should result is important not least because the patient's local health-care system takes on the responsibility and funding for post-operative care including treatment for complications and to remedy any side effects of poor care abroad. The British Association of Plastic, Reconstructive and Aesthetic Surgeons have argued, for example, that increasing numbers of outward-bound UK medical tourists are subsequently requiring treatment by the NHS for complications arising from poor care provided overseas (Jeevan and Armstrong 2008). (The overall cost to the public purse is not clear, nor how the situation compares with domestic private surgery that goes awry with cost implications for the NHS).

There are also some in-depth case studies of poor outcomes from surgery abroad incurring significant public costs to rectify poor treatment (Cheung and Wilson 2007). Birch *et al.* (2010) highlights the case of medical-tourist patients who sought bariatric surgery and required urgent surgical management at a tertiary care centre in Canada. For dental treatment abroad, there are reported cases of complications having to be dealt with by the home health system (Milosevic 2009; Barrowman *et al.* 2010).

Does medical tourism break the cycle of care?

The medical-tourist treatment pathway may be analysed through a number of stages, each carrying potential risks (Figure 2.3).

1 There is a period prior to travelling, and if this involves travel to a country with a tropical or a sub-tropical climate such as Thailand or India, where the disease ecosystem and disease profiles are different, then this should be a consideration for the home system.
2 There may be issues around pre-counselling and informed consent for procedures being contemplated. Individuals may have a pre-existing illness (e.g. diabetes mellitus, cardiovascular deficiency, respiratory disease, renal failure, HIV disease) or be taking significant medications prior to travelling, which health-care professionals will need to integrate into treatment plans.
3 There may be shortcomings of communication surrounding immediate treatment processes. Canales *et al.*'s (2006) study of kidney transplants, for example, concludes there was inadequate communication of information – immunosuppressive regimens and preoperative information. Similar gaps may be evident in other services.
4 The medical traveller/tourist may become ill while overseas, perhaps in a way quite unrelated to their primary reason for becoming a medical traveller, or they might develop complications or side effects related to their treatment. The quality of post-operative care can vary dramatically depending on the

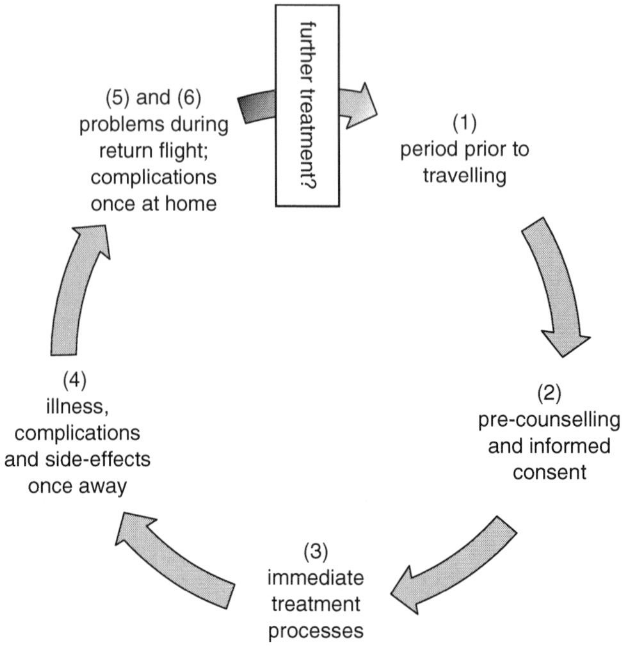

Figure 2.3 Medical tourism and continuity of care.

Source: Authors.

health-care facility and country of destination and may be different from the United States or Western European standards.

5 Problems can develop during the return flight, such as deep venous thrombosis and pulmonary thromboembolism, or a myocardial infarct. The journey home following treatment can be difficult and painful, especially after complex surgery. Despite medical tourism involving air travel, there is no reliable evidence on travel risk resulting from medical tourism, for example, with regard to thrombosis on long flights.

6 Subsequent to arriving home, complications, side effects and post-operative care become the responsibility of the home medical care system, and patients may encounter problems accessing adequate health care. For example, physicians in the United States may be uncomfortable dealing with patients who had travelled overseas to another country and undergone an operation to implant a kidney they had purchased (Boschert 2007).

Globalising infection and spread of pathogens?

The public health aspects of medical tourism raise a number of issues. Of significance is the potential for hazardous micro-organisms transferring between hospitals located in different parts of the world on the body of a medical tourist (Green 2008; Hall and James 2011; see also Chapter 13). These could include antimicrobial resistance, and dangerous pathogens, such as Severe Acute Respiratory Syndrome. The rapid spread of North American "swine" flu out of the United States and Mexico to the rest of the world in 2009 and after illustrates the ease with which micro-organisms can be transported across borders. Instances of infection outbreaks arising from treatment of US citizens at overseas 'medical-tourist' facilities have been reported in the literature (Newman *et al.* 2005). The lack of any routine data means there is little idea of how prevalent infections among medical tourists are or how they compare with rates from non-medical tourists.

The overseas and private nature of delivery explains why there is such a dearth of information relating to clinical outcomes, post-operative complications, lapses in safety and poor professional practice. Presently, there is a lack of comparative quality and safety data, and knowledge of infection rates for overseas institutions and reporting of adverse events is lacking. Bodies like the World Health Organization have yet to publish any firm guidance on this, and there does not appear to be any immediate intention to do so. For some, a lack of transparency on quality is a barrier to the development of a mature market in medical tourism (Ehrbeck *et al.* 2008: 6).

External quality assessment and accreditation

There are a range of organisational dimensions related to the quality and safety of medical treatment abroad. Many of these are not necessarily unique to medical tourism in that health care is replete with information asymmetries and potential threats to the quality and safety of patient-care pathways. Medical tourism adds a new dynamic to this element of risk, due to the overseas travel involved and the shift in legal jurisdiction. Choosing an overseas treatment centre may bring a number of challenges – difficulties in assessing comparative quality and performance of alternative providers, differences in legal liability and knowledge concerning the processes of how to pursue complaints and receive redress (MacReady 2007).

Optimising quality and minimising risk are two key ingredients for creating better and safer health-care services, whether they are providing services for domestic consumption or for medical travellers. This can only be accomplished through the setting up of appropriate forms of clinical governance framework within the hospital or clinic designed to assess quality, identify risk and deal with all relevant issues, and at the same time promoting a culture of remaining vigilant. At the present time, medical tourism services remain largely unregulated. Concerns over the quality and safety of the medical care provided overseas have also emerged due to the lack of robust clinical governance arrangements and quality-assurance procedures in provider organisations (Zahir 2001). There have also been questions over the training, qualifications, motivations and competence of health-care professionals.

External Quality Assessment (EQA) – the introduction of a trusted third party to assure quality control – contain the potential for increasing the information flow, especially exchange of good practice between organisations, and transparency within organisations. A number of EQA models exist that have possible relevance for medical tourism:

- statutory inspection (including licensing);
- public sector educational programs for training and testing private providers;
- industry-based assessments;
  - ISO certification;
  - evaluation (usually internal) against the 'business-excellence' framework;
- health-care-based assessment through peer review;
  - reciprocal visiting;
  - increase regulation and monitoring of private providers;
  - self-directed quality-improvement tools;
  - licensure, certification and accreditation (Green 2009).

In response to such concerns, a range of independent accreditation schemes have been established with the aim of assuring the care of medical tourists in a way that avoids potential conflicts of interest. There are a range of international accreditation bodies such as the Joint Commission International from the United States, Accreditation Canada International, the Australian Council on Healthcare Standards and QHA Trent Accreditation.

Accreditation is a form of EQA where surveying is carried out by a third-party conformity assessment body using a combination of self-assessment and external peer review led by a team of external peer reviewers. Accreditation is generally accepted to apply to organisations rather than individuals, although it can apply as readily to a dental clinic as to a full hospital. The process has come to be thought of as a 'stamp of approval' verifying the authenticity and quality of the services provided. Common characteristics of all accreditation schemes include: surveys and reviews that are conducted by professional peers with appropriate training; the means that are in place by which problems can be identified prospectively; and a mechanism within the accreditation process for ensuring follow-up action on any recommendations that arise from the survey and for correcting any problems identified by the measurement process. Finally, the assessment process should be repeated periodically, usually between 2–4 years (Green 2009).

Accreditation may be of particular interest to the medical tourism market in three ways. First, the offer of assurance to commercial interests of the quality and safety of the product they are selling to the public, which in turn may reduce their liability and minimise adverse publicity in the future. Second, as signals to potential access to funding from overseas sources. In the United States, accreditation schemes such as the Joint Commission on Accreditation of Healthcare Organisations are routes to US Medicare participation and this approach could conceivably be broadened to international travel and provider choice. Third, attracting business, given potential customers for medical tourism may scrutinise whether or not a hospital has accreditation, and hospitals can advertise their accredited status (Green 2009).

Potential problems with accreditation for the medical-tourism industry include that the commercial needs and aspirations of the accreditation schemes may become ends in themselves. Indeed, many accreditation schemes operating internationally are private companies or corporations. Less well-off countries that are often heavily involved in medical tourism may have no access to the accreditation process, or engaging in accreditation may lead to financial hardship. There may be a considerable amount of marketing 'hype' and manipulation of the accreditation market. Further, accreditation processes may not tackle ethically contentious areas, such as organ trafficking, payment issues around organ and tissue donation, selective gender abortion, surrogate pregnancy, unnecessary operations and use of unproven therapies.

Currently, there is no universal 'official agency/group', such as the World Health Organization or World Tourism Organization. engaged in either the delivery of accreditation, the co-ordination of delivery of accreditation or licensing or studying the existing schemes that deliver accreditation. Mandatory accreditation may appeal to governments and commercial health-care purchasers such as third-party payers (e.g. insurance companies and occupational health-care providers). Accreditation has most often been used as a marketing tool by wealthier provider hospitals, medical tourism facilitators and the governments of provider countries seeking to grow their share of the medical-tourism business (see the example of Brazil in Box 2.2).

Box 2.2 **Plastic surgery in Brazil**

The Brazilian medical-tourism market is largely an import market centred on cosmetic surgery (Ramírez de Arellano 2007; Edmonds 2011) with a reported 50,000 visitors every year (Brazilian Institute of Tourism 2005). While cost is a key motivation for medical travel to Brazil – a procedure is likely to cost around 50 per cent of what it would in the United States – it is clearly not the sole driver. Writers have identified the patient-centred nature of care in Brazil, the willingness to offer procedures not available elsewhere and the reputation for quality are key pull-factors (Barron 2008; Edmonds 2011). This perceived high level of quality is undoubtedly aided by the proportion of accredited clinics (more facilities accredited than any country other than the United States) and partnerships with organisations such as the International Hospital Corporation, which is based in the United States (Herrick 2007; International Hospital Corporation 2011; JCI 2011).

Regulating global medical tourism?

Within the market for medical tourism, considerations of quality and risk are important. There is clearly the potential for supplier-induced demand, whereby the supplier determines the need for the service as well as being funded for delivering the service. This may include unnecessary or multiple treatments being offered to patients. There are also treatments where there are more likely to be associated psychological factors than with the broader population – such as those seeking cosmetic surgery who may have associated conditions such as body dysmorphic disorder (Phillips and Crino 2001; Grossbart and Sarwer 2003). That said, we know relatively little about the development of European and international industries and markets trading in medical tourism.

Difficult ethical questions are raised by medical tourism. Should a patient's local health-care system take on the responsibility and foot the bill for post-operative care including treatment for complications and side effects for patients returning from overseas private surgery? Some discussions in the United States, United Kingdom and Australia have all pointed towards costs being imposed on publicly funded health systems and the implications for local population health (e.g. exacerbating waiting lists even further) (Cheung and Wilson 2007; Jeevan and Armstrong 2008; Barrowman *et al.* 2010). However, the scale and extent of adverse complications is not clear.

Given commercialisation and commodification, the range of treatments knows few limits. Human stem-cell therapies are a controversial procedure and scientifically are of unproven value, especially as beauty therapies. Within the medical tourism field there are examples of countries offering stem-cell therapies targeted at specific conditions including Parkinson's, stroke and brain infections. Here there are no clinical trials to assess efficacy and effectiveness (Murdoch and Scott 2010).

A major policy issue for governments therefore is whether and how best to safeguard medical tourists abroad and to ensure redress when they return. One solution is to do nothing beyond a warning of *caveat emptor* – buyers beware! If governmental agencies do see a responsibility, possible interventions (both national and transnational) range from those that provide more information (although by whom and at what points is not clear) to those that restrict choice of potential consumers (either directly prohibited or through discouragement) to attempts to restrict supply (whether approving or licensing provider or intermediaries). There are also interventions that may aim to offer consumer protection around poor-quality treatments which could involve encouraging independent holistic accreditation by recognised schemes, advising that clinicians responsible for delivering services take out personal medical indemnity which would compensate their patients in the event of problems occurring as a consequence of their seeking health care, or requiring medical tourists to take out insurance coverage (Cohen 2010). Source health systems may attempt to shift risk onto individual medical tourists, for example, with disclaimers to prevent medical tourists from seeking to rectify poor outcomes at cost to the public purse.

If patients experience poor-quality treatment which results in adverse outcomes and wish to bring a civil or criminal case, they face a potential legal minefield. A combination of services may contribute towards the medical-tourist experience (see Figure 2.2) including product advertising, initial Internet consultation, a brokerage service, surgery itself and various mixes therein. With regards to advertising and promotional material, there are typically national and European restrictions of what can be advertised, but given the role of the Internet in promoting medical tourism this may be difficult to regulate.

In the United Kingdom, signed informed consent prior to an elective procedure is considered best practice and ensuring that patients are fully informed as to the benefits and adverse effects of a procedure or treatment they are being advised to undergo is a standard requirement, and patients also have the opportunity to ask questions and seek answers (GMC 2008). This may not be available every time in the medical-tourism setting, and it is possible that medical tourists may come to regret this if there are failings in professional or clinical practice (Pennings 2004, 2007; Barclay 2009; Jeevan *et al.* 2011). How patient information flows across national boundaries and the safeguarding of IT information by professionals are further questions for the regulation of the medical-tourism industry.

There are complexities regarding who can be subject to legal proceedings, the jurisdiction of hearing any case and the country's law that should govern any case (Svantesson 2008; Vick 2010). There are unanswered questions about who to sue and whether medical tourists dissatisfied with their care should be able sue the individual surgeon, the clinical team, the hospital or even the broker that may have arranged the treatment. Medical tourists may be encouraged to sign legal disclaimers prior to receiving treatment that restrict where any subsequent case will be held, the law that will cover it and include further liability limitation or exclusion clauses.

Travelling to an overseas country to pursue a legal case involves potential language and cultural difficulties of courtroom understanding. A favourable judgement handed down in an overseas jurisdiction may be difficult to enforce or any financial award may be limited – one reason U.S. health care is so expensive is the size of malpractice premiums. Beyond the liability of brokers, surgeons and clinics, what are potential liability issues for Health Maintenance Organisations that decide to include overseas providers within their suite of referrals? Under such circumstances, should they be expected to credential physicians, and are they likely to be subject to vicarious liability?

Conclusion

Medical tourism is an emerging form of health trade with a range of supply and demand drivers influencing the emerging markets and treatment choices. At the centre lie the prospective medical traveller and his or her decision to seek treatment overseas. The potential benefits that accrue – choice, price and improved outcomes and quality of life – must be balanced against the risks of surgical treatment. As with all health care, there are quality and safety concerns surrounding the provision of treatments to medical tourists. As an emerging field of academic study, we do not yet know enough about core concerns of quality, safety and risk and how problems might be best addressed. As the field continues to develop, both primary research and its implications for policy and practice must make contributions to the ongoing debate.

References

Barclay, E. (2009) 'Stem-cell experts raise concerns about medical tourism', *The Lancet*, 373: 883–884.

Barron, N.C. (2008) 'Seeking beauty, cutting costs: why so many Americans go under the knife abroad', *Print Journalism (M.A)*, University of Southern California.

Barrowman, R.A., Grubor, D. and Chandu, A. (2010) 'Dental implant tourism', Australian Dental Journal, 55: 441–445.

Bertinato, L., Busse, R., Fahy, N., Legido-Quigley, H., McKee, M., Palm, W., Passarani, I. and Ronfini, F. (2005) *Cross-border Health Care in Europe*. Copenhagen: WHO.

Birch, D.W., Vu, L., Karmali, S., Stoklossa, C.J. and Sharma, A.M. (2010) 'Medical tourism in bariatric surgery', *The American Journal of Surgery*, 199: 604–608.

Boschert, S. (2007) Treating 'transplant tourists' after the fact. Internal Medicine News. [Online]. Available at: http://www.entrepreneur.com/tradejournals/article/print/178448629.html (accessed 15 June 2007).

Brazilian Institute of Tourism (EMBRATUR) (2005) *Annual Abstract of Statistics*. Brasília: EMBRATUR.

Burge, P., Devlin, N., Appleby, J., Rohr, C. and Grant, J. (2004) 'Do patients always prefer quicker treatment?: a discrete choice analysis of patients' stated preferences in the London Patient Choice Project', *Applied Health Economics and Health Policy*, 3: 183–194.

Canales, M.T., Kasiske, B.L. and Rosenberg, M.E. (2006) 'Transplant tourism: outcomes of United States residents who undergo kidney transplantation overseas', *Transplantation*, 82: 1658–1661.

Carrera, P. and Bridges, J.F.P. (2006) 'Globalization and healthcare: understanding health and medical tourism', *Expert Review of Pharmacoeconomics and Outcomes Research*, 6: 447–454.

Carrera, P. and Lunt, N. (2010) 'A European perspective on medical tourism: the need for a knowledge base', *International Journal of Health Services*, 40: 469–484.

Chee, H.L. (2007) Medical tourism in Malaysia: international movement of healthcare consumers and the commodification of healthcare. *ARI Working Paper*, 83. [Online]. Available at: http://www.ari.nus.edu.sg/docs/wps/wps07_083.pdf

Cheung, I.K. and Wilson, A. (2007) 'Arthroplasty tourism', *Medical Journal of Australia*, 187: 666–667.

Cohen, I.G. (2010) 'Protecting patients with passports: medical tourism and the patient protective-argument', *Iowa Law Review*, 95: 1467–1567.

Cormany, D. and Baloglu, S. (2010) 'Medical travel facilitator websites: an exploratory study of web page contents and services offered to the prospective medical tourist', *Tourism Management*, 32(4): 709–716.

Crooks, V., Kingsbury, P., Snyder, J. and Johnston, R. (2010) 'What is known about the patient's experience of medical tourism? A scoping review', *BMC Health Services Research*, 10: 266.

Davis, P., Lay-Yee, R., Briant, R; Schug, S; Scott, A., Johnson, S. and Bingley, W. (2003) 'Adverse events in New Zealand public hospitals', in E. Coiera, S. Chu, and C. Simpson (eds) HIC 2003 RACGP12CC: Proceedings. Brunswick East, Victoria: Health Informatics Society of Australia (HISA); Royal Australian College of General Practitioners.

Edmonds, A. (2011) 'Almost invisible scars': medical tourism to Brazil. *Signs: Journal of Women in Culture and Society*, 36: 297–302.

Ehrbeck, T., Guevara, C. and Mango, P.D. (2008) 'Mapping the market for medical travel', *The McKinsey Quarterly* [Online]. Available at: https://www.mckinseyquarterly.com/Mapping_the_market_for_travel_2134 (accessed 9 April 2012).

Glinos, I.A., Baeten, R. and Boffin, N. (2006) 'Cross-border contracted care in Belgian hospitals', in M. Rosenmöller, R. Baeten and M. McKee (eds) Patient Mobility in the European Union: Learning from Experience. Denmark: European Observatory on Health Systems and Policies.

Glinos, I.A., Baeten, R., Helble, M. and Maarse, H. (2010a) 'A typology of cross-border patient mobility', *Health & Place*, 16: 1145–1155.

Glinos, I.A., Baeten, R. and Maarse, H. (2010b) 'Purchasing health services abroad: practices of cross-border contracting and patient mobility in six European countries', *Health Policy*, 95: 103–112.

GMC (2008) *Consent: Patients and Doctors Making Decisions Together*. London: General Medical Council.

Green, S.T. (2008) 'Medical tourism – a potential growth factor in infection medicine and public health', *The Journal of Infection*, 57: 429.

Green, S.T. (2009) Quality control and accreditation of health service providers and facilities. Paper prepared for World Health Organization 'Workshop on the movement of patients across international borders – emerging challenges and opportunities for health care systems', Kobe, Japan, 24–25 February.

Grossbart, T.A. and Sarwer, D.B. (2003) 'Psychosocial issues and their relevance to the cosmetic surgery patient', *Seminars in Cutaneous Medicine and Surgery*, 22: 136–147.

Hall, C.M. (2011) 'Health and medical tourism: kill or cure for global public health?' *Tourism Review*, 66(1/2): 4–15.

Hall, C.M. and James, M. (2011) 'Medical tourism: emerging biosecurity and nosocomial issues', *Tourism Review*, 66(1/2): 118–126.

Herrick, D.M. (2007) *Medical Tourism: Global Competition in Health Care, NCPA Policy Reports*. Dallas, TX: National Center for Policy Analysis.

Hurwitz, B. and Sheikh, A. (2009) *Health Care Errors and Patient Safety*. Chichester: Wiley-Blackwell.

Institute of Medicine (2001) Crossing the Quality Chasm: A New Health System for the 21st Century, Committee on Quality of Health Care in America, Institute of Medicine, Washington, DC: National Academy Press

International Hospital Corporation (2011) VITA Hospitals. [Online]. Available at: http://www.internationalhospital.com (accessed 1 June 2011).

JCI (2011) *JCI Accredited Organizations*. Joint Commission International. [Online]. Available at: http://www.jointcommissioninternational.org/JCI-Accredited-Organizations (accessed 14 March 2011).

Jeevan, R. and Armstrong, A. (2008) 'Cosmetic tourism and the burden on the NHS', *Journal of Plastic, Reconstructive & Aesthetic Surgery*, 61: 1423–1424.

Jeevan, R., Birch, J. and Armstrong, A.P. (2011) 'Travelling abroad for aesthetic surgery: informing healthcare practitioners and providers while improving patient safety', *Journal of Plastic, Reconstructive & Aesthetic Surgery*, 64: 143–147.

Legido-Quigley, H., McKee, M., Nolte, M. and Glinos, I.A. (2008) *Assuring the Quality of Health Care in the Europe Union: A Case for Action*. Denmark: European Observatory on Health Systems and Policies.

Lowson, K., West, P., Chaplin, S. and O'Reilly, J. (2002) Evaluation of Patients Travelling Overseas: Final Report. York: York Health Economics Consortium.

Lunt, N. (2006) 'Global social policy', in T. Fitzpatrick, M. Manning, J. Midgely and G. Pascale (eds) *International Encyclopaedia of Social Policy*. London: Routledge.

Lunt, N. (2008) Boats, planes and trains: British migration, mobility and transnational experience. *Migration Letters*, 5: 151–165.

Lunt, N. and Carrera, P. (2010) 'Medical tourism: assessing the evidence on treatment abroad', *Maturitas*, 66: 27–32.

Lunt, N. and Carrera, P. (2011) 'Advice for prospective medical tourists: systematic review of consumer sites. *Tourism Review*, 66: 57–67.

Lunt, N., Hardey, M. and Mannion, R. (2010) 'Nip, tuck and click: medical tourism and the emergence of web-based health information', *The Open Medical Informatics Journal*, 4: 1–11.

MacReady, N. (2007) 'Developing countries court medical tourists', *The Lancet*, 369: 1849–1850.

Milosevic, A. (2009) 'Dental tourism—a global issue?' *Journal of Esthetic and Restorative Dentistry*, 21: 289–291.

Murdoch, C.E. and Scott, C.T. (2010) 'Stem cell tourism and the power of hope', *The American Journal of Bioethics*, 10(5): 16–23.

Newman, M.I., Camberos, A.E. and Ascherman, J. (2005) '*Mycobacteria abscessus* outbreak in US patients linked to offshore surgicenter'. *Annals of Plastic Surgery*, 55: 107–110.

Pennings, G. (2004) 'Legal harmonization and reproductive tourism in Europe', *Human Reproduction*, 19: 2689–2694.

Pennings, G. (2007) 'Ethics without boundaries: medical tourism', In R.E. Ashcroft, A. Dawson and J.R. McMillan (eds) *Principles of Health Care Ethics*. Chichester: John Wiley & Sons.

Phillips, K.A and Crino, R.D. (2001) 'Body dysmorphic disorder', *Current Opinion in Psychiatry*, 12: 113–118.

Ramírez de Arellano, A.B. (2007) 'Patients without borders: the emergence of medical tourism', *International Journal of Health Services*, 37: 193–198.

Reisman, D. (2010) *Health Tourism: Social Welfare through International Trade*. Cheltenham: Edward Elgar.

Rosenmöller, M., McKee, M. and Baeten, R. (eds.) (2006) *Patient Mobility in the European Union: Learning from Experience*, Denmark. European Observatory on Health Systems and Policies.

Sapir, A. and Winter, C. (1994) *Service Trade*. Brussels: Universite Libre de Bruxelles.

Sari, A.B.-A., Sheldon, T.A., Cracknell, A. and Turnbull, A. (2007) 'Sensitivity of routine system for reporting patient safety incidents in an NHS hospital: retrospective patient case note review', *British Medical Journal*, 334: 79.

Smith, R.D., Lee, K. and Drager, N. (2009) 'Trade and health: an agenda for action', *Lancet*, 373(9665): 768–773.

Svantesson, D.J.B. (2008) 'From the airport to the surgery to the courtroom – private international law and medical tourism', *Commonwealth Law Bulletin*, 34, 265–276.

Terry, N.P. (2007) 'Under-regulated health care phenomena in a flat world: medical tourism and outsourcing', *Western New England Law Review*, 29: 421.

Vick, L. (2010) 'Medical tourism: legal issues', in *Destination Health Medical Tourism Conference*. Olympia, London: Michelmores Solicitors.

Vincent, C., Neale, G. and Woloshynowych, M. (2001) 'Adverse events in British hospitals: preliminary retrospective record review', *British Medical Journal*, 322: 517–519

Weingart, S.N., Wilson, R.M., Gibberd, R.W. and Harrison, B. (2000) 'Epidemiology of medical error', *British Medical Journal*, 320: 774–777

Whittaker, A. (2008) 'Pleasure and pain: medical travel in Asia', Global Public Health: An International Journal for Research, Policy and Practice, 3: 271–290.

Zahir, K. (2001) *Clinical Governance in the UK NHS*. London: Department for International Development Health Resource Centre.

3 The four modes of medical tourism

Economic, social and institutional impediments

Lydia L. Gan

Introduction

Rising health-care costs, ageing of baby boomers, and loss of employer-based insurance coverage by consumers in advanced economies all have one thing in common: they are catalysts to the rising popularity of travelling outside the country's border for medical care, commonly known as 'medical tourism' or 'medical outsourcing' (see Chapter 1; see also Hall 2011). Some view this as a negative trend, posing a threat to the domestic health-care providers by capturing significant market share for particular medical procedures, even though a study found it has negligible impact on the US health-care industry, responsible for only less than 2 per cent of non-cosmetic health-care expenditure (Milstein and Smith, 2006). However, Keckley and Underwood (2008, 2009) projected that the medical tourism industry in the United States would grow from three-quarter million travellers in 2007 to 1.6 million by 2012 and to 10 million by 2017 with the corresponding spending doubling from a projected annual US$15 billion in 2012 to US$30 billion per year by 2017 (Keckley and Underwood 2008). It is therefore not surprising that some see the opportunity to take advantage of the globalisation of health care.

The four transactional modes of medical tourism

The development and growth of medical tourism is rapidly changing the model in which consumers and producers of the global health-care market interact with each other. The four transactional modes of medical tourism (Gan and Frederick, 2011a) (see Figure 3.1) are briefly described as follows:

Mode 1. Medical tourism arranged by domestic consumers with foreign health-care providers.

Mode 2. Medical tourism arranged by domestic medical tourism facilitators (MTFs).

Mode 3. Medical tourism induced and arranged by domestic health insurers or employers.

Mode 4. Medical tourism (formally) referred and arranged by domestic health-care providers.

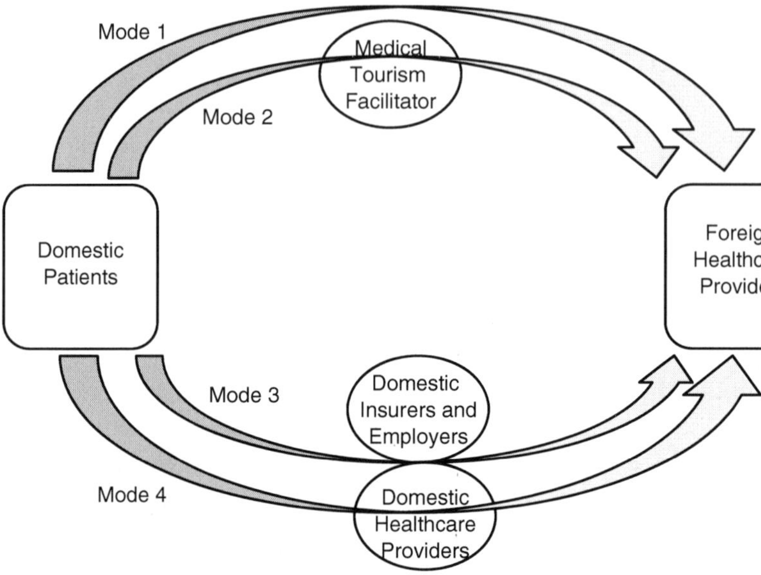

Figure 3.1 Four transactional modes of medical tourism.

These patterns as well as their economic, social and institutional aspects of impediments faced by players in each mode will be described and analysed, followed by a brief discussion on constraints faced by destination economies and the conclusion.

Mode 1: Medical tourism arranged by domestic consumers with foreign health-care providers

This is the simplest and earliest mode of medical tourism. Consumers who use this mode engage in medical tourism directly with foreign health-care providers. The consumers are typically somewhat familiar with foreign hospitals and would arrange their travel and medical procedures either on their own or through friends and families who reside in some of these destination countries. They usually contact the international patient centres of their pre-selected hospital directly or through the marketing offices of the hospital located in developed nations. The consumers typically consist of diasporic groups and consumers who have prior experience with medical travel, who are likely to be underinsured and uninsured from developed nations. They are most likely to seek maintenance or preventive treatment such as routine physical examination and dental procedures, but they also seek elective treatments popularly sought by medical tourists such as cardiovascular, orthopaedic, bariatric and cosmetic surgeries.

Economic impediment

One of the major economic impediments faced by consumers in this mode is coming up with sufficient financial means to cover both treatment and travel expenses, especially among the underinsured (e.g. those with pre-existing conditions) and the uninsured. It is not uncommon for the American uninsured to sell their homes so they can afford a coronary artery bypass graft (CABG) that could cost up to US$200,000 in the United States. For the insured, they are concerned about the portability of insurance coverage across borders and whether they will be reimbursed when they return home. There are hosts of literature reviews that single out significant cost savings (typically 70–90 per cent) as one of the major motivating forces that influence potential consumers to travel (Demicco and Cetron, 2006; Mattoo and Rathindran, 2006; American Medical Association 2007). As a growing number of third-party sponsors such as employers and insurers begin to adopt medical tourism, financial inducements in the form of cash incentives and bonuses, paid leaves, waiver of deductibles and co-payments would simply be another reason to attract potential consumers to travel abroad for treatment. However, since quality and continuity of care are important and legitimate concerns for most potential consumers (American Medical Association 2007; Vitalis and Milton 2009), some argued that the difficulties of having the domestic health-care system deal with complications, side effects, and post-operative care could be so large that they outweigh the cost savings from medical tourism. For that matter, it pays for consumers in this mode to do their pre-trip research on the prospective physicians and hospitals. Some foreign hospitals and more established MTFs such as Medvoy and Global Surgery Network do offer 'complication' insurance to consumers to ensure their peace of mind. Similarly, consumers in this mode would want to ensure the destination country has a sound legal system in cases of medical negligence or malpractice. If something goes wrong, the potential litigation costs could be so high that they may offset the cost savings in the first place.

Social impediments

Aspects of the geo-political climate, such as social and political instability of a country can certainly impede potential consumers from travelling to a particular country (Dhariwal 2005; Bookman and Bookman 2007). Prospective tourists are also likely to stay away from countries that are prone to natural disasters (Fernandez *et al.* 2002; Huan *et al.* 2004) and epidemics (Tata 2007). Because potential consumers may face cultural and language barriers when they travel, social and cultural compatibility (Seddighi *et al.* 2001; Lee and Davis, 2004) of a country are deemed important when selecting a destination country. The familiarity of one's domestic environment in terms of medical needs and quality of care can also be a psychological hindrance (Carrera and Bridges 2006).

The hassle of travel and travel risk are additional aspects of impediment for medical tourists. The hassle of travel includes airline and hotel reservations, visa application, leave application, airport transiting, and even packing for the trip, which have high opportunity costs on the part of travellers. Travel risk means taking extra precautionary safety measures when travelling outside the country. When taking a long flight, dehydration and immobility may cause patients to suffer from deep-vein thrombosis (Carabello 2008) and pulmonary emboli.

Institutional impediments

There are also social and institutional impediments faced by consumers, which may include ethical and moral issues that revolved around medical complications (Jones and McCullough 2007; Birch *et al.* 2010). The availability of alternative treatments such as stem cell therapy, organ transplantation, surrogate pregnancy, late-term abortion and euthanasia may encourage some to travel to seek such treatments but it may also deter some from travelling to countries that uphold these bioethical legislations. Additionally, the absence of HIPAA (*Health Insurance Portability and Accountability Act*) compliance by the foreign hospitals and consequently the lack of treatment confidentiality may also deter consumers who seek 'highly sensitive' treatments (e.g. drug rehabilitation, plastic surgery, sex change) to travel abroad for treatment. Unfortunately, despite the privacy of medical records protected under HIPAA, courts and insurance companies are among those who can still access these records if required. As mentioned, another major impediment regards whether the legal system in a destination country is in place for medical malpractice and the redress of grievances if they are needed.

Mode 2 Medical tourism arranged by domestic MTFs

This mode represents consumers who use the service of a middleman known as an MTF. Consumers in this mode rely completely on the expertise of the MTF to locate suitable foreign hospitals, arrange treatment, air transportation and lodging during recuperation. A typical consumer in this mode is best described as a middle-aged, middle-income earner, underinsured or uninsured, and may not have prior experience with medical travel. Consumers in this mode tend to seek popular elective treatments sought by medical travellers (e.g. CABG, knee or hip-replacement, gastric bypass, dental surgeries), and cosmetic or plastic surgeries.

Economic impediments

Due to insufficient knowledge, lack of prior experience, and information overloading from the Internet, potential consumers in this mode are more likely to face asymmetric information and experience a higher search cost than consumers in mode 1. While most have a specific treatment in mind, decisions concerning which country and hospital to choose can be daunting, as can quality and cost comparison across hospitals or countries. A potential consumer without prior experience who attempts to communicate directly with a foreign physician or hospital is likely to experience an intensive search on the hospitals' websites, possibly followed by several email exchanges or even international phone calls.

Language and communication are likely to add to another layer of complexities. In order to overcome asymmetric information and high search cost, consumers in this mode engage in the service of an MTF.

Although hiring an MTF will add another layer of cost to medical tourism, most would consider it marginal given the expected benefits. Some MTFs bundle their services and charge a fixed price, while others unbundle their services à la carte and charge each 'add-on' service accordingly. The 'all-inclusive' pricing usually covers medical costs (including hospitalisation, physician fees, medicine, nursing care and therapy outside the hospital), travel costs (mainly airfares) and hotel expenses. Some charge a flat concierge fee of approximately US$200 plus the treatment costs, and some charge a commission as a percentage of the cost of services they arrange, while others simply receive finder's fees directly from the foreign hospitals. A wise consumer should find out what each 'package' would comprise before committing to the service of an MTF.

Institutional impediments

The MTF industry in the United States is currently unregulated and there is a lack of standardisation. Although there has been an effort by the Medical Tourism Association, an industry self-regulated organisation, to certify MTFs, only five are successfully certified at the time of writing (Medical Tourism Association 2011). The industry is largely characterised by wide differentiation of packaged products and services. Gan and Frederick (2011a) found three emphases among MTFs in the United States: (1) physician-focused, (2) travel-agent focused and (3) country-selection focused. While having a physician on staff can add credibility to the service of an MTF, they also noted a high exit rate among these companies, so Internet-exposed MTFs are not necessarily firms consumers can rely on. Although it is in the best interest of MTFs to network with foreign health-care providers or even partner with third-party sponsors, prudent MTFs should conduct their own research concerning the foreign health-care providers prior to partnership. The foreign hospitals whom the MTFs network with are often, though not always, noted for quality of care (e.g. successful surgical outcomes, high nurse–patient ratio) (Demicco and Cetron 2006), recognised accreditation such as Joint Commission International (JCI) (Gan and Frederick 2011a, 2011b), highly recognised certification of their health professionals (Mattoo and Rathindran 2006) and advanced medical technology and equipment (Demicco and Cetron 2006). Some foreign hospitals have their own international patient centres or marketing offices in developed nations which compete directly with MTFs. As such, MTFs should differentiate their product and services to attract consumers.

Once again, legal liability is of major concern to MTFs regarding their responsibility as a middleman. An MTF is likely to use a disclaimer disclaiming its liability for any wrongdoing related to the referral process or for any care given by foreign health-care provides. Whether that disclaimer is upheld is likely to be determined by the individual state (American Medical Association 2007). A liability product known as MedTour Pro has been made available to both MTFs and third-party payers since 2008 – it covers damages caused by any actual or alleged negligent act, error or omission while arranging or providing medical tourism. The maximum limits are US$1 million with a minimum premium of US$2,225 (Insurance Journal 2008).

Mode 3 Medical tourism induced and arranged by domestic health insurers or employers

Consumers in this mode are induced to travel abroad for treatment by the third-party sponsors who are required to meet their ERISA (*Employee Retirement Income Security Act*) fiduciary duty when managing the group plans. As medical tourism becomes widely recognised, and in an effort to contain cost, some third-party payers have begun to provide incentives for covered employees to seek medical care abroad. Similarly, some managed-care health plans have included foreign hospitals on their lists of approved providers as a way to reduce costs. Consumers in this mode are likely to be middle income, middle aged and possibly moderately educated and are likely to seek popular elective treatments (excluding cosmetic surgeries) mentioned earlier that are covered by their health plans.

Economic impediments

Third-party payers have been suffering from health-care liabilities and regulations that continue to raise their costs. Recent policies threaten to put more pressure on employers by requiring them to provide health-care benefits for their employees, thereby imposing additional costs. Examples are Massachusetts' universal health plan and San Francisco's Health Access Program (Ernst 2006). Insurance companies such as Anthem Wellpoint, Blue Cross Blue Shield of South Carolina, Blue Shield and Health Net and United Group Programs, Inc. have already come up with programmes to reimburse treatments performed outside the United States. It was reported that sending a patient to Thailand for a heart bypass operation would save the employers or the insurers approximately US$60,000–US$70,000 (Ernst 2006). Pro-medical tourism regulation such as West Virginia House Bill 4359 (West Virginia House of Delegates 2006) and Colorado House Bills 1143 (Colorado House of Representatives 2007), if they had passed, would have added another economic incentive for the state employees to participate in medical travel.

Before endorsing medical tourism, third-party sponsors should weigh the pros and cons of doing so. Other than the substantial cost savings for the companies, employers will also face a rising absenteeism cost of employees, which may offset the savings. Potential employers and health insurers would need to work out the logistics of the coverage such as the types of treatment to be covered and the entire benefits package. These benefits would typically include waivers for deductibles and co-payments, bonuses and rebates, paid leave and airfares for the employee and a companion. They may even include travel and 'complications' insurance as parts of the package or as riders. They would want to find out whether the cash incentives they offer to their employees are considered as parts of health-care costs and thus non-taxable. Satori World Medical, an MTF, has developed a plan for insured workers with high deductibles but no co-payment and the employer would share a portion of the savings by putting it in a tax-free health saving account, which allows the employees to spend on other health-care needs (Rhea 2009). Furthermore, third-party sponsors would face the complexity of dealing with an international billing system which can include the conversion of foreign exchanges, and perhaps learning a different measurement standard such as the metric system. In order to come up with a unique product or incentive package, the third-party sponsors may wish to add in their budget the hiring and outsourcing of new expertise required, for instance, legal service, risk management, software solutions, or even partner with an established MTF. Presumably, the higher the incentives offered, the higher the inherent legal risks assumed by the third-party sponsors (Marlowe and Sullivan 2007).

Institutional impediments

One of the impediments faced by third-party sponsors in the United States is whether an ERISA health plan can outsource its medical service needs to health-care providers outside the country. For those who have resolved this issue, quality of care and patient safety would no doubt rank high among their fiduciary responsibilities. While quality of care covers quality assurance, control procedures, clinical practice and facility operation (García-Altés 2005), patient safety often involves travel risk and surgical risk. It is not easy to compare the quality between the domestic hospitals and international hospitals. For one thing, unlike hospitals in countries like Singapore and other destination countries, the hospitals in the United States do not report surgical outcomes or participate in international performance measurement systems (Milstein and Smith 2006). Even if treatment outcomes are readily available in these countries, some argue that there may be substantial variations across JCI-accredited foreign hospitals, just as mortality and complication rates can vary across accredited hospitals in the same city in the United States (Marlowe and Sullivan 2007). The JCI and the World Health Organization (WHO) jointly developed international standards for patient safety in 2005 (WHO, 2005). Other than JCI, accreditation standards recognised outside the United States are International Society for Quality and Safety in Healthcare (IsQua), Trent Accreditation Scheme (United Kingdom), the Accreditation Canada International (ACI) and Australian Council on Healthcare Standards (ACHS). Even so, there is currently no regulation of health insurance that covers medical tourism, and some argue that the Congress should encourage international accrediting procedures for destination hospitals that market medical tourism to American consumers (Burkett 2007).

In addition, the third-party sponsors would want to ensure that the foreign hospitals comply with information privacy policies such as the one required by HIPAA in the United States. The purpose of the Act is to protect patient information and restrict the use and the sharing of information. Failure to follow the regulation can result in civil penalties of US$100 per case (up to US$25,000 per year). Criminal penalties may also be imposed on someone who 'knowingly obtains and discloses individual identifiable health information' (Forgione and Smith 2007).

Some potential consumers are motivated to go abroad for medical procedures that are still under clinical trials in their home countries. For instance, hip resurfacing is a common procedure in Asia and Europe but is unavailable in the United States. Some believe hip resurfacing, a simpler medical procedure, can replace approximately 20 per cent of hip-replacement surgeries (Fisher 2006). However, due to the cumbersome approval process by the Food and Drug Administration (FDA), only a selected few hospitals in the United States are participating in clinical trials. In the case of Duke Medical Center, the demand for this procedure has far exceeded its supply by five times. Most insurance companies are unwilling to cover the procedure due to its 'experimental' state in the United States and the fact that it can cost up to approximately US$40,000.

Third-party sponsors may also consider including foreign hospitals in their network of health-care providers directly or through the service of a MTF. In order to contain health-care cost and control the quality, they may prefer to establish a long-term relationship with a selected few foreign health-care providers to whom they can channel their covered employees or subscribers. Examples of such partnerships are Hannaford Brothers (insured by Aetna) with Parkway group of hospitals in Singapore and Serigraph (insured by Wellpoint) with Apollo hospitals in India. In order to limit any potential fiduciary liability, they may wish to conduct their own research concerning the prospective hospitals, for instance, if they are accredited and if their physicians and staff have the proper credentials and outcomes data. More prudent third-party sponsors may even visit the facilities and talk to the staff before including them in their preferred provider network.

Just as with patient safety and quality of care, third-party sponsors are equally concerned with their legal responsibility for any malpractice abroad. Before endorsing medical tourism, they would want to be assured of any existing regulatory framework in the destination countries to deal with malpractice liability as well as to be informed of the expected rewards sum.

One reason that explains the significant cost difference between some of these destination countries and the United States is the difference in malpractice insurance premiums. For instance, in the United States, a specialist would pay an annual premium of up to US$150,000 for medical malpractice insurance, whereas it only cost US$5,000 annually for the average physician in Thailand (Roth 2006). Similarly, a surgeon in India would pay only 4 per cent of what a practicing surgeon in New York would pay (Lancaster 2004). The lower insurance premiums paid by physicians in these countries translate into lower awards caused by malpractice damages. For instance, in 2007, the average malpractice award payout was US$308,000–US$1,000,000 in the United States as compared to US$100,000, the largest medical malpractice award in Thailand during the same period (Roth 2006). The lower sum in damages is due mainly to the fact that the laws in Asia, including Thailand, do not account for pain and suffering. Another reason for the substantial cost savings in these countries is the lack of involvement in third-party payments. Most medical tourists who travel to these countries pay cash for treatment without the involvement of insurance and their related administrative and processing fees, which can be as high as 10 per cent in the United States (Weisser and Gengler 2006). Third-party sponsors who are contemplating the endorsement of medical tourism should take all these circumstances into consideration when offering an incentive package to their employees. Moreover, employers may face opposition from unions for participation in medical tourism (McLean 2007), as in the case of Blue Ridge Paper, Inc. in North Carolina. In order to save potential costs of US$80,000 for treatment in the United States, the company offered to pay for treatment and airfares expenses plus US$10,000 cash to one of its union employee to travel to India for gallbladder removal and rotator-cuff surgeries. The union served an injunction and forced the company to abandon their plan.

Mode 4 Medical tourism (formally) referred and arranged by domestic health-care providers

Consumers in this mode experience the exchange of international medical care, formally referred and arranged by domestic health-care providers. This is an extension of the common practice of hospitals outsourcing medical services internationally. A good many JCI-accredited foreign hospitals participating in medical tourism are actually owned and managed by, or are affiliated with, prestigious US hospitals such as Harvard Medical International or John Hopkins International. Some US health-care providers with international presence are already sharing their management protocols with foreign hospitals (H and HN 2004). For instance, Johns Hopkins has developed consulting and referral relationships with their affiliated hospitals in India and Singapore. These arrangements generate revenues through fees and often result in patient referrals.

Economic–social–institutional impediments

Currently there is no law that prevents international medical travel, and American Medical Association (AMA) (2008), American College of Surgeons (ACS) (2009), and American Dental Association (ADA) (2009) have all issued statements recognising the patient's rights to choose his or her own physicians and hospitals. All three associations emphasise the importance of post-care and their related financial responsibilities. ACS specifically supports the view that third-party payers should be responsible for the coordination and reimbursement of post-care in the United States, including the management of complications, readmission, rehabilitation and long-term care.

Although some may highlight greater consumer sovereignty as one of the political benefits (Burkett 2007), the outflow of patients to foreign countries, nevertheless represents a substantial loss of revenues for the domestic health care professions and eventually the domestic health-care systems. This may result in resistance by US health-care professionals, for instance, by refusing to participate in a Preferred Provider Network that includes foreign providers or by boycotting insurers that cover foreign treatment (thereby denying services to their subscribers). The trend may also result in some innovative structural change such as the emergence of hospitals that offer discounted bundled care for certain procedures by specialising in them, and doing them in high quality and high volumes (Rhea 2009). A good example is Galichia Heart Hospital in Wichita, Kansas, which offers a flat fee of US$10,000 for CABG without complication (Atwater 2008) – a price comparable with those offered by popular destination countries. The intention is to keep patients and eventually the health-care revenues within the domestic health-care system.

Furthermore, the domestic health-care providers are often involved in pre-care and post-care directly or indirectly. Patients may be given the option of undergoing a preliminary evaluation or care planning as well as follow-up care with the domestic health-care providers after they have returned home. In some cases, ethical and moral issues may arise, first as a result of medical complications due to surgery performed by physicians from foreign countries, and secondly by imposing an additional responsibility of the domestic doctors to treat these ill returning patients (Jones and McCullough 2007; Birch *et al.* 2010). This could place constraints on the domestic health-care system. For instance, in the United Kingdom, treating complications resulting from plastic surgery performed by doctors outside the country increased the waiting time in the National Health Service (NHS) for treatment for other more acute and urgent procedures such as oncology and trauma (Jeevan and Armstrong 2008).

The emergence of medical tourism may put pressure on US health-care providers to reduce prices and may force greater transparency in pricing and surgical outcomes, and even an upgrade to more efficient health-care delivery methods in the domestic health-care system. The pressure to lower the price may result in longer waiting lines and lower quality given (due to less time spent) by some domestic health-care providers in order to compete. It may even reduce the number of potential doctors entering the profession or even affect patient care.

From an institutional perspective, proponents of medical tourism say regulation would help ensure access to quality care for Americans by maintaining a health-care alternative in low-cost international hospitals, and to reduce some of the strain on public resources for the uninsured as some procedures become more affordable (Burkett 2007). From economic and social view points, outsourcing elective health care might also relieve the demand pressure in the domestic health-care system, allowing the latter to serve the urgent health-care demand of ageing baby boomers, for instance, in long-term care and retirement home. All these may result in a greater cooperation between domestic and foreign hospitals through affiliations and formal patient referrals.

Impediments to destination economy

Since most medical tourism destinations are developing economies, opponents of medical tourism highlight social issues such as health equity and ethics, and the political sovereignty of these economies. From these economies' perspective, some are concerned whether the more 'affluent' international patients would actually constrain the resources of the local communities, making health care less affordable for the less affluent local patients (Hazarika 2010; Vijaya 2010). Proponents of medical tourism argue that medical tourism will reduce the external brain drain among health professionals of developing economies, and the revenues thus earned can be reinvested into the economies to attract better trained physicians and to better serve international and local patients who otherwise would have limited access to modern medical facilities and services (Horowitz and Rosensweig 2008). A case in point was when Thailand's Bumrungrad hospital helped the Thai economy during the economic crisis of 1997 and brought in 600,000 international patients in 2004 (Burkett 2007). In addition, medical tourism serves as a major source for foreign exchange and employment generation for other related sectors such as tourism, transportation, hotels and pharmaceuticals in these developing economies (Ramirez de Arellano, 2007). A downside of that was the internal brain drain from the public to private hospitals within countries such as India or Thailand (Tata 2007; Hazarika 2010), resulting in a two-tier system for health-care delivery that may increase the inequality in health-care access between private and public systems (Ramirez de Arellano 2007).

Conclusion

The economic, social, and institutional impediments encountered by consumers and producers of medical tourism in each transactional mode discussed earlier may prevent the efficient exchange of global health-care resources. On the one hand, as the 79 million (DeNavas-Walt *et al.* 2010) baby boomers in the United States become eligible for Medicare, it may have a negative impact on the medical tourism industry because Medicare's discounted prices would be more comparable to those offered by most destination economies. The *Patient Protection and Affordable Care Act* (PPACA) of 2010 presumably will reduce the number of uninsured in the United States, thus reducing the number of potential medical tourists. However, the universal health care under the new PPACA is also likely to increase the demand on an already strained domestic health-care system and may result in longer waits for treatments. This may increase the likelihood of high-income patients seeking access to quicker care abroad (Rhea 2009). It is unlikely that the outflow of patients will ever be sufficient to solve the US health-care problems. Nevertheless, as the growth of medical tourism continues and becomes sustainable in the long run, it may result in a smaller pool of patients demanding treatment from the domestic health-care system. This may even lead to higher prices due to possible physician-induced demand or the manifestation of economies of scale, and eventually resulting in a concerted effort to upgrade the quality of care in the domestic health-care system.

Acknowledgement

The author wishes to thank James Frederick for his helpful comments.

References

American College of Surgeons (2009) 'Statement on medical tourism and surgical tourism', *Bulletin of the American College of Surgeons*, 94(4). [Online]. Available at: http://www.facs.org/fellows_info/statements/st-65.html (accessed 17 May 2011).

American Dental Association (2009) 'ADA findings on dental tourism trends', 5 January [Online]. Available at: http://www.ada.org/news/1161.aspx (accessed 17 May 2011).

American Medical Association (2007) 'Medical care outside the United States', [Online]. Available at: http://www.ama-assn.org/ama1/pub/upload/mm/372/a-08cms1.pdf (accessed 17 May 2011).

American Medical Association (2008) 'New AMA guidelines on medical tourism', [Online]. Available at: http://www.ama-assn.org/ama1/pub/upload/mm/31/medicaltourism.pdf (accessed 17 May 2011).

Atwater, A. (2008) 'Galichia Heart Hospital's $10K bypass jolts industry', *The Wichita Eagle*, 24 February.

Birch, D.W., Vu, L., Karmali, S., Stoklossa, C.J. and Sharma, A.M. (2010) 'Medical tourism in bariatric surgery', *The American Journal of Surgery*, 199(5): 604–608.

Bookman, M. and Bookman K. (2007) *Medical Tourism in Developing Countries*, New York: Palgrave MacMillan.

Burkett, L. (2007) 'Medical tourism: concerns, benefits, and the American legal perspective', *The Journal of Legal Medicine*, 28(2): 223–245.

Carabello, L. (2008) 'A medical tourism primer for U.S. physicians', *Medical Practice Management*, 23(5): 291–294.

Carrera, P.M. and Bridges, J.F.P. (2006) 'Globalization and healthcare: understanding health and medical tourism', *Expert Review of Pharmacoeconomics Outcomes Research*, 6(4): 447–454.

Colorado House of Representatives (2007), *House Bill 1143: A Bill for an Act concerning the Option of a Covered State Employee under a Self-insured Group Benefit Plan to Obtain Medical Care in an Accredited Foreign Health Care Facility*, Denver, CO: Colorado House of Representatives.

Demicco, F.J. and Cetron, M. (2006) 'Club medic', *Asia Pacific Biotech News*, 10(10): 527–531.

DeNavas-Walt, C., Proctor, B.D. and Smith, J.C. (2010) *Income, Poverty, and Health Insurance Coverage in the United States: 2009, Current Population Reports: Consumer Income Series Report no. P60-238*, Washington, DC: U.S. Census Bureau.

Dhariwal, R. (2005) 'Tourists arrivals in India: how important are domestic disorders?', *Tourism Economics*, 11(2): 185–205.

Ernst, D. (2006) 'Medical tourism: why Americans take medical vacations abroad', *Pacific Research Institute*, 15 September, 4(9): 1–4.

Fernandez, L.S., Byard, D., Lin, C.C., Benson, S. and Barbera, J.A. (2002) 'Frail elderly as disaster victims: emergency management strategies', *Prehospital and Disaster Medicine*, 17(2): 67–74.

Fisher, J.P. (2006) 'Hip patients find surgeons overseas', *The News & Observer*, 10 April: A1.

Forgione, D.A. and Smith, P.C. (2007) 'Medical tourism and its impact on the US health care system', *Journal of Health Care Finance*, 34(1):. 27–35.

Gan, L. and Frederick, J.R. (2011a) 'Medical tourism facilitators: patterns of service differentiation', *Journal of Vacation Marketing*, 17(3): 1–19.

Gan, L. and Frederick, J.R. (2011b) 'Medical Tourism in Singapore: a structure conduct performance analysis', *Journal of Asia-Pacific Business*, 12(2): 141–170.

García-Altés, A. (2005) 'The development of health tourism services', *Annals of Tourism Research*, 32(1): 262–266.
H and HN (2004) 'Competition circling the globe', [Online]. Available at: http://www.hhnmag.com (accessed 17 May 2011).
Hall, C.M. (2011) 'Health and medical tourism: kill or cure for global public health?' *Tourism Review*, 66(1/2): 4–15.
Hazarika, I. (2010) 'Medical tourism: its potential impact on the health workforce and health systems in India', *Health Policy and Planning*, 25(3): 248–251.
Horowitz, M.D. and Rosensweig, J.A. (2008) 'Medical tourism vs. traditional international medical travel: a tale of two models', *International Medical Travel Journal*, [Online]. Available at: http://www.imtj.com/articles/2008/medical-tourism-vs-traditional-international-medical-travel-a-tale-of-two-models/ (accessed 1 January 2012).
Huan, T.C., Beaman, J. and Shelby, L. (2004) 'No escape natural disaster: mitigating impacts on tourism', *Annals of Tourism Research*, 31(2): 255–273.
Insurance Journal (2008) 'U.S. Risk launches MedTour Pro for medical tourism industry', 29 May [Online]. Available at: http://www.insurancejournal.com/news/national/2008/05/29/90432.htm (accessed 17 May 2011).
Jeevan, R. and Armstrong, A. (2008) 'Cosmetic tourism and the burden on the NHS', *Journal of Plastic, Reconstructive and Aesthetic Surgery*, 61(12): 1423–1424.
Jones, J.W. and McCullough, L.B. (2007) 'What to do when a patient's international care goes south?' *Journal of Vascular Surgery*, 46(5): 1077–1079.
Keckley, P.H. and Underwood, H.R. (2008) *Medical Tourism: Consumers in Search of Value*, Washington, DC: Deloitte Center for Health Solutions, [Online]. Available at: http://www.deloitte.com/assets/Dcom-Croatia/Local%20Assets/Documents/hr_Medical_tourism(3).pdf (accessed 17 May 2011).
Keckley, P.H. and Underwood, H.R. (2009) *Medical tourism: Updates and implications*, Washington, DC: Deloitte Center for Health Solutions. [Online]. Available at: http://www.deloitte.com/assets/Dcom-Greece/Local%20Assets/Documents/Attachments/Health/Medical_tourism09.pdf (accessed 17 May 2011).
Lancaster, J. (2004) 'Surgeries, side trips for 'medical tourists': affordable care at India's private hospitals draws growing number of foreigners', *Washington Post*, 21 October: A1.
Lee, O.F. and Davis, T.R.V. (2004) 'International patients: a lucrative market for U.S. hospitals', *Health Marketing Quarterly*, 22(1): 41–56.
McLean, T.R. (2007) 'Commentary: the industrialization of medical tourism and the Blue Ridge Paper claim', *Journal of Controversial Medical Claims*, 14(1): 18–19.
Marlowe, J. and Sullivan, P. (2007) 'Medical tourism: the ultimate outsourcing', *Human Resource Planning*, 30(2): 8–10.
Mattoo, A. and Rathindran, R. (2006) 'How health insurance inhibits trade in health care', *Health Affairs*, 25(20): 358–367.
Medical Tourism Association (2011) Certified facilitators, [Online]. Available at: http://www.medicaltourismassociation.com/en/certified-facilitators.html (accessed 17 May 2011).
Milstein, A. and Smith, M. (2006) 'America's new refugees: seeking affordable surgery offshore' *The New England Journal of Medicine*, 355(16): 1637–1640.
Ramírez de Arellano, A.B. (2007) 'Patients without borders: the emergence of medical tourism', *International Journal of Health Services*, 37(1): 193–198.
Rhea, S. (2009) 'Still packing their bags', *Modern Healthcare*, 27 July, 39(30): 28.
Roth, M. (2006), 'A cheaper medical alternative – for those with minimal health insurance, getting surgery abroad may be a sound option', *Pittsburgh Post-Gazette*, 10 September: G-1.

Seddighi, H., Nuttall, M. and Theocharous, A. (2001) 'Does cultural background of tourists influence the destination choice? An empirical study with special reference to political instability', *Tourism Management*, 22(2): 181–191.

Tata, S. (2007) *Medical travel in Asia and the Pacific: Challenges and opportunities*, Bangkok: United Nations Economic and Social Commission for Asia and the Pacific, [Online]. Available at: http://www.unescap.org/ESID/hds/lastestadd/MedicalTourismReport09.pdf (accessed 17 May 2011).

Vijaya, R.M. (2010) 'Medical tourism: revenue generation or international transfer of healthcare problems?' *Journal of Economic Issues*, 44(1): 53–70.

Vitalis, J.E. and Milton, G.A. (2009) 'Medical travel: threat or opportunity for U.S. providers? It depends on your perspective', *Journal of the Center for Health Innovation*, Winter: 10–13. [Online]. Available at: http://noblis.com/MissionAreas/HI/private/Documents/horizons2009.pdf (accessed 17 May 2011).

Weisser, C. and Gengler, A. (2006) '50 Ways to cut your health – care costs', *CNN Money*, 1 November, [Online]. Available at: http://money.cnn.com/popups/2006/moneymag/healthcare/index.html (accessed 17 May 2011).

West Virginia House of Delegates (2006). *House Bill 4359*. Committee on Health and Human Resources then the Judiciary, West Virginia.

World Health Organization (WHO) (2005) 'World Health Organization partners with Joint Commission and Joint Commission International to eliminate medical errors worldwide', *News Release*, 23 August, [Online]. Available at: http://www.who.int/patientsafety/newsalert/WHO_final.pdf (accessed 17 May 2011).

4 Medical tourism, xenotourism and client expectations

Between bioscience and responsibilisation

Peta S. Cook, Gavin Kendall, Mike Michael and Nik Brown

Introduction

Tourism brings together a number of themes of late-modern society: rich Westerners, no longer meaningfully tied to economies of production, entertain themselves by consuming experiences of 'otherness' – an entertainment which in a globalised world, cheap and rapid international travel and international hotels and motels have made possible in a heightened way (Urry 1990). However, such flows are not recent developments. Theilmann (1987) suggests that medieval forms of tourism were connected to religion, especially through the practices of pilgrimage, which was actively encouraged when it might connect to medical treatment. Health-related travel and pilgrimage can be traced even further back. For example, Douglas (2001) indicates that the ritual and sacred use of water occurred during the Neolithic and Bronze ages. Similarly, the Ancient Mesopotamians saw an intimate connection between climatic change and health (Kevan 1993), and throughout their provinces, the Ancient Romans constructed thermal spas, including Baden-Baden in Germany and Vichy in France (Douglas 2001; Bookman and Bookman 2007). In addition, the rapid urbanisation wrought by industrialisation aggravated the unsanitary and poor living environments in Britain and some sections of Europe and led to a concern for health and an interest in sun-seeking and 'taking the waters' (Holden 2006; Swarbrooke and Horner 2007). In short, what emerges from the above is the close historical connection between tourism, health and medicine.

Stimulated by globalisation, health care has become an international marketplace with emerging, developing and developed nations competing for patients (known increasingly as clients or 'health consumers'). This global industry was estimated to be worth US$60 billion in 2007, and is growing by 20 per cent per year (MacReady 2007). It is forecast that 15.8 million Americans will receive medical treatment internationally by 2017 (Mitka 2009). Such economic incentives for the state has led to increasing options for Western medical tourists, who have more disposable incomes and in some cases portable health-insurance policies. In addition, some nation-states are making it easier for medical tourists to access services. The large number of options and destinations open to medical tourists has also spawned a new industry of medical brokers, who act as intermediaries to match patients and health-care providers (Westlund 2000). While medical tourists predominately come from the developed world, medical-tourist sites are found globally, with many medical tourists flowing to world-class facilities in the developing world.

Despite the social, political and economic importance of medical tourism, there has been little critique and examination of the tensions that arise for the health consumer under the impress of neoliberalism (see Chapter 1, see also Hall 2011). In this chapter, we explore these tensions specifically through the lens of xenotransplantation (XTP; the transplantation of animal parts into humans) and xenotourism. We begin with a brief overview of existing accounts of medical tourism; in the process, identifying some of the key concerns in the field. We then move on to focus on xenotourism, where additional issues become prominent. As we argue, XTP is potentially dangerous both for the individual undergoing the procedure, but also, not least because of the risks posed by endogenous retroviruses, for human populations at large. Central to the latter is the lack of global regulation of such procedures within a globalised health market. In this context, we describe how the contemporary health consumer faces a complex array of problems in a situation where there is no definitive authority on the medical, technical and social uncertainties of xenotourism. We then go on to discuss how, as a potentially dangerous carrier of disease, the xenotourist presents a range of profound challenges to ill-equipped health-care systems which have been fundamentally reshaped by neoliberal policies. We end by considering some of the possible reactions to this state of affairs where, for instance, consumer culture increasingly becomes conflated with surveillance society.

Medical tourism

The term 'medical tourism' or 'health-care tourism' needs some clarification, as its treatment in the literature is ambiguous (see chapter 1, see also Hall 2011). Definitions of health care and medical tourism tend to focus on either the perspective of supply (provider) or demand (consumer). For example, Goodrich and Goodrich (1987) take the supply angle, defining health-care tourism as

> the attempt on the part of a tourist facility (e.g. hotel) or destination (e.g. Baden, Switzerland) to attract tourists by *deliberately* promoting its health-care services and facilities, in addition to its regular tourist amenities
>
> (Goodrich and Goodrich 1987: 217, original emphasis)

Schofield (2004: 137) combines demand and supply, highlighting health tourism as involving the promotion of health services and 'restoring physical, mental and social well-being while using health service facilities outside of the tourists' permanent place of residence or work'. Most definitions, however, are concerned with demand. This perspective privileges the perceived desires or motivations of the consumer. In turn, some authors differentiate between health-care and medical tourism. For Connell (2006a: 1093–94), health tourism is concerned with general health and well-being, involving spa treatments and recreational activities such as sport. In contrast, medical tourism is the movement of people who, in addition to holidaying as a tourist, undergo medical, dental and surgical intervention. Similarly, Carrera and Bridges (2006: 447, 449) consider medical tourism to be a subset of health tourism, being 'the organized travel outside of one's natural healthcare jurisdiction for the enhancement or restoration of the individual's health through medical intervention'. All these factors seeking medical treatment for a pre-existing health condition(s), moving across borders for treatment and seeking tourist experiences – are combined in the following definition of medical tourism:

> Medical tourism is defined as the sum of all the relationships and phenomena resulting from a journey by people whose primary motive is to treat or cure a medical condition by taking advantage of medical intervention services away from their usual place of residence while typically combining this journey with a vacation or tourism elements in the conventional sense (Voigt *et al.* 2010: 36)

Based on these definitions, we view medical tourism as the phenomenon of patients travelling to foreign or international locales with the motivation to receive invasive medical treatment, usually because cost or availability confers some financial or personal advantage. For example, Mitka (2009) reports that heart-valve surgery in the United States costs US$200,000 but is significantly cheaper in India at US$9,500. Even with the added costs of airfare, accommodation and tourist activities (which could already be accounted for in a medical-tourism package), the savings are substantial. This is illustrated by the case of Eileen Clemenzi, who was quoted US$48,000 for a hip replacement which, in Malaysia, cost a total of US$11,000 including all travel expenses (York 2008: 100). Thus, the term can include the practice of packaging together holidays with medical treatments. The marketing of medical tourism often concentrates on nearby attractions and/or vacation packages. However, the increasing focus on tourism does allow more expensive locations, such as the United States and Australia, to be part of the medical tourism industry. In this latter meaning of the term, the treatments are more likely to be cosmetic or life enhancing rather than lifesaving, for the obvious reason that those with chronic and acute illness are unlikely to be well enough to engage in much tourism, especially post-surgery. Elective procedures – for example, dental surgery, laser eye surgery, rhinoplasty, liposuction, blepharoplasty, facelifts and breast augmentation – can be purchased at an increasing number of venues around the world. Specific destinations have also become known for relatively inexpensive treatments. Poland and Hungary are common destinations for dental treatment 'tours' for citizens from Germany and the UK. Primarily, however, South America, Russia and Asia, especially Thailand, are meccas for medical tourism, with India often identified as the centre. From these remarks, we suggest there are two ways of further understanding medical tourism.

Extending from the above considerations, our second understanding of medical tourism – the idea of combining medical treatment with a holiday – is one which, we suggest, is becoming increasingly fuzzy around the edges, precisely because medical treatment is merging into the tourist experience, and also because it is sometimes hard to see the boundary between body modification and medical treatment. People investigating laser eye surgery might opt to pay the same amount as in their industrialised Western nation, but have the procedure in South America with a free holiday thrown in. This highlights a connection to cost and availability, where the procedural costs at home do not include tourist 'retreats' and recovery in often luxurious surrounds. As these procedures become increasingly marketed and mundane, they potentially become more an impulse purchase rather than part of planning a holiday (or life). Medical treatment is both an addition to the traditional tourist sightseeing experience (Goodrich and Goodrich 1987) and potentially, a significant motivating factor for travel. However, it has been questioned whether the 'tourism' of medical tourism is merely a slogan; an advertising tool for the industry (Connell 2006a).

Our first understanding of medical tourism – which focuses on medical tourism undertaken primarily on the grounds of cost or availability and independent of traditional tourist experiences – is the one on which we wish to concentrate. Whole organ transplantation and cardiac bypass surgery fall into this category. These medical interventions are often available in the patient's home country, but may be hard to access because of waiting times, a lack of resources, and exorbitantly high prices. Thus, serious medical interventions are the basis of what is rapidly becoming a multi-billion dollar global health-care business. Transplant tourism, for example, occurs because (i) the long waiting lists for kidney transplants in the developed world may lead to death before an individual can receive a transplant, and (ii) there exists an (apparent) willingness on the part of people in the developing world to sell their kidneys. This also indicates that some forms of medical tourism cater to very ill-health consumers, who may require long recuperation times or be too sick to engage in typical tourism experiences. Alternatively, medical tourism can facilitate the bypassing of national restrictions. As outlined in English *et al.* (2001), this has occurred in the UK with fertility treatments, where individuals wanting to be inseminated with their dead partner's sperm or wanting to select the sex of their baby, have chosen to travel to continental Europe to have their medical and social desires fulfilled. Similarly, physicians may want to establish floating clinics in international waters in order to provide treatments that are illegal in some countries, such as abortion or euthanasia (English *et al.* 2001).

Treatment by (frequently Western-trained) doctors in developing nations becomes a much desired solution for health consumers to the health crisis faced in many developed countries. While the slogan of this industry might be 'first-world treatment at third-world prices', the industry must come to terms with other factors that may negate its pricing advantages, not least concerns about medical standards (Connell 2006b). Attempts to allay such fears in medical-tourism marketing campaigns often involve reference to physician training undertaken at Western locations, certification and accreditation from Western bodies (such as the Joint Commission International (JCI), which is endorsed by the World Health

Organization), and the high quality of advanced medical facilities. This advertising additionally focuses on affordability, quantity and quality of care, the absence of waiting times and, of course, location. Despite the interest in accreditation, however, there is no effective global regulation of the medical industry. As a result, it seems likely that assuaging the health consumer's real or imagined concerns through marketing campaigns is, and will continue to be, a major feature of the medical-tourism industry. Evaluative concerns of medical-tourism providers and services are largely restricted to the individual patient, the health consumer, who is given the responsibility for estimating the multitude of risks involved. Drawing on the case study of xenotourism, it is this concern to which we now turn.

Xenotourism

A contemporary development in medical tourism, known as xenotourism, connects to XTP, the transplantation of living animal cells, tissues or organs into a human recipient. One example of XTP is the transplantation of porcine insulin-producing cells from the pancreas, known as the islets of Langerhans, into an individual with Type-1 diabetes. The aim of such animal transplant therapy is to obtain better metabolic control for the human transplant recipient by reducing their insulin dependency, or possibly facilitating insulin independence. The potential of XTP becoming available to international patients as medical tourism has raised some concern (e.g. D'Apice in Armstrong 2004; Sykes *et al.* 2004a). While xenotourism possesses obvious similarities to transplant tourism, xenotourism raises far more dangers for the international community. One of these dangers is trans-species viral infection. The new intimacies created by XTP could mean viruses not previously capable of infecting humans would become infectious, and create new diseases capable of generating human epidemics (Bloom *et al.* 1999; Gold and Adams 2002). Of particular concern have been endogenous retroviruses, which are spread to subsequent generations through their germ line integration. While these are normally dormant in the host species, they can be activated in a different species. In pigs, the animal source of choice for XTP, these are called porcine endogenous retroviruses (PERV). After Patience *et al.* (1997) established PERV could infect human cells in vitro, concerns were raised about animal-to-human and subsequent human-to-human in vivo spread. This has remained a highly contentious subject. However, it is now argued that PERV does not infect humans (e.g. Armstrong 2004; Fishman and Patience 2004). Endogenous retroviruses, however, are not the only concern. XTP also poses the risk of unknown infections. As in the case of other human infections of animal origin, such as human swine influenza (H1N1), viruses are not constrained by geopolitical (or species) borders, meaning XTP produces local, national and global angst (Gold and Adams 2002).

However, the infectious risk posed by XTP is considered by some to be theoretical rather than real problem. For advocates of XTP, the risk is selective in nature, dependent on where in the world the clinical trials or xenotourism therapies are being performed, and by whom. Interestingly, the increased threat of a global pathogen is perceived to relate to inappropriate national and international regulatory frameworks that deal with XTP's potential (negative) outcomes (McKenzie *et al.* 2002; Sykes *et al.* 2003a, 2003b, 2004a, 2004b). Such locations are typically labelled 'xeno-havens'. In other words, it is the location at which xenotourism occurs which is seen to mobilise risk, and not XTP as a medico-scientific endeavour (and experiment). Consequently, there is much discussion around the need to establish international guidelines and/or collaboration and surveillance strategies (e.g. Buhler 2005; Sykes 2005; Sykes *et al.* 2003b, 2004b; O'Connell 2004).

These concerns, however, also relate to economic benefit and loss. We might speculate that envy plays a role in activating risk, as some can use xenotechnologies to acquire the consequent fiscal and reputational benefits of xenotourism. In addition, xeno-havens and xenotourism providers may use intellectual property rights to prohibit access to knowledge, as highlighted in the cloning and stem cell debates (Cohen 2002). In this light, developing nations would derive economic benefits through xenotourism, while developed nations would not. Critics thus believe the present stringent regulations of varying degrees on XTP in the Western world (for example, Australia, New Zealand, United Kingdom and United States) not only deny individuals hope, choice and a desired treatment (note the focus here is placed on the 'responsiblised' health consumer), but also jeopardise investments of time and economic resources and, in turn, potential economic benefits (Barton 2005; Sykes 2005). This brings us to xenotourism.

At the Laboratorio de Xenotrasplantes (Mexico), under the leadership of paediatric surgeon Dr Rafael Valdés, research was being conducted on using porcine insulin-producing cells, mixed with sertoli (testicular) cells to treat Type-1 diabetes. As sertoli cells are believed to shield against immunological rejection, it was proposed this co-XTP might provide the immunological conditions for the porcine islet cells to function and grow in the foreign human environment. The results were promising. Valdés (in Armstrong 2004; Secretary's Advisory Committee on Xenotransplantation and L.A.D. Reporting Company 2004) reported that some patients no longer required insulin injections, while others had a reduced insulin requirement (Barton 2005; Buhler 2005; Check 2002). Despite the procedure being approved as therapy in August 2004 by the Department of Health and National Center for Transplant (Mexico), Valdés' work was subject to condemnation on a number of grounds, including a lack of preclinical studies, issues of informed consent among the trial participants, a need for more experimental trials and questions on the control and monitoring of infectious disease (Check 2002; D'Apice in Armstrong 2004; Buhler 2005).

These criticisms took on a new urgency as xenotourism became a reality. Jiménez (2006) reports that two international patients from Canada (a woman and a boy), received xenotherapy in Mexico. The cost of the treatment was reported to be approximately US$30,000 (Armstrong 2004), which did not include pre-transplant appointments and out-of-hospital expenses such as airfares and accommodation. But these xenotourism examples are no more: pressure from the International Xenotransplantation Association (IXA) led to a review by Mexico's

National Committee of Bioethics, which asserted that the therapy should not continue on grounds of ethics and safety (Jiménez 2006; Sykes *et al.* 2007). Xenotourism, however, has recently resurfaced, now offered in Russia in the form of DiabeCell®, from the Australian-based biotechnology company Living Cell Technologies (2010).

The case of xenotourism demonstrates that within medical tourism, tourism and health care may be distinct. Even though travel is involved, this does not mean the journey involves the combination of luxurious accommodation and tourist packages. Importantly, xenotourism relies on the unavailability of the treatment in other parts of the world and the desperation of particular health consumers. The drawcard is not the location or the tourist experience. Xenotourism currently does not work the association between medicine and tourism. Any tourist experience – if it does occur – is arranged independent of and experienced separately from the medical institution and the medical procedure. It should be further noted that while the past and current offerings of xenotourism target relatively healthy patients living with a chronic life-long disease (Type-1 diabetes), future offerings may target more frail health consumers, such as those requiring whole (animal) organ transplants. Tourist 'extras' are unlikely to be valued by such vulnerable patients.

It has been suggested that tourism is a pleasurable activity that is distinguishable and different from everyday reality. This means that 'tourism results from a basic binary division between the ordinary/everyday and the extraordinary' (Urry 1990: 11). As a result, tourism is a passive, leisurely pursuit that stands in stark contrast to labour and work (e.g. Boorstin 1963; MacCannell 1973, 1976; Urry 1990). Medical tourism, however, can be considered work, as '[i]t is doubtful that many people would define surgery [and the consequent recuperation] as pleasurable' (Cook 2010: 141). On the other hand, metaphors commonly associated with tourism can be more appropriately linked to XTP itself. For example, the medical procedure of mixing human and animal is itself exotic, strange and extraordinary; over and beyond – and more intimate – than any cultural or tourist experience. At the same time, the individual's ordinary and everyday reality is at the forefront of the xenotourism experience, being the singular focus and purpose of travel. This is because unlike many other forms of medical tourism where pleasure and luxury is part of a medical package, xenotourism simply offers a surgical experience that will possibly provide improved quality of life by alleviating diabetic symptoms and insulin dependence. In this light, the pleasurable experience of xenotourism is connected to the potential result of an unpleasant xenotourism experience. The religious pilgrimage of early medical tourism has changed to a commodified pursuit, although both embrace medical healing and cures that are centralised in a 'sacred' site. Such movement can be connected to a history of cure seeking, where 'healthy holidays' and a 'change of climate' have been perceived to provide positive health outcomes (Kevan 1993).

Medical and bodily commodification is evidenced by xenotourism's exclusive relationship between local medicine and the international marketplace, where humans are reduced to commodities (Scheper-Hughes 2002) and medical diagnoses. At this early stage of xenotourism, it is primarily an economic activity based on the local cost of the medical procedure(s) and the unavailability of this medical intervention in other parts of the world. This allows procedures offered through medical tourism – and in particular xenotourism – to create 'niche' markets, which facilitate and exacerbate divisions between the developed and the developing world, between rich and poor, and between the haves and the have-nots (Pettman 1997; Scheper-Hughes 2002). As the literature on reproductive and sex tourism demonstrates, these disparate communal and individual bodies, the other and the self, are intimately mixed through such practices (Pettman 1997). Xenotourism expands this hybrid process by distinguishing animals from humans (using one to benefit the other), while crossing the species divide to fuse these bodies. While tourism has traditionally been conceptualised as entertainment through the consumption of 'otherness' (Urry 1990), the consumption of otherness in xenotourism is literal and embodied. The extraordinary becomes transformed into the everyday, mundane reality.

We must also question whether post-xenotransplant monitoring is feasible. Patients have already received the procedure and have returned to their home countries. Additionally, people with Type-1 diabetes, such as Peter Thompson (in Barton 2005) and Graeme Collinson (in 'Pig-cell transplant treatment denied', *New Zealand Herald*, 2005), warn they will travel to seek 'cures' despite national XTP restrictions in their home countries and will take advantage of a lack of international and national infrastructures to deal with xenotourists. The paradox here is that despite the implicit desire for global regulation, individual responsibility for health is fostered and encouraged by neoliberal health-care policies and, in some cases, the international pliability of private health insurance. The links between national regulations and the nation-state are not clear-cut. Despite national restrictions on XTP, residents can travel to another country to receive a xenotransplant: the individual may visit several countries with varying XTP regulations, before returning to their home country. XTP and its potential consequences, then, move across geopolitical boundaries and territories. As a result, national boundaries become fluid and flexible, making it even more likely that a turn to global standards is a likely response; but as Barry (2001: 63) argues '[t]he ideal of standardization is the fantasy of a smooth and homogenous technological zone'. Through standardisation, XTP might become internationally structured but, without any global political and legal body to undertake such decisions that can overturn or override the nation-state, such a call is utopian. We are therefore left with tricky questions: how can we monitor XTP recipients? Can and should national regulations prevent the movement of people with xenotransplants?

The responsibilised health consumer

Caught up in all of these global/local medical controversies is, of course, the individual health consumer who has to make sense of it all, and increasingly has to take responsibility for the management of their own health regime. It has become a commonplace in political sociology that neoliberal political regimes have worked to strip back welfare systems and their associated safety nets, and increasingly to insist that citizens make private arrangements to safeguard their (and, in many instances, their family's) health, education, retirement and so forth (e.g. Rose 1996). Neoliberalism has reshaped health and health-care provision, where reform has focussed on replacing publicly funded health care with a private, user-pays system. The citizen has become the health consumer. Such strategies are being enacted globally, and are backed by policies in institutions such as the International Monetary Fund (IMF) and the World Bank. As recounted in Meghani (2011: 23-24), the enforcement from IMF and the World Bank of neoliberal reform in India has led to a heavily privatised health-care sector that has exacerbated the local divide between rich and poor. Many hospitals in India are built with medical tourists in mind; this industry is supported by the Indian government through subsidies, and by providing medical tourists and their companions with medical visas which are valid for one year (Chinai and Goswami 2007). The upshot of this is that poorer or less developed nations are developing medical tourism industries that typically have no benefit to their own citizens.

While the more robust versions of neoliberalism see little wrong with individuals pursuing their goals and imagine that an unfettered market can only be a good thing, xenotourism provides a stark reminder of the inescapable problem: the citizen's inalienable right to do what he or she wants may conflict with the interests of other citizens and, ironically, that of the neoliberal nation-state. Thus, the neoliberal paradigm of cost-effective and consumer-friendly private markets falls short of consumer welfare and public good. For example, the encouragement of medical tourism in India has resulted in the indirect and direct redirection of health-care monies from the health care of locals who are comparatively poor (Meghani 2011). In the case of xenotourism, the proactive management and pursuit of personal health – now commodified and marketed – may be at the expense of infecting other people or, in the worst-case scenario, a global epidemic. To what extent is one free to unleash PERVs or other infectious viruses on the rest of one's species? The conflicts emerging here are between private and public health, and choice and responsibility. These complexities fall on the health consumer's shoulders. Of course, there may be a simple Hobbesian solution to this dilemma: accept the necessary evils of the Leviathan that is state regulation. The problem, however, is that in an international context, there really are no effective mechanisms of global regulation that can cope with global threats. Although risk society has 'gone global' (Beck 1999), there are no 'World Police' that mimic this spread of influence. This raises a number of areas of concern.

First, in the context of a global medical market, the marketing of new treatments still needs to draw on some criteria around efficacy, safety and so on. Where are these sought by neoliberal health consumers? Where can they go to get reassurance? Who counts as trustworthy? Or does desperation trump any such considerations? The neoliberal solution to this, one might anticipate, is a series of benchmarking operations: perhaps in time we shall see league tables of international medical tourism and XTP centres so that the informed consumer can choose with confidence.

Second, and following on from this, attempts to monopolise the setting of standards by certain Western actors through such central organisations as the

United Nations might seem desirable. However, there is currently no international body with the legal ability or capacity to make such decisions, or to override the nation-state. Therefore, while the WHO endorses the JCI accreditation system, this system does not control decisions at the nation-state level or shut down 'rogue' medical-tourism providers. It could be viewed as an example of Western hegemony, where Western standards are imposed. However, would health consumers even be aware of any international standardisation? If such standardisation does occur, will it meet the *actual* interests and needs of the health consumer, or that of the medical industry?

Even if it were the case that patients/patient groups became aware of Western demands for global regulatory standardisation, this might well aggravate the individualised pursuit of therapy abroad. For example, the patient may perceive international treatments, offered at cheaper prices and/or with a holiday, as increasingly safe due to the internationalisation of Western medical guidelines and certifications. At the same time, this would no doubt partly be the upshot of a reaction against what is seen as unwarranted Western biomedical monopolisation. However, it is also likely to be informed by counter-rhetorics from the periphery (the destinations of xenotourism, or medical tourism more broadly) that Western demands for global governance are in actuality a ploy to impress upon local (that is, Western) regulatory authorities that they must be more amenable to local research/trials. The aim of such strategies would be to keep patients at home rather than allow them to be tempted to go to other countries, which may have less stringent regulations. This highlights another conundrum. The need for national regulations on medical tourism demands consideration of what is available internationally in order to provide health care on a cost-effective basis to local patients. In this scenario, the nation-state's restrictions on XTP or other medical therapies become reactionary to the regulations – or lack thereof – in other nation-states. Consequently, the demand for and assessment of risk is not simply a consideration of (selected) citizens. Rather, it is an economic and strategic decision by the nation-state so as not to be 'left behind'.

Third, there is a curious trend in the regulation of medicines, procedures and services. Regulatory authorities are increasingly seeing themselves as having a role in the licensing of private clinical laboratories for quality control (hygiene, cleanliness, data management) rather than being concerned with clinical efficacy (Salter and Jones 2002). There is, then, increased scope for the privatisation of relationships between health consumers and medical services. In this sense, regulation is downscaling in its scope: an example of state-organised irresponsibility (Beck 1999). This contributes to the important tension in the xenotourism case between an increasingly privatised set of priorities (personal health) advancing at the expense of public health priorities (disease management).

In short, the globalisation of medicine throws up all kinds of problems for patients who are only really enmeshed in nation-state safety nets, many of which are close to atrophied. One point we stress here is that the neoliberal paradigm struggles to deal effectively with problems which exhibit the following traits: first, if a problem has a large technical component (and this will often be characteristic of medical procedures), it becomes almost impossible for individuals to make informed choices; second, when a problem has global ramifications (in the case of XTP and xenotourism, possible infectious spread and/or an epidemic), there are no effective global regulatory mechanisms to temper the rash actions of certain 'dangerous individuals' or 'dangerous places', nor completely and effectively to deal with any consequences such as an outbreak; third, the paradigm of self-responsible patients only encourages individuals to seek desired treatments that could be 'irregulated'; and finally, how do we deal with xenotourists (or other health consumers) who have engaged in 'risky' consumption practices when returning to a country that has a moratorium, ban or stringent regulations on the procedure?

Conclusion

Medical tourism can be analysed as a practical example of the increasing commodification of the body. It seems sensible to us to distinguish two types of medical tourism: travelling to get access to medical treatment, and travelling to get medical treatment as well as engaging in other tourist practices. It may well be that in the global development of the latter, the former is a necessary first stage. The example we have discussed in this chapter – XTP – is, so far, an example of a treatment that is becoming available in the first modality of medical tourism but not (yet?) the second. Xenotourism throws up a number of difficult, maybe insoluble, problems.

First, the unusual dangers of the medical procedures such as XTP draw our attention to the inadequacies of our existing mechanisms of global regulation. If the market becomes the only arbiter of whether such treatments will be offered, surely no one should be amazed if there are a few nasty surprises. Second, the globalisation of the market in medical treatment goes hand in hand with an increasing individualisation of patients. Patients now have much more responsibility for researching treatments and deciding how to weigh up expertise, where they can save money, and so forth. Again, no one should be surprised if patients cannot effectively play these roles.

What we are witnessing is a reconfiguration of patients as consumers, mediated through an unregulated globalised market, enacted through the mobility of relatively privileged patients. The hegemony of Western rationality does not solely determine what science is safe and unsafe, as patients are actively constructing medical tourism. As a result, xenotourism becomes a political issue. For example, we might envisage the following scenarios. First, in a further twist to the correlation between increasing individualisation and increasing surveillance (the conflation of consumer culture and surveillance society), we might expect to see Western states implementing still more stringent border-control systems (e.g. medical details encoded in passports). Second, it is possible to imagine that in a context of lax global regulation, non-governmental organisations (NGOs) will take on a global quasi-regulatory role. Being unencumbered by the market forces to which national medical and regulatory actors are subject, and insofar as they are skilled at making connections and coordinating transnational interventions against biomedical initiatives, NGOs will become the 'global police' of risky biomedicine. On this score, xenotourism is an important continuing case study of the sorts of reactions that arise to the increasingly fluid and globalised biomedical market.

References

Armstrong, A. [producer]. Garrett, K. [executive producer] (2004) 'Pig parts: xenotransplantation', *ABC Radio National, Radio broadcast*, 11 July. [Online]. Available at: http://www.abc.net.au/radionational/programs/backgroundbriefing/pig-parts-xenotransplantation/3421282 (accessed 22 May 2012).

Barry, A. (2001) *Political Machines: Governing a Technological Society*, London/New York: The Athlone Society.

Barton, C. (2005) 'Pig cells offer hope of miracle cure', *The New Zealand Herald*, 21 May. [Online]. Available at: http://www.nzherald.co.nz/index.cfm?a_id=36&;ObjectID=10126647 (accessed 4 July 2011).

Beck, U. (1999) *World Risk Society*, Cambridge: Polity.

Bloom, E.T., Moulton, A.D., McCoy, J., Chapman, L.E. and Patterson, A.P. (1999) 'Xenotransplantation: the potential and the challenges', *Critical Care Nurse*, 19(2): 76–83.

Bookman, M.Z. and Bookman, K.R. (2007) *Medical Tourism in Developing Countries*, New York: Palgrave Macmillan.

Boorstin, D.J. (1963) *The Image, or What Happened to the American Dream*, Harmondworth, Middlesex: Penguin Books.

Buhler, L. (2005) 'Balancing potential benefit and risks of clinical trials in xenotransplantation: what should be done?' *Insulin-Free Times*, [Online]. Available at: http://www.insulinfreetimes.com/05_summer/buhler.htm (accessed 1 September 2005).

Carrera, P.M. and Bridges, J.F.P. (2006) 'Globalization and healthcare: understanding health and medical tourism', *Expert Review Pharmacoeconomics Outcomes Research*, 6(4): 447–454.

Check, E. (2002) 'Diabetes trial stirs debate on safety of xenotransplants', *Nature*, 419(6902): 5.

Chinai, R. and Goswami, R. (2007) 'Medical visas mark growth of Indian medical tourism', *Bulletin of the World Health Organization*, 85(3): 164–165.

Cohen, P. (2002) 'The race for a cure', *New Scientist*, 173(2334): 6.

Connell, J. (2006a) 'Medical tourism: sea, sun, sand and … surgery', *Tourism Management*, 27(6): 1093–1100.

Connell, J. (2006b) 'Medical tourism: the newest of niches', *Tourist Recreation Research*, 31(1): 99–102.

Cook, P.S. (2010) 'Constructions and experiences of authenticity in medical tourism: the performances of places, spaces, practices, objects and bodies', *Tourist Studies*, 10(2): 135–153.

Douglas, N. (2001) 'Travelling for health: spa and health resorts', in N. Douglas, N. Douglas and R. Derrett (eds) *Special Interest Tourism: Contexts and Cases*, Milton, Ontario: John Wiley and Sons.

English, V., Gardner, J., Romano-Critchley, G. and Sommerville, A. (2001) 'Ethical briefings', *Journal of Medical Ethics*, 27: 284–285.

Fishman, J.A. and Patience, C. (2004) 'Xenotransplantation: infectious risk revisited', *American Journal of Transplantation*, 4(9): 1383–1390.

Gold, E.R. and Adams, W.A. (2002) 'Reconciling private benefit and public risk in biotechnology: xenotransplantation as a case study in consent', *Health Law Journal*, 10: 31–75.

Goodrich, J.N. and Goodrich, G.E. (1987) 'Health-care tourism – an exploratory study', *Tourism Management*, 8: 217–222.

Hall, C.M. (2011) 'Health and medical tourism: kill or cure for global public health?' *Tourism Review*, 66(1/2): 4–15.

Holden, A. (2006) *Tourism Studies and the Social Sciences*, London: Routledge.

Jiménez, M. (2006) 'Diabetes patients, therapy undergo trial by fire', *Globe and Mail*, 5 September: A4.

Kevan, S.M. (1993) 'Quests for cures: a history of tourism for climate and health', *International Journal of Biometeorology*, 37(3): 113–124.

Living Cell Technologies (2010) LCT's DIABECELL® registered for sale and use in Russia. [Online]. Available at: http://www.lctglobal.com/html/blob.php/LCT's%20Diabecell%20Registered%20for%20Sale%20and%20Use%20in%20Russica_101210.pdf?attach=0&documentCode=2409&elementId=20084.

MacCannell, D. (1973) 'Staged authenticity: arrangements of social space in tourist settings', *American Journal of Sociology*, 79(3): 589–603.

MacCannell, D. (1976) *The Tourist: A New Theory of the Leisure Class*, New York: Schocken.

McKenzie, I.F.C., D'Apice, A.J.F. and Cooper, D.K.C. (2002) 'Xenotransplantation trials', *Lancet*, 359(9325): 2280–2281.

MacReady, N. (2007) 'Developing countries court medical tourists', *Lancet*, 369(9576): 1849–1850.

Meghani, Z. (2011) 'A robust, particularist ethical assessment of medical tourism', *Developing World Bioethics*, 11(1): 16–29.

Mitka, M. (2009) 'Surgical tourism: some us patients travel abroad for less costly surgery', *Journal of the American Medical Association*, 302(14): 1519.

New Zealand Herald (2005) 'Pig-cell transplant treatment denied', *The New Zealand Herald*, 21 May. [Online]. Available at: http://www.nzherald.co.nz/index.cfm?c_id=5&;ObjectID=10126694 (accessed 4 July 2011).

O'Connell, P. (2004) 'International Xenotransplantation Association (IXA) minutes of the business meeting held in Glasgow, 2003', *Xenotransplantation*, 11(3): 222–223.

Patience, C., Takeuchi, Y., and Weiss, R.A. (1997) 'Infection of human cells by an endogenous retrovirus of pigs', *Nature Medicine*, 3(5): 282–286.

Pettman, J.J. (1997) 'Body politics: international sex tourism', *Third World Quarterly*, 18(1): 93–108.

Rose, N. (1996) 'Inventiveness in politics', *Economy and Society*, 28(3): 467–493.

Salter, B. and Jones, M. (2002) 'Regulating human genetics: the changing politics of biotechnology governance in the European Union', *Health, Risk and Society*, 4(3): 325–340.

Scheper-Hughes, N. (2002) 'The ends of the body: commodity fetishism and the global traffic in organs', *SAIS Review*, 12(1): 61–79.

Schofield, P. (2004) 'Health tourism in the Kyrgyz Republic: the Soviet salt mine experience', in T.V. Singh. (ed.) *New Horizons in Tourism: Strange Experiences and Stranger Practices*, Wallingford: CAB International.

Secretary's Advisory Committee on Xenotransplantation and L.A.D. Reporting Company (2004) *Transcript: Sixth Meeting of the Secretary's Advisory Committee on Xenotransplantation*, 24 February. [Online]. Available at: http://www4.od.nih/oba/sacx/Feb2004/Feb2004transcript.pdf (accessed 1 September 2005).

Swarbrooke, J. and Horner, S. (2007) *Consumer Behaviour in Tourism*, 2nd edn, Oxford: Butterworth-Heinemann/Elsevier.

Sykes, M. (2005) 'Commentary: World Health Assembly Resolution 57.18 on Xenotransplantation', *Transplantation*, 79(6): 636–637.

Sykes, M., D'Apice, A. and Sandrin, M. (2003a) 'The ethics of xenotransplantation. Position paper of the Ethics Committee of the International Xenotransplantation Association', *Xenotransplantation*, 10(3): 194–203.

Sykes, M., Sandrin, M. and D'Apice, A. (2003b) 'Guidelines for xenotransplantation', *New England Journal of Medicine*, 349(13): 1294–1295.

Sykes, M., Sandrin, M. and Cozzi, E. (2004a) 'International cooperation on xenotransplantation', *Nature Medicine*, 10(2): 119.

Sykes, M., Sandrin, M., Cozzi, E. and Rees, M.A. (2004b) 'Commentaries: World Health Organization resolution on xenotransplantation', *Xenotransplantation*, 11(3), 224–225.

Sykes, M., Cozzi, E., D'Apice, A.J.F., Pierson III, R.N., O'Connell, P., Cowan, P., Dorling, A., Hering, B., Soulillou, J-P., and Sandrin, M. (2007) 'Response to Valdes-González 'clinical trial of islet xenotransplantation in Mexico"'. *Xenotransplantation*, 14(1), 90–91.

Theilmann, J.M. (1987) 'Medieval pilgrims and the origins of tourism', *Journal of Popular Culture*, 20(4): 93–102.

Urry, J. (1990) *The Tourist Gaze: Leisure and Travel in Contemporary Societies*, London: Sage.

Voigt, C., Laing, J., Wray, M., Brown, G., Howat, G., Weiler, B. and Trembath, R. (2010) *Health Tourism in Australia: Supply, Demand and Opportunities*, Gold Coast: CRC for Sustainable Tourism.

Westlund, K. (2000) 'Medical tourism: a growing trend in the Americas', *Latin Trade*, 8(1): 62–63, 66.

York, D. (2008) 'Medical tourism: the trend toward outsourcing medical procedures to foreign countries', *Journal of Continuing Education in the Health Professions*, 28(2): 99–102.

Part III

National and regional policy, regulatory and competitive settings

5 Impacts of health policy on medical tourism in Germany

Christof Pforr and Cornelia Locher

Introduction

Like in many other developed nations, the traditional German health-care system has come under increasing pressure over the past few decades. After the Second World War, it was, in particular, a growing number of people with health-care cover and a rapid expansion of health services that raised initial concerns about its viability, but at that stage the country's booming post-war economy was able to provide the necessary growth and employment to cope (Gerlinger 2010). However, faced with issues like a slowing economy, globalisation pressures, demographic change towards an increasingly ageing population and their growing expectation to age well, technological advancements and rising costs of medical services, it became an obvious necessity for political and administrative decision makers to adjust the system to better cope with these new developments (Felder 2010; Funk 2010; Gerlinger 2010; Golz 2010). The immense pressure on Germany's health-care system is illustrated by the dramatic increase in public spending on health from approximately €159 billion (9.6 per cent of GDP) in 1992 to €278 billion (11.6 per cent of GDP) in 2009, which translates into an increase in total expenditure on health per capita from €1,970 to €3,400 (Statistisches Bundesamt 2011).

Between the mid-1970s and the early 1990s rising health-insurance premiums and cost containment were the main strategies adopted, but since these measures turned out to be insufficient to rein in spiralling health-care costs, a string of wide-ranging reforms have since been introduced to the German health-care system, which have all strongly focused on increasing competition within the health-care sector and on the modernisation of its traditional structures. These developments have also gone hand in hand with a push for higher individual financial contributions towards the actual costs of medical services (Gerlinger 2010). The contribution of private households and private organisations to total health expenditure has increased in the decade 1995–2005, for example, from €19 billion (10.2 per cent) to €32.2 billion (13.5 per cent) (Robert Koch-Institut 2009).

At least seven major reforms as well as a number of smaller reforms have been implemented in the German health-care system over the past 25 years. They had wide-ranging effects on the way health care is organised, funded and regulated.

Modernisation and rationalisation, first steps away from collective solidarity towards the 'privatization of the costs of illness' as well as increased competition and market regulation are all characteristics of these reform agendas (Böckmann and Gerlinger 2009; Pannowitsch 2009; Gerlinger 2010). Interestingly, but not surprisingly, the process adopted was that of an institutionalised reform of incremental steps where each newly introduced reform provided the platform for another round of change (Pannowitsch 2009). As will be outlined in more detail in a later section of this chapter when focusing on the German medical wellness market in the country's traditional spas and health resorts, some of the particular measures taken had a direct influence, but by and large the full set of health-care system reforms that has taken place since the early 1990s provides the backdrop to an understanding of the current status of medical tourism in Germany. These reforms are therefore briefly outlined in the next section after a general introduction to the country's health-care system. The chapter then moves on to illustrate how these policy changes have impacted Germany's medical-tourism market which, considering the size of the health sector as a whole, is currently still marginal but expected to grow further.

Germany's health-care system

The health-care sector's greater financial needs compared to other industry sectors are reflected in a significant increase in health-related expenditure and its percentage of GDP over the past decades across all OECD (Organisation for Economic Co-operation and Development) countries. In Germany, the annual growth in health related expenditure over the past 35 years was 7.5 per cent and its percentage of GDP has increased by 78 per cent since 1970 (Felder 2010).

Interestingly, this trend does not seem to be greatly influenced by the way health care is organised and financed (Wehkamp 2006; Funk 2010). Probably more than any other policy field, the health sector seems to be dominated by national traditions and structures so that across Western industrialised countries a range of different health care systems have developed over time. Although hybrid models are increasingly common, three different fundamental approaches to health care can be observed (Wehkamp 2006). Health care in the United States, for example, is founded on a strongly market-driven approach. In this case, demand, supply and available financial means determine the individual level of medical care (Wehkamp 2006). The second model is the so-called Beveridge system, where health policy is fully financed through taxes and as such stands in direct competition with every other policy field. As a consequence, health care under this system tends to be cheaper, but not necessarily more effective. This approach, which is very popular across Europe and currently implemented to varying degrees, for example, in the United Kingdom, Denmark, Sweden, Italy, Greece and Spain, is characterised by a single national health service acting as the country's sole health-insurance fund. Under this system, medical claims normally do not incur a cost for the patient; however, there is a high level of bureaucracy and subsequently long waiting lists. The United Kingdom, for instance, where the

Beveridge system is implemented in its purest form, is plagued by the longest waiting lists in Europe for certain medical procedures. This has led to the development of a two-tiered medical system, where those who can and want to, either take out additional private health-insurance cover or travel to other countries to access medical care faster (Wehkamp 2006). In the context of inbound medical tourism, we will revert to this point in the later part of this chapter.

Known as the 'Bismarck Model', the third general approach to health care is to date only adopted (to varying degrees) in Germany and France. It is arguably the most expensive approach as it offers no real incentives for cost containment and at the same time impacts heavily on labour costs. However, it is also claimed that in this system the type and extent of medical services is dictated by medical best practice and patient needs rather than by economic considerations (Wehkamp 2006). In the following section, the main characteristics of this system, as it evolved over time in Germany, will be discussed in more detail.

Alongside insurance schemes for retirement, accidents and unemployment, health care is an important column of the German welfare state. These welfare pillars are in the main founded on the initiatives of Otto von Bismarck, the first German Chancellor of the German Empire (Handel 2009). For instance, in 1883 he established the German health-insurance system on a national level. Its key characteristics are collective solidarity, subsidiarity and various levels of corporatism (Green and Irvine 2001; Wehkamp 2006; Henderson 2009). With only some input from general taxation and a limited amount of consumer co-payments, the most important financial footing of health care is health-insurance funds (Jakubowski and Busse 1998; Green and Irvine 2001). Principally, these funds offer either compulsory cover as statutory insurance, which applies to almost 90 per cent of the population and is offered by about 250 different funds (Gerlinger 2010), or private insurance with premiums influenced by risk and a larger range of packages and differentiated premiums (Böckmann 2009). To potentially have private health insurance not only as a supplement to what is covered by the public system (as do about 9 per cent of Germans), but as a complete alternative to statutory insurance is a very unique feature of German health care which sets it apart from most other European systems and indeed most other industrialised nations around the world (Böckmann 2009). The option of a fully private health-insurance cover is only open to public servants, those who are self-employed and some high-income earners who have the opportunity to opt out of the compulsory statutory insurance scheme (Gerlinger 2010).

Despite fundamental differences, there is an important element common to both the public and the private health-insurance system, health-insurance premiums (based on a fixed percentage of taxable income in the case of the public system or on the respective private health-insurance package) are paid in almost equal parts by the employee as well as his/her employer (Green and Irvine 2001; Böckmann 2009; Gerlinger 2010). In the case of the statutory system, this arrangement reflects a social partnership based on collective solidarity as those who are on higher incomes ultimately face higher contributions (Ulrich 1996). Public and private health insurance in Germany covers not only the member but also his/her spouse and any children under the age of 18 (or under 23 if not employed/under 25 if still studying) and ensures access to a wide range of health-care services as well as the payment of sickness benefits. Germans thus enjoy the benefits of a health-care system which is arguably among the best in the world (Green and Irvine 2001; Breske 2004).

However, in view of its financing model of almost equal employer–employee contributions, it is obvious that the German health-insurance system is strongly dependent not only on a booming economy and high employment, but also significantly impacted by broader socio-economic factors like demographic change towards an increasingly aging society. In turn, it also has the potential to hinder Germany's international competitiveness by increasing labour costs (Gerlinger 2010). Against this backdrop, to ensure the health-care system's financial viability and at the same time its ability to provide a high standard in services, is therefore a formidable challenge and one of the main drivers of health-care system reform that has taken place since the late 1980s. The key tenets of the various reform measures are briefly outlined in the following section.

Health-care system reforms

The *Health Care Reform Act* (Gesundheitsreformgesetz) of 1989 as the major first step in a series of ensuing reforms (Table 5.1) was strongly influenced by a traditional cost-containment approach (Perschke-Hartmann 1994), as evident in its emphasis on preventative measures, early diagnosis and health promotion. It also set in motion the trend of privatising treatment costs that has been ongoing since with increasing consumer co-payments for a wide range of health-care services (e.g. for prescriptions, hospitalisation, dental and orthodontic treatments, optometrist services). Today, these amount to 10 per cent of total treatment costs within set minimum and maximum payments (Gerlinger 2010). In the light of exploding health-care costs, first measures towards more competition among health-insurance funds were introduced with the *Health Care Structure Act* (Gesundheitsstrukturgesetz) in 1993. It abolished the rather rigid traditional system of allocating members to particular funds depending on their occupation and offered the public free choice among the various statutory insurance funds. As intended, this move intensified competition and also significantly reduced fund numbers due to strategic mergers (Green and Irvine 2001; Gerlinger and Schönwälder 2007; Robert Koch-Institut 2009) but despite some inbuilt safeguards (a risk adjustment between the various funds known as 'Risikostrukturausgleich'), this also created a rather distorted market. Insurers started to compete for 'low-risk' members at the expense of those who suffered or were at risk of serious or chronic diseases and thus caused substantially higher treatment costs (Gerlinger 2010). Only with the introduction of additional corrective measures, such as incentives for providing special disease-management programs for the chronically ill, was it possible to ensure the continuing proper operation and also the legitimacy of the public health-insurance system (Gerlinger 2010).

Other reforms (e.g. *Promotion of Growth and Employment Act* and *Contribution Relief Act*, both in 1997) targeted, among other areas, rehabilitation measures and severely cut support through the health-care system for traditional 'Kur' treatments in Germany's spas and health resorts. As will be outlined at a later stage in this chapter, these reforms in particular had a substantial impact on the development of medical wellness tourism in the country.

In 2004, another major reform, the *Statutory Health Insurance Modernization Act*, 2004, aimed to reduce labour costs and therefore increase Germany's global competitiveness by, for the first time, watering down the traditional principle of equal employer–employee contributions to health-insurance premiums. It burdened members with 0.9 per cent more of the total costs but this was only a stepping stone towards the more radical changes implemented with the most recent reform package, the *Statutory Health Insurance Competition Strengthening Act*, 2007. Commencing in 2009, it dictated the same premiums for all statutory health-insurance funds (15.5 per cent of taxable income), but notably with higher employee (8.2 per cent) than employer (7.3 per cent) contributions. To maintain competition, depending on their financial situation, the option of an additional charge of up to 1 per cent for all members or a partial reimbursement of their contributions has been granted to the statutory insurance funds. There is now also the possibility within the statutory system of offering lower premiums to members in exchange for higher co-contributions to treatment costs, options which have previously been only available to those covered by private health insurance (Gerlinger 2010). These most recent reforms also continued to emphasise preventative measures and the need for more personal responsibility. Members with public health insurance are now, for example, required to regularly see their doctor to be screened for risk factors, for instance, for chronic diseases (e.g. diabetes, hypertension) and for various forms of cancer (Landeszentrale für politische Bildung Baden-Württemberg 2007; Robert Koch-Institut 2009).

It is obvious particularly with the latest reform measures that they might just be another step on the path towards a complete decoupling of health-insurance costs from taxable income. Currently, the liberal-conservative government coalition advocates the introduction of the same flat-rate premium for everyone independent of income ('Kopfpauschale'/Gesundheitsprämie'), whereas Labor and the Greens see the future of German health care in a system where everyone is covered by the same insurance ('Bürgerversicherung') and individual premiums are calculated not only on income but also on other assets (Allinger 2006; Spies 2006; Gerlinger 2010).

But no matter where the path of institutionalised health-care reform in Germany will ultimately lead to, there is no doubt that the various steps that have been taken over the past 30 years have led to intensified competition as well as a substantial privatisation of treatment costs, shifting the burden of sickness from the collective to the individual (Ewert 2009). Thus, economisation and marketisation have been the main impetus for health-care system reform in Germany. The former is evident in the way the health-care system now deals with its limited resources, namely more efficiency in many areas but also a less generous and more controlled distribution of its services. Tendencies towards marketisation, on the other hand, are obvious not only in the stronger competition which has been

Table 5.1 Main reforms to German health care

	Main measures
Health Care Reform Act (Gesundheitsreformgesetz), 1989	• Introduction of or increase in consumer co-payments for prescriptions, hospitalisation, dental and orthodontic treatments, optometrist services • Promotion of preventative measures, early diagnosis and health promotion
Health Care Structure Act (Gesundheitsstrukturgesetz), 1993	• Further increases to consumer co-payments (particularly regarding dental and orthodontic treatments) • Free choice among statutory insurance funds • Risk adjustments between funds depending on member structure (Risikostrukturausgleich)
Promotion of Growth and Employment Act (Wachstums- und Beschäftigungsförderungsgetz), 1997	• Duration of 'Kur' treatments reduced from 4 to 3 weeks
Contribution Relief Act (Beitragsentlastungsgesetz), 1997	• Higher consumer co-payments for prescriptions • Sickness benefit payments reduced from 80% to 70% of taxable income • Higher co-payments and cuts to services covered during 'Kur' treatments
Health Care Structure Reform Act (Gesundheitsreform), 2000	• Incentives for providing special disease management programs through statutory insurance funds • Further promotion of prevention and rehabilitation measures
Statutory Health Insurance Modernization Act (Gesetz zur Modernisierung der Krankenversicherung), 2004	• Employees pay extra 0.9% for health insurance (but no increase to employer contribution) • €10 payment per quarter when seeing a doctor • 10% co-payments (min €5, max €10) for prescriptions • €10 per day for hospital in-patients (to a maximum of 28 days)
Statutory Health Insurance Competition Strengthening Act (Gesetz zur Stärkung des Wettbewerbs in der gesetzlichen Krankenversicherung), 2007	• Same premium for all statutory health funds but with higher employee than employer contributions • Funds can charge members up to 1% more of their contributions or partially reimburse them • Flexible packages can be offered by statutory insurance funds (e.g. lower premiums but higher co-contribution to treatment cost)

Sources: Adapted from Lisac 2006 and Robert Koch-Institut 2009.

created within the system, but also in other market instruments such as a much greater role of demand and supply in the diversification of health-care products and services on offer, the outsourcing of particular services or the introduction of efficiency benchmarks (Ewert 2009).

One important consequence of these fundamental changes to the health-care system is a shift in consumer behaviour. As Ewert (2009: 22) highlights,

> While an economized health-care system favors cost containment policies and compliant users above all, the emergence of a health-care market with various tailored products and services forces users to act as experts on their own behalf, or rather as health consumers.

It is in particular this new 'breed' of health consumers which drives recent developments in Germany's health-tourism activities. With the onus of greater personal responsibility and faced with steady increases in co-payments and out-of-pocket expenses for health-care services no longer covered by the statutory funds, Germans become very aware of the choices they make.

Germany's health economy

These developments have fuelled a massive expansion of Germany's 'second health-care market', a market sector which covers a diverse range of health-care products and services that are fully paid by consumers. These range from sport and fitness offerings, wellness and alternative medical treatments to over-the-counter medication, preventative health measures and also a range of health-related tourism activities. The sheer size of this constantly expanding second health-care market, worth approximately €64 billion in 2008 (Kartte and Neumann 2008), is certainly a main contributor to the growth in Germany's health economy, which has transformed itself into a key industry sector, providing 11.5 per cent of total employment in 2008, despite decades of reforms aimed at reining in spiralling health-care costs (Bundesministerium für Gesundheit (BMG) 2011). With this has come a slow but steady change in the public and political perception of health care. Instead of a burden, it is now commonly seen as an opportunity for the national economy. Its transformation into a 'health economy' has been fuelled by demographically driven higher demand, by advancements in medical and pharmaceutical technology and by a generally greater health awareness across all sectors of society. Germany's health economy today is also characterised by a high level of cross-sectoral expansion beyond its core primary health-care sector and traditionally associated industries like the pharmaceutical industry and medical technology. Many more products and services conducive to the preservation and restoration of health, such as sport and fitness activities, balanced nutrition and healthy lifestyle options as well as health and wellness tourism are all contributing to the flourishing health economy (Institute for Work and Technology (IWT) 2010).

Health tourism in Germany

The expansion of the second health-care market has created new prospects for health tourism as a growing segment of Germany's health economy. Dörpinghaus (2009) highlights that a study on health tourism in Germany conducted by the

Institute for Leisure Economics found that between 2002–2007 the interest in this tourism-market segment rose by 31 per cent. Based on their findings, the Institute predicts a further increase of 82 per cent until 2020. Opaschowski (2010) reported that 35 per cent of all Germans were interested in wellness tourism and 10 per cent in medical and Kur tourism.

The blending of health with tourism is, however, not a new phenomenon (see Chapter 1; see also Hall 2011). In the eighteenth century, as Wesley and Pforr (2009) highlight, for instance, visitors were attracted to coastal destinations due to the apparent medicinal properties of seawater and sea air. In Lohmann's (2010) view, health tourism even constitutes the roots of modern tourism. The sector's attractiveness is thus only an incessant trend but, as Bennett *et al.* (2004) predict, one that is likely to continue well into the future. The rapidly expanding health-tourism market, which is fuelled by a very diverse range of needs and expectations, does not constitute a homogenous market segment, but embraces significantly different streams of special interest health tourism with respect to medical tourism (essential and elective medical treatment) and wellness tourism (beauty spa visitation, lifestyle resort visitation, spiritual retreat visitation), with an overlap between the two fields with respect to 'medical wellness' (Voigt *et al.* 2010). The notion health tourism can refer to leisure activities focusing on mental and physical wellness, to indulgence and pampering and also to preventative treatments and travel for the purpose of essential or elective hospital treatments or surgery (Rulle *et al.* 2010). Consequently, the market covers a continuum that ranges from medical tourism to wellness tourism spanning across spa treatments, spiritual retreats, sport holidays, medical wellness or 'Kur' visits. The latter, a specific medical prevention, reconvalescence and rehabilitation program or treatment for a particular chronic disease by highly qualified health professionals, is very popular in Germany's more than 300 certified spas and health resorts. More details on the impacts of health-care system reform on this particular health-tourism segment are discussed further below.

Kaspar (1996, in Mueller and Lanz-Kaufmann 2001: 7) attempts to highlight the broadness of the umbrella term 'health tourism' with his definition of

> the sum of all the relationships and phenomena resulting from a change of location and residence by people in order to promote, stabilise and, as appropriate, restore physical, mental and social wellbeing while using health services and for whom the place where they are staying is neither their principle nor permanent place of residence or work.

At one end of the health-tourism continuum, wellness tourism can then be seen as

> the sum of all the relationships resulting from a journey by people whose primary motive is to maintain or promote their health and well-being and who stay at least one night at a facility that is specially designed to enable and enhance people's physical, psychological, spiritual and/or social well-being.
>
> (Voigt 2008, in Voigt *et al.* 2010: 8)

On the other end of the spectrum, medical tourism can be differentiated as

> the sum of all the relationships and phenomena resulting from a journey by people whose primary motive is to treat or cure a medical condition by taking advantage of medical intervention services away from their usual place of residence while typically combining this journey with the consumption of tourism products and services.
>
> (Voigt *et al.* 2010: 8)

In essence, the global phenomenon of medical tourism is thus driven by more or less ailing people's motivation to improve their health status away from their usual place of residence. Reflecting this understanding are the terms 'patient tourism' (*Patiententourismus*) and 'hospital tourism' (*Spitaltourismus*), which in a German-speaking context are far more commonly used than medical tourism (Rulle *et al.* 2010). The notion of 'patient tourism' has a long-standing tradition in Germany and Switzerland, for instance, where it was quite common based on both country's excellent reputation and health facilities for international elites to travel to in order to receive particular medical treatments. Horowitz and Rosensweig (2007, 2008) refer to this as 'traditional international medical travel'. This form of medical tourism is aptly described in a classic piece of German literature, *The Magic Mountain* by Thomas Mann (1924), in which the son of a wealthy Hamburg merchant family who suffers from tuberculosis spends many years in a sanatorium in Davos in the Swiss Alps seeking a cure from his ailment. Today, high-end inbound medical tourism to Germany, where the cost of treatment is no obstacle, is still often driven by the country's reputation of providing health care of the highest standards (Germann 2009; Albaner and Grozea-Helmenstein 2002).

However, most instances of inbound medical tourism have their roots in failures in the health-care systems of the source markets. Reasons for this can be manifold: in countries like Canada and the UK waiting lists for particular types of medical intervention are a major problem; in less advanced countries, the health-care system might be underdeveloped and hence particular treatments not generally available, whereas in other countries, particularly where a privatised medical system dominates (e.g. United States), certain treatment option are simply too expensive for a majority of the population to afford (Albaner and Grozea-Helmenstein 2002; Kumar 2009). Horowitz and Rosensweig (2007, 2008) refer to these developments as 'new medical tourism'. Hubs for this modern form of medical tourism are concentrated in South and South East Asia and here in particular in India as well as Singapore, Thailand and Malaysia (see Chapters 11 and 12; Turner 2007; Cohen 2010).

German inbound medical tourism

Germany's source markets are mainly within Europe, particularly from its neighbours Netherlands, France, Austria and Poland as well as the United Kingdom. Beyond European borders, patients travel to Germany for medical services from

Russia and the United States as well as Middle Eastern countries, particularly Saudi Arabia, Kuwait and the United Arab Emirates (von Bandemer *et al.* 2009). A typical characteristic of inbound medical tourism in Germany is its concentration in only a few very specialised medical centres which are mainly located in Munich, Berlin, Hamburg, Frankfurt, Rastatt and Heidelberg (von Bandemer *et al.* 2009). There are large variations between different German clinics, on average 0.4 per cent of all patients are from outside Germany, but in some of the clinics specialised in treating international medical tourists (e.g. with expertise in orthopaedics, cardiology, paediatrics), this figure might be up to 40 per cent (Spielberg 2009). They have facilities catering specifically to the needs and expectations of this international clientele (e.g. competent and discrete treatments, airport transfer and translating services, specific tour packages for accompanying family members and/or patients, prayer rooms, particular dietary arrangements) (von Bandemer *et al.* 2009; Spielberg 2009) and solicit mainly in networks, for instance, with the help of a centralised organisation such as the 'Kuratorium' (German Curatorship for the Promotion of German Medicine Abroad). Its main purpose is information management, liaising with international partner organisations as well as quality control (Albaner and Grozea-Helmenstein 2002). In 2009, about 50 German hospitals advertised for international patients, for instance, via Internet, personal references and contacts, professional agencies, embassies and consulates as well as during international health conferences (Spielberg 2009).

In contrast to the newly emerging global hubs, medical tourism in Germany is a very small niche market at best (Juszczak 2006; Hajen 2009; Hinsken 2009; von Bandemer *et al.* 2009; Rulle *et al.* 2010; Deutsche Zentrale für Tourismus (DZT) 2011). Reports on actual numbers differ, but tend to range, in 2007 for instance, between only 58,800 (von Bandemer *et al.* 2009) and 80,000 (DZT 2011) medical tourists. Taking the more conservative figure into account, this translates into only 0.35 per cent of all treatment cases in Germany in that year, 0.26 per cent of the total income of all hospitals and also into only 0.24 per cent of all international tourist arrivals (von Bandemer *et al.* 2009; DZT 2008). Interestingly, a closer examination of the most common medical treatments of international patients reveals that in about 80 per cent of all cases their hospitalisation must have been unplanned, reflecting either an accident or medical emergency while holidaying in the country (e.g. cerebral haemorrhage, alcohol poisoning, acute myocardial events, premature birth and fractures). Strictly speaking, these cases, although related to international tourism, do not meet the definition of medical tourism per se, since the primary travel motivation was not to treat or cure a medical condition. How 'soft' data on international patients treated in Germany are, is also highlighted by Wismar *et al.* (2011) who found that in 2004, for example, 4,816 patients with permanent residency in France were treated in German hospitals, however, only 1,160 of them were accounted for officially via cross-border health-insurance reimbursement schemes. A more reliable indicator for the current status of Germany's medical tourism might therefore be the System of Health Accounts. According to these, the export volume of health products and services for foreigners travelling to Germany specifically for the purpose of obtaining these, thus for medical tourists in line with our narrow definition earlier, is with less than US$ 8 million indeed negligible (OECD 2009).

Most likely, the low volume of inbound medical tourism in Germany is directly related to the country's relatively high costs for medical treatments. In an international comparison of OECD countries, annual per capita health-related expenditure in Germany is above average, for example, in 2006, Germany with US$ 3,371 was well behind the United States with US$ 6,714, but was substantially more than in the United Kingdom (US$ 2,760), Italy (US$ 2,614) or Japan (US$ 2,578) (Niehaus and Finkenstädt 2009; Robert Koch-Institut 2009).

German outbound medical tourism

Considering the very low export volume of health products and services for foreigners travelling to Germany according to the System of Health Accounts, it is interesting to explore whether the country's import volume differs markedly; in other words, if Germans tend to travel to other countries to obtain medical care. There is certainly a lot of hype in printed and digital media about this phenomenon, but specific figures which help to seize this trend are difficult to come by. According to the System of Health Accounts, the country's import figures for health-related travel were at US$ 1.5 billion also very low, accounting for only about 0.5 per cent of all health-related expenditure in 2007. Interestingly, however, the trend is upwards with a 13 per cent increase over the period 2004–2007, making Germany the clear leader among 21 OECD countries for health-related travel (OECD 2009).

There are two principal reasons for this increase in outbound medical tourism and both are directly linked to the major reforms to German health care that have taken place in recent decades. With the privatisation of many treatment costs that has shifted the burden of sickness from the collective to the individual, Germans are faced with steadily increasing co-payments and substantial cuts to the number of medical products and services covered by the statutory insurance funds. Subsequently, patients are now forced to also adopt the role of a consumer in the health economy. The evolving second health-care market certainly fuels growth in the industry on a national level, but to a smaller degree also outside the country. In particular, in the areas of dental prosthesis and implants, 'Kur' treatments as well as the purchase of medication, price conscious consumers look beyond Germany's borders for cheaper options (Merten 2004). Rehabilitation care in the Czech Republic, for example, tends to be 30–40 per cent cheaper compared to Germany (Wismar *et al.* 2011).

On the other hand, faced with increasing competition, particularly since the latest round of health-care reform in 2007, which allows statutory insurance funds to reimburse their members for parts of their premiums, public health insurers are forced to be more economical in their operations. They, thus, have also started to search outside the country for cheaper health-service options for their members. A free flow of patients within the European Union would sit well with its principles of unrestricted movement of people, goods, services and capital. However, cross-border contracting poses many administrative, political and legal challenges, considering for instance that in most cases (as high as 93 per cent according to a study conducted by a German statutory insurance fund in 2003) patients are not even medical tourists in the narrow sense, but travellers who require medical attention while holidaying (Merten 2004). Based on rulings of the European Court of Justice on cross-border care, reforms to German health care in 2004 put in place a framework which allowed statutory insurance funds to arrange contracts with other European health-care providers. Tight regulations were, nonetheless, put in place, for example, only those health-related goods and services that were covered by statutory insurance funds in Germany could be obtained via cross-border contracting, they could only be obtained from the foreign public health-care system and the contracts had to be in accordance with German law (Nebling and Schemken 2006).

Driven by several decisions of the European Court of Justice, the Council of the European Union approved on 28 February 2011 a new EU Directive on cross-border health care. The intention is to facilitate the movement of patients across EU member states and to strengthen inter-state cooperation in a number of health-care areas (NHS European Office 2011; Council of the European Union 2011). The Directive 'provides clarity about the rights of patients who seek health care in another member state and supplements the right that patients already have at EU level through the legislation on the coordination of social security schemes' (Council of the European Union 2011: 1). Specifically, by October 2013 member states will have to make provisions in their national legislations to allow patients to receive health-care products and services in another EU country and be reimbursed for them to the same extent as they would be in their home country. Alternatively, payment for these services can be arranged directly between the member states. There must also be national contact points put in place which assist patients in making an informed choice on potentially obtaining cross-border health care. These have to provide, for example, the necessary information on rights, entitlements, quality, safety and practicalities (Council of the European Union 2011). Hailed as 'the first genuine example of EU legislation specifically in the area of health care services, which are traditionally the sole preserve of national governments' (NHS European Office 2011: 6–7), the EU Directive will undoubtedly pose an enormous challenge for the member states in organising the national logistics of this free flow of patients, particularly for hospital treatments and procedures which involve very expensive medical infrastructure and/or highly skilled operating personnel. Questions like how to plan for an uncertain number of additional patients or a potentially significant outflow need to be addressed. On the other hand, further growth in national health economies, including more employment opportunities, can be expected (Spielberg 2006).

As mentioned above, reliable figures on the number of Germans currently obtaining health-care products and services outside the country are difficult to find. It is estimated that the number is between 270,000–300,000 per annum (GEO 2011), mainly to Poland, the Czech Republic and Hungary. In 2007, the EU Commission estimated expenditure on cross-border health care with approximately €10 billion to be around 1 per cent of public-health spending (Hajen 2009). In 2004, the estimate for Germany was €455.8 million, which equates to an average of only €9 of the total per capita spending of €2,764 or 0.3 per cent of public health spending in that year (Nebling and Schemken 2006). Interestingly, this percentage was relatively stagnant (0.35–0.44 per cent) between 1992–2002 (van Ginneken and Busse 2011). With the new Directive in place, these numbers can be expected to increase, although it needs to be seen to what extent. In the light of ongoing health-care reform with a strong emphasis on marketisation and economisation, the attractiveness of cross-border health care for German patients and statutory insurance funds alike is likely to increase.

Domestic medical tourism

In the light of the currently still low volume of German inbound and outbound medical tourism, it is travel within the country for medical and more recently increasingly also for wellness purposes, which forms the basis for Germany's health-tourism market. It takes place in particular in its more than 300 certified spas and health resorts, which include mineral and moor spas (*Mineral- und Moorheilbäder*), climatic resorts (*heilklimatische Kurorte*), seaside spas and resorts (*Seeheil- und Seebäder*) and Kneipp spas and resorts (*Kneippheilbäder und Kneippkurorte*) depending on their particular natural resources (e.g. soil, sea, climate) (Deutscher Heilbäderverband (DHV) 2009a). Among them are internationally renowned thermal spa destinations like Baden-Baden and Aachen, which date back to the Roman era (Erfurt-Cooper and Cooper 2009). In 2010, more than 20 million visitors spent 102.8 million nights (about one-third of all visitor nights) in these spas and health resorts (DHV 2009b), they generated approximately 10 per cent of GDP (€30 billion) and offered employment for about 350,000 people, figures which underline the importance of this particular health-tourism segment for the country (DZT 2011).

A key characteristic of these destinations are the previously mentioned 'Kur' treatments, which have to a large, but in the light of ongoing health-care reform diminishing, degree been funded by statutory insurance funds. In line with the government's focus on economisation and marketisation in the health-care system, the *Contribution Relief Act* (*Beitragsentlastungsgesetz*) in 1997, for example, cut the standard duration of a 'Kur' from 4 to 3 weeks, allowed its prescription only every 4 years instead of every 3 years and more than doubled the daily patient co-contribution. It was also no longer possible to have a 'Kur' treatment funded purely for preventative purposes. The *Health Care Structure Reform Act* (Gesundheitsreform), 2000, with its stronger emphasis on prevention and rehabilitation measures in the context of outpatient care (instead of in-patient treatments in a facility away from home), also proved detrimental for the often rural official spas and health resorts, which relied strongly on domestic 'Kur' travel. To make matters even worse, other destinations particularly within Europe have started to market their own 'Kur' treatments, which might not be as well reputed but are often substantially cheaper than those offered by their German counterparts (Landtag von Baden-Württemberg 2008). These offers attract not only self-funding guests but also statutory insurance funds which now often include these international 'Kur' programs into their standard product offerings.

It needs, however, to be highlighted that not all implemented health-care system reform measures had a negative impact on Germany's certified spas and health resorts. In particular, the generally stronger promotion of prevention and rehabilitation measures played into the hands of these destinations, but mainly outside their traditional 'Kur' business. Subsequently, most of them have started to broaden their operations with the inclusion of health promotion and wellness products and services as a second business platform alongside the traditional 'Kur' treatments (Kliegel 2007). With this move, they have started to rejuvenate their image by successfully blending tradition with innovation. Certified spas and health resorts are well placed to tap into the growing, privately funded medical wellness market by promoting their existing infrastructure, expertise and reputation (DHV 2009b). Together with a number of newly emerging wellness destinations, they now compete for a growing number of well-informed and price-conscious health consumers, who currently fuel Germany's expanding second health-care market. In 2008, in some of the officially recognised 'Kur' destinations up to 80 per cent of guests self-funded their visit. This figure indicates that spas and health resorts will in the future rely less and less on statutory insurance funds for their business (Kurdirektion Bad Wörishofen 2008). Changes in market profile are, for example, reflected in visitation numbers for these destinations. Between 1999–2008 arrival numbers increased by 23.6 per cent, but visitor nights were relatively stagnant (plus 4.1 per cent), which indicates that price sensitive self-funding health and wellness tourists tend to prefer shorter but also more frequent visits (DHV 2009b).

Conclusion

Against some key tenets of the German health-care system as background, the chapter highlighted how decades of policy changes with their focus on economisation and marketisation, and here in particular on more competition and higher individual financial contributions, have influenced medical tourism in Germany. In our discussion, we have adopted three perspectives, inbound, outbound and domestic tourism. The former is driven by Germany's long-standing reputation of providing high-quality medical services in a timely manner. Due to the country's relatively high costs of health-care services, its export volume for health-related goods and services is currently, though increasing, nonetheless very small. A similar situation was noted for outbound medical tourism, where patients, often encouraged by their health funds, opt to access medical services abroad, mainly in neighbouring EU countries. This process has certainly been facilitated by the European liberalisation of cross-border health care. In particular, the latest EU Directive (2011), once fully implemented by all EU member states, can be expected to further facilitate outbound medical tourism. But again, despite steady increases, the number of Germans currently travelling abroad is still very small. So at present, medical tourism is mainly a domestic phenomenon, concentrated in the main on the country's certified spas and health resorts, which are specialised in specific medical prevention, reconvalescence and rehabilitation programs. The funding of these 'Kur' treatments and thus their popularity was strongly affected by health policy, particularly by specific reform measures in 1997 and 2000. As was illustrated earlier, the crisis response by many of the traditional 'Kur' destinations has been to concentrate strongly on the development of medical wellness as a second business platform. By tapping into the growing self-funded second health-care market, they have started to broaden their traditional customer base. What made this move successful in many instances has been an ability to offer specialised, differentiated and authentic products and services built on endogenous potentials, most importantly a tradition of health competence.

In conclusion, it can be clearly stated that, at present, medical tourism in Germany, particularly with respect to inbound and outbound activities, is a very small tourism niche. It is difficult to accurately seize the market, not only because there is very little scholarly documentation, but also since data vary quite considerably, reflecting that it can be difficult to differentiate between medical tourism in a narrow sense as opposed to health tourism in general and also the treatment of patients who just happen to be international tourists to the country. Nonetheless, the trend lines certainly point upwards and in some instances significant growth rates have been reported. This might explain why medical tourism currently receives a considerable amount of media and government attention, but any report on growth needs to be seen in the context of a very low base level. Nonetheless, it can be expected that a continuing liberalisation in Germany's health-care system, further cuts to services covered by the statutory system and thus a further privatisation of the risk of illness will fuel further growth in this sector although its volume might remain limited in the medium term.

References

Albaner, J. and Grozea-Helmenstein, D. (2002) *Bestandsaufnahme der Entwicklungspotenziale im Gesundheitstourismus*, Wien: Bundesministerium für Wirtschaft und Arbeit. BMWA.

Allinger, H.J. (2006) *Bürgerversicherung und Kopfpauschale Haben Vieles Gemeinsam – Anmerkungen zu einer Reform der Gesetzlichen Krankenversicherung* (Passauer Diskussionspapiere: Volkswirtschaftliche Reihe), Passau: Gruppe der volkswirtschaftlichen Professoren, Universität Passau.

Bennett, M., King, B. and Milner, L. (2004) 'The health resort sector in Australia: a positioning study', *Journal of Vacation Marketing*, 10(2): 122–36.

Böckmann, R. (2009) 'The private health insurance: demarketization of a welfare market?' *German Policy Studies*, 5(1): 119–40.

Böckmann, R. and Gerlinger, T. (2009) 'Health policy and marketization: introduction', *German Policy Studies*, 5(1): 1–2.

Breske, F. (2004) *Leistungskatalog des Gesundheitswesens im Internationalen* Vergleich, Kiel: Institut für Gesundheits-System-Forschung.

Bundesministerium für Gesundheit (BMG) (2011) *Daten des Gesundheitswesens 2010*, Berlin: BMG.

Cohen, E. (2010) 'Medical travel – a critical assessment', *Tourism Recreation Research*, 35(3): 225–37.

Council of the European Union (2011) *Directive on cross-border health care adopted* (Press Release). [Online]. Available at: http://www.consilium.europa.eu/uedocs/cms_data/docs/pressdata/en/lsa/119514.pdf (accessed 18 June 2011).

Deutsche Zentrale für Tourismus (DZT) (2008) *Incoming Tourismus-Deutschland*, Frankfurt: DZT.

Deutsche Zentrale für Tourismus (DZT) (2011) *Leitfaden Gesundheitstourismus*, Frankfurt: DZT.

Deutscher Heilbäderverband (DHV) (2009a) *Die Kur in Deutschland*, Berlin: DHV.

Deutscher Heilbäderverband (DHV) (2009b) *Jahresbericht 2009*, Berlin: DHV.

Dörpinghaus, S. (2009) *Medical Wellness – Zukunftsmarkt Mit* Hindernissen, Gelsenkirchen: IAT.

Erfurt-Cooper, P. and Cooper, M. (2009) *Health and Wellness Tourism. Spas and Hot Springs*, Bristol: Channel View Publications.

Ewert, B. (2009) 'Economization and marketization in the German health care system: how do users respond?', *German Policy Studies*, 5(1): 21–44.

Felder, S. (2010) 'Ökonomie des gesundheitswesens: genese und optimierung', *Das Parlament*, 45. [Online]. Available at: http://www.das-parlament.de (accessed 18 March 2011).

Funk, K. (2010) 'Gesundheitspolitik in internationaler perspektive', Das Parlament, 45. [Online]. Available at: http://www.das-parlament.de (accessed 18 March 2011).

GEO (2011) *Gesund Reisen – Medizintourismus*. [Online]. Available at: http://www.geo.de (accessed 12 June 2011).

Gerlinger, T. (2010) 'Health care reform in Germany', *German Policy Studies*, 6(1): 107–42.

Gerlinger, T. and Schönwälder, T. (2007) *Gesundheitsreformen in Deutschland 1975-2007* (Themen), Berlin: Bundeszentrale für politische Bildung. [Online]. Available at: http://www.bpb.de/themen/ (accessed 10 April 2010).

Germann, M. (2009) *Potential des Internationalen Medizintourismus am Sempacher See*, Siders: STF.

Golz, H.-G. (2010) 'Editorial', *Das Parlament*, 45. [Online]. Available at: http://www.das-parlament.de (accessed 18 March 2011).

Green, D.G. and Irvine, B. (2001) *Health Care in France and Germany: Lessons for the UK*, London: Civitas.

Hajen, L. (2009) 'Europäischer wachstumsmarkt. Gesundheitsdienstleistungen zwischen vision und realität'. Paper presented at the Symposium *Gesundheitsdienstleistungen im Europäischen binnenmarkt*, Johan Wolfgang Goethe Universität Frankfurt, 24–25 November 2009.

Hall, C.M. (2011) 'Health and medical tourism: kill or cure for global public health?' *Tourism Review*, 66(1/2): 4–15.

Handel, G. (2009) *Social Welfare in Western Society*, New Brunswick, NJ: Transaction Publishers.

Henderson, J.W. (2009) *Health Economics and Policy*, Mason, OH: Cengage Learning.

Hinsken, E. (2009) 'Greetings from Germany – offer of first class health tourism', *Medical Tourism*, 12(9/10): 70.

Horowitz, M.D. and Rosensweig, J.A. (2007) 'Medical tourism – health care in the global economy', *Physician Executive*, 33(6): 24–30.

Horowitz, M.D. and Rosensweig, J.A. (2008) 'Medical tourism vs. traditional international medical travel: a tale of two models', *International Medical Travel Journal*, 1–14. [Online]. Available at: http://www.imtjonline.com (accessed 30 May 2011).

Institute for Work and Technology (IWT) (2010) Structure of the health economy. [Online]. Available at: http://www.iatge.de/ (accessed 19 March 2010).

Jakubowski, E. and Busse, R. (1998) *Health Care Systems in the EU. A Comparative Study (Public Health and Consumer Protection Series, SACO 101 EN)*, Brussels: European Parliament, Directorate General for Research.

Juszczak, J. (2006) 'Medizintourismus als chance für die tourismusindustrie'. Paper presented at ITB Hochschulforum, Berlin, 8 March 2006.

Kartte, J. and Neumann, K. (2008) *Der Gesundheitsmarkt*. Berlin: Roland Berger Strategy Consultants.

Kliegel, I. (2007) 'Der markt der gesundheit. Daten, fakten, trends', *Focus Marktanalysen*, 1–43.

Kumar, R. (2009) *Global Trends in Health and Medical Tourism*, New Delhi: SBS.

Kurdirektion Bad Wörishofen (2008) *Kur- und Tourismusbericht 2008*, Bad Wörishofen: Kurdirektion Bad Wörishofen.

Landeszentrale für politische Bildung Baden-Württemberg (2007) *Die Gesundheitsreform 2007 (Dossiers)*. Stuttgart: Landeszentrale für politische Bildung Baden-Württemberg. [Online]. Available at: http://www.lpb-bw.de/gesundheitsreform.html (accessed 22 March 2010).

Landtag von Baden-Württemberg (2008) *Förderung Öffentlicher Tourismuseinrichtungen (Drucksache 14/3414)*, Stuttgart: Landtag von Baden-Württemberg.

Lisac, M. (2006) *Health Care Reform in Germany: Not the Big Bang*, Gütersloh: Bertelsmann Stiftung.

Lohmann, M. (2010) Nachfragepotenziale im Gesundheitstourismus – Chancen und Herausforderungen im Quellmarkt Deutschland (ÖGAF/ITF – Expertengespräch), Wien, 25 November.

Mann, T. (1924) *The Magic Mountain (Der Zauberberg)*. Berlin: S. Fischer Verlag.

Merten, M. (2004), 'Patientenmobilität in Europa. Von tourismus keine spur', *Deutsches Ärzteblatt*, 101(27), 1942–44.

Mueller, H. and Lanz-Kaufmann, E. (2001) 'Wellness tourism: market analysis of a special health tourism segment and implications for the hotel industry', *Journal of Vacation Marketing*, 7(1): 5–17.

Nebling, T. and Schemken, H.-W. (2006) 'Cross-border contracting: the German experience', in M. Rosenmöller, M. McKee and R. Baeten (eds) *Patient Mobility in the European Union*, Copenhagen: WHO.

NHS European Office (2011) Patient choice beyond borders. Implications of the EU Directive on cross-border healthcare for NHS commissioners and providers (Briefing), 7: 1–8. [Online]. Available at: http://www.nhsconfed.org/Publications/briefings/Pages/Patient-choice-beyond-borders.aspx (accessed 22 June 2011).

Niehaus, F. and Finkenstädt, V. (2009) *Deutschland – Ein im Internationalen Vergleich Teures Gesundheitswesen? (WIP Diskussionspapier 12/09)*, Köln: Wissenschaftliches Institut der PKV.

Opaschowski, H.W. (2010) 'Wohin geht die reise?', *Diercke Weltatlas Magazin*, 2: 4–5.

Organisation for Economic Co-operation and Development (OECD) (2009) *Health at a Glance 2009-OECD Indicators*, Paris: OECD.

Pannowitsch, S. (2009) 'Institutionalized healthcare reform in Germany? Error correction or political strategy?', *German Policy Studies*, 5(1): 141–68.

Perschke-Hartmann, C. (1994) *Die Doppelte Reform. Gesundheitspolitik von Blüm zu Seehofer*, Opladen: Leske and Budrich.

Robert Koch-Institut (2009) Ausgaben und Finanzierung des Gesundheitswesens (Gesundheitsberichterstattung des Bundes, Heft 45), Berlin: Robert Koch-Institut.

Rulle, M., Hoffmann, W. and Kraft, K. (2010) *Erfolgsstrategien im Gesundheitstourismus. Analyse zur Erwartung und Zufriedenheit von Gästen*, Berlin: Erich Schmidt Verlag.

Spielberg, P. (2006) 'Kommission auf schmusekurs', *Deutsches Ärzteblatt*, 103(47): 3162.

Spielberg, P. (2009) 'Individuelle rundumbetreuung erwünscht', *Deutsches Ärzteblatt*, 106(47): 2361.

Spies, T. (2006) *Die Bürgerversicherung - Zukunftsfähig und Gerecht*, Frankfurt: VAS-Verlag.

Statistisches Bundesamt (2011) *Gesundheitsausgaben 2009 (Tabelle Gesundheitsausgaben in Deutschland in Mio. €)*, Berlin: DSTATIS.

Turner, L. (2007) 'Medical tourism: family medicine and international health-related travel', *Canadian Family Physician*, 53(10): 1639–41.

Ulrich, V. (1996) 'Health care in Germany: structure, expenditure, and prospects', in W. McArthur, C. Ramsay and M. Walker (eds) *Healthy Incentives: Canadian Health Reform in an International Context*, Vancouver: The Fraser Institute. [Online]. Available at: http://www.oldfraser.lexi.net/publications/books/health_reform/germany (accessed 12 May 2010).

van Ginneken, E. and Busse, R. (2011) 'Cross-border health care data', in M. Wismar, W. Palm, J. Figueras, K. Ernst and E. van Ginneken (eds) *Cross-Border Health Care in the European Union*, Copenhagen: WHO.

Voigt, C., Laing, J., Wray, M., Brown, G., Howat, G., Weiler, B. and Trembath, R. (2010) *Health Tourism in Australia: Supply, Demand and Opportunities*. Gold Coast: STCRC.

von Bandemer, S., Salewski, K. and Schwanitz, R. (2009) *Die Internationalisierung der Gesundheitswirtschaft*, Gelsenkirchen: IWT.

Wehkamp, K.-H. (2006) 'Balanceakt zwischen Bismarck und Beveridge', *Das Parlament*, 50. [Online]. Available at: http://www.das-parlament.de (accessed 18 March 2011).

Wesley, A. and Pforr, C. (2009) 'Historical dimensions of coastal tourism', in R. Dowling and C. Pforr (eds) *Coastal Tourism Development*, New York: Cognizant Communication Corporation.

Wismar, M., Palm, W., Figueras, J., Ernst, K. and van Ginneken, E. (2011) Cross-border Health Care in the European Union, Copenhagen: WHO.

6 Thermal medical versus surgical medical tourism in Hungary

The challenges of reconciling public and private sector policies

Melanie Smith, László Puczkó and Ivett Sziva

Introduction

This chapter focusses on the relationship between thermal tourism and surgical medical tourism in Hungary and the policies of more than 50 years which have influenced their development. Most of Hungary's thermal bath complexes were not constructed until after the Second World War, with the exception of some of the renovated Turkish baths in Budapest. They were therefore developed during the state socialist period (1945–1989), when tourism was mainly limited to domestic and intra-regional (Central and Eastern European) tourism, and the focus was predominantly on thermal medical tourism. The main aim of policy during this time was for the State to support medical trips to thermal destinations.

After 1989, post-socialist governments continued to support domestic thermal medical tourism in the form of holiday vouchers (from the early 1990s), but by the 2000s, especially after Hungary's European Union (EU) accession in 2004, policy started to focus more on surgical medical tourism. This started mainly with clinics and hospitals offering surgical procedures within thermal medical locations, but has gradually extended to non-thermal destinations (e.g. dentistry in Sopron and Magyaróvár). Policy priorities included attracting medical tourists from Europe, so medical and thermal hotels were improved and Destination Management Organisations began to be developed by 2006. The government, elected in 2010, plans to replace the Holiday Voucher System, which provides state-supported thermal medical trips for domestic tourists, to focus on dentistry and provide incentives for state hospitals to open up to private patients for other surgical treatments.

Overall, thermal medical tourism has largely been supported by the state and used by domestic tourists, whereas surgical medical tourism is predominantly provided by the private sector and used by international tourists. International tourists do use the thermal waters, but usually for leisure or recreational reasons, and only because they happen to be an attraction of the location (e.g. the heritage baths in Budapest). Many international visitors are not familiar with the evidence-based healing properties of medical waters and may not trust them anyway. The exception to this would be Central and Eastern European visitors, but they are more likely to visit medical thermal baths in their own countries where they are given state support for domestic tourism.

There have therefore been relatively few attempts to reconcile public and private sector policies for thermal medical and surgical medical tourism until recently. This chapter will critically analyse the challenges of doing so in region and a country where collaboration, partnerships and clustering are fairly new concepts. The data in this chapter is derived from a content analysis of health-tourism resources as listed on the Hungarian National Tourist Office's website; 294 personal interviews with health tourists in Békés County Health Tourism Cluster (Hungary); a website analysis of 200 private surgical medical clinics, and desk-based research looking at secondary sources such as government and research agency statistics, strategies and policies.

Overview of health tourism in Hungary

Health tourism in Hungary is inextricably connected to its thermal baths and historic bathing culture. Hungary has some of the richest geothermal water resources in the world. Bathing culture (sometimes referred to as 'spa culture') is nearly 2,000 years old, going back to pre-Roman Celtic times and including the Turkish occupation in the sixteenth century, which left a legacy of (Turkish) baths especially in Budapest. Because bathing culture is based on natural resources, thermal and medical tourism have always played an important role in Hungarian tourism, and attracted international medical tourists and domestic tourists. Thermal or medical waters can be found in over 80 per cent of Hungary. Nearly 300 thermal springs are used for bathing and in 385 settlements all over Hungary there are baths/spas with healing water (VITUKI-MAFI-Aquaprofit 2006). The National Health Tourism Development Strategy in 2007 identified 17 baths of international significance, 60 baths of regional significance and a further 110 baths of local significance. About 130 mineral and medicinal springs are located in the capital, Budapest. There are 13 Hungarian settlements with 'health-resort' qualification: Balf, Bük, Kékestető, Lillafüred, Balatonfüred, Debrecen, Eger, Gyula, Hajdúszoboszló, Harkány, Hévíz, Parád and Zalakaros.

Much of the time, medical tourism in Hungary typically involves a tourist using thermal or medical baths under the supervision or prescription of a doctor. Like in many other Central and Eastern European countries, the state historically supported domestic tourists' visits to medical waters, often for several weeks at a time. Hungary has around 31 medical hotels, which must have doctors and trained medical staff on site and provide medical treatments (typically based on natural healing assets, i.e. thermal waters). These hotels are located in the greater thermal-hubs of Hungary, namely the northwest and northeast, but some of them are positioned mainly for international tourists in Budapest. Medical hotel status can only be gained from the National Public Health and Medical Officer Service that has strict criteria for any applicant. The Hotel Association of Hungary had an initiative, which would have been aimed at hotels wanting to become medical hotels, but the new medical hotel standards did not become operational.

Hungary is also becoming relatively well-known for its surgical medical tourism, especially dental treatments, plastic surgery and orthopaedic surgery. Hungarian medical science and research has achieved a high international profile in the areas of orthopaedics (backbone surgery), cardiology (invasive surgery), treating disabled people (Pető-method) or in vitro fertilisation (IVF; Kaáli-method). The Medical Tourism Association (2009) also states that Hungarian surgeons are held to much stricter educational standards than those in the United Kingdom or the United States. However, until recently, this form of medical tourism was not as actively promoted by the government as thermal medical tourism, despite the fact that Youngman (2009) estimated that the number of medical touristic arrivals in Hungary is as high as in some Asian countries. In addition, few Hungarian clinics possess international accreditation, according to the list of the accreditation institutions (JCI [Joint Commission International], Tempos, ACHS [Australian Council for Healthcare Standards]), and only 15 per cent of a sample of 200 clinics analysed by the authors have TÜV/International Organization for Standardization (ISO) accreditation.

There are no exact statistics for the surgical medical tourist market, but according to some estimates (e.g. the Hungarian Healthcare Research Institution; ESKI 2009), the private sector is responsible for most of the turnover. The turnover of the total market (private and public sectors) is estimated at around 36–56 billion HUF (1 EUR = 265 HUF), 90 per cent of which is offered by private service providers. Nearly 300,000–400,000 medical tourists arrive in Hungary yearly, and around 50–60 per cent of them are treated at private clinics. There are around 600–800 private clinics for surgical medical tourism, most of which offer dentistry (80 per cent), cosmetic surgery, eye surgery, IVF and a small amount of obesity surgery. Public clinics or hospitals tend to focus on gynaecology, cancer, cardio-vascular treatments and eye surgery.

In order to provide a more detailed overview and analysis of the current health-tourism resources and facilities in Hungary, the authors undertook a content analysis on the online communication materials of health-tourism suppliers. The sample was selected from the official Hungarian National Tourist Office (HNTO 2009) list of health-tourism providers and was based on a stratified, random sample (every fifth site on average was analysed). In some cases (e.g. the mofetta, caves, aquapark) only one example was taken as there are very few of these sites available:

- 85 thermal baths;
- 92 locations with wellness baths;
- 107 wellness hotels;
- 52 spa hotels;
- 10 spa hospitals;
- 8 aquaparks;
- 5 thermal water caves;
- 1 mofetta or carbon dioxide healing bath.

The analysis aimed to show the main orientation of service providers (i.e. medical, wellness, leisure, beauty), as well as typical facilities and treatments. This resulted in the analysis detailed in Table 6.1 (% indicates the number of sites in the sample with these facilities or services).

It is clear from the analysis in Table 6.1 that the main focus of most of the health-tourism attractions in Hungary is on medical tourism. There are relatively

Table 6.1 Content analysis of Hungarian health-tourism sites and resources

Type of facility	*Number in sample*	*Main orientation*	*Typical facilities*
Mofetta	1	Medical	Carbon dioxide bath, physiotherapy, massages, hydrotherapy
Cave	1	Medical	Climate for healing respiratory organs, no special treatments
Aquapark	1	Leisure Medical	Mediterranean atmosphere, child-world Treatments based on healing water, physiotherapy Some wellness services (e.g. for new mothers)
Spa hospitals	2	Medical Main specialisation: rehabilitation, rheumatology, angiology, clinical services (e.g. gastroenterology, gynaecology, healing infertility)	Healing-water bath In-patient departments
Spa hotels	10	Medical services (90%) Main specialisation: rehabilitation, locomotive diseases Preventive or complex medical wellness services (70%)	Healing water baths, balneo-physiotherapeutic treatments, diagnostic sections, dental clinics, traditional massages Wellness treatments (50%)
Wellness baths	15	Medical services (100%) Wellness elements (70%)	Thermal bath (100%), medical supervision + balneo-physiotherapy (50%) Wellness services: sauna (70%) traditional massages (50%)
Thermal baths	17	Medical Leisure	Thermal bath (100%); balneo-physiotherapy (45%), wellness services (45%)
Wellness hotels	25	Wellness Beauty Leisure	Sauna world (76%), massage (76%), beauty (64%), bath world (60%), sports (44%), balneotherapy (36%), lifestyle consultation (24%), ayurveda (20%), occupational wellness (4%)

few privately owned and managed leisure facilities with only a handful of aquaparks and hotels specifically serving families with children. In some cases, operators have made the mistake of trying to attract three generations simultaneously, whose interests may be mismatched or conflicting (i.e. some spas were built with aquapark type facilities for kids alongside traditional medical facilities for the elderly). This suggests that medical thermal tourism and recreational thermal tourism do not mix. Medical wellness is a feature of some spa hotels, which means a medical practitioner-supervised wellness programme.

Overall, health tourism in Hungary yields an income of EUR 368 million. Medical tourism in particular has a significant economic impact. The registered market of tourism based on medicinal waters – including the domestic and international turnover – was estimated at about EUR 147 million in 2008. Dental tourism alone yields a similar sum of revenue (ESKI 2009).

The markets for medical tourism in Hungary

International health tourists visit four main types of medical and wellness tourism services in Hungary: medical hotels for typical balneotherapy (water-based medical therapies), dental clinics, wellness hotels and historic baths in Budapest. Foreign visitors tend to prefer modern, purpose-built bath complexes and historic facilities (e.g. the Turkish baths in Budapest, Art Nouveau or Baroque-style baths). However, there are a growing number of international medical tourists who appreciate the high-quality medical services and the good price/quality ratio (in relation to the prices of similar services and treatments in Western European countries and elsewhere). These tourists mainly come for surgical medical tourism rather than thermal-bath–based medical tourism. Medical services based on natural assets such as thermal waters (so-called 'evidence-based medicine') are not approved in many countries, which has created a permanent challenge to attract foreign tourists. On the other hand, Hungarian statistics show that domestic tourists happily use any thermal (often medical) waters, regardless of their impacts or contraindications. 64.4 per cent of Hungarians consider their thermal/medical baths to be world famous and 59.3 per cent believe that these waters and related services can cure or prevent illnesses (Halassy 2007).

Recent statistics show that there are around 0.6 million health tourists in Hungary, which represents 4.6 per cent of all tourists. Approximately half of these are international. The main sender countries are Germany (36 per cent), Austria (14 per cent) and Russia (6 per cent). Domestic tourists tend to spend around $US 41 per day whereas international tourists spend double that ($US 82 per day). There are around 1.2 million guest nights in medical hotels, which are roughly split between international tourists (300,000 visits in 2009) and domestic tourists (400,000 visits in 2009) (Hungarian Central Statistical Office (HCSO) 2009). Domestic tourism clearly plays an important role in Hungarian health tourism, especially for thermal/medical water-based tourism. This can be explained by the fact that the state subsidises medical treatments and trips (ten different medical treatments can be used by prescription per year).

After the Second World War, in socialist Central and Eastern Europe (CEE) medical treatments in spas were largely sponsored by the state or trade unions. After the end of the socialist period in 1989, some governments in CEE (e.g. Hungary, Czech Republic, Slovakia) started to invest large sums in the development and upgrading of traditional medical spa resorts. The state still provides large subsidies for medical treatments and trips in the form of 'social tourism'. Following this model, Hungary introduced the system of holiday cheques as part of a social tourism scheme on January 1st, 1998. These can be purchased by companies for their employees or can

Table 6.2 The expansion of the range of services covered by holiday cheques in Hungary, 1998–2009

1998–2003	*2004–2006*	*2007–2008*	*2009*
Accommodation	Accommodation	Accommodation	Accommodation
	Eating out	Eating out	Catering/eating out
	Fishing permits	Fishing permits	Fishing permits
	Cultural programmes, festivals, zoo	Cultural programmes, festivals, zoo	*(in a new category)*
	Fuel	Fuel	N/A
	Travelling by train, coach and ship	Travelling by train, coach and ship	Travelling by train, coach and ship
	Visiting thermal baths	Visiting thermal baths	Visiting thermal baths
		Cultural attractions, sightseeing	Visiting zoos and botanical gardens
		Health conservation and illness prevention	Cultural services
		Leisure sports (e.g. fitness, wellness)	Health conservation and illness prevention
			Swimming pool services and spa treatment
			Sport and cultural services (including Formula-1 and BNV Exhibition Centre)
			Renting equipment
			Pleasure flights
			Motorway tickets
			Cinema tickets
			Internet subscription
			Domestic travel insurance

Source: Derived from HNFR, 2009.

be received by disadvantaged groups (e.g. pensioners, young people). Holiday cheques are more and more popular from year to year, and can be mentioned as one of the main driving forces of the increase in domestic travel of Hungary, as well as domestic health tourism (Puczkó and Rátz 2011). In 2008, 35 billion HUF worth of holiday cheques (+24 per cent to 2007) were redeemed at different service providers, and an amount of 14 billion HUF at hotels. The cheques used for health preservation services (treatments, massages) showed a dynamic increase: 896 million HUF was spent on such services in 2008 (a 460 per cent increase from 2007) (HCSO 2009). Table 6.2 shows the proliferation of possible services for which cheques could be used, including visits to thermal baths.

However, one major barrier to the use of health-tourism services is still the fact that they tend to be too expensive for citizens with average earnings and there is a general lack of information about available services (the average earning is $US 630 per person per month). The research of the HNTO (Halassy 2007) showed that 49.5 per cent of the respondents find Hungarian medical baths expensive. The rest of the respondents even with average yearly income would need a discount of nearly 40 per cent so as to afford health services, and around 24 per cent would need a 25 per cent discount. The main target segments of health tourism seem to be the age groups of 18–24 years and 41–50 years (although this also includes wellness tourism. It should be noted that thermal medical tourists on average tend to be aged 55 or over). In both age groups, those who are particularly interested in health trips are better educated, have a higher than average income, are living in towns, and travelling in three-member families.

The HNTO ran a themed Year of Waters in 2007 for the domestic market. The communication focussed on both thermal and fresh waters. Surveys were conducted before and after the themed year about their travelling habits including health and wellness motivations. The results show that health preservation became more popular between 2006–2008. In 2006, 5.6 per cent of respondents said that the main motivation for domestic trips was health preservation, whereas in 2008 the same proportion was 15.1 per cent (HNTO–M.Á.S.T. 2008). This is a positive indication that the propensity to travel for reasons of preventative healthcare is increasing, albeit relatively slowly.

Policy and planning for health tourism in Hungary

It seems that thermal bath tourism, which is mainly public-sector supported, and surgical medical tourism, which is mainly private-sector supported, need to be analysed separately. However, a growing number of private spas and hotels make use of thermal waters, and some public hospitals and clinics have started to become involved in surgical tourism to improve their financial situation. There is no official data on the involvement of public hospitals in privately funded surgical procedures. However, it is assumed that surgeons tend to use public facilities and staff for their privately funded operations (i.e. a private patient can be operated on in a public hospital, but the fees are paid to the surgeons directly).

In terms of policy and strategy, the Government's Széchenyi Tourism Development Plan (2000) and the 10-year Health Tourism Development Programme (2000–2010) gave priority to health-tourism development supporting both medical and wellness tourism developments. An estimated 31 billion HUF was invested in projects connected to medical and thermal bath construction or reconstruction between 2001–2003 in 9 regions, in 57 towns and in 90 spas and hotels (100 billion HUF investment) (Ministry of Local Government, 2007). The 10-year Health Tourism Development Programme's strategic aim was to gain a leader position in the European medical tourism market by the end of 2010.

In the National Development Plan II (2007–2013), 100 billion HUF subsidies were separated to develop health tourism in Hungary: 40 per cent of the amount is for developing attractions and services, and 60 per cent is for developing accommodation facilities (wellness, medical hotels). The 6-year (2007–2013) National Health Tourism Development Plan was finalised in 2007. It defined seven priority areas:

1 the conscious product-development of baths with international significance;
2 strengthening the contact of traditional medicine and tourism;
3 product-development at wellness services;
4 capacity-development of medical and wellness hotels;
5 development of marketing activity in the area;
6 development of education system for wellness and medical service providers;
7 developing of national and regional operating system of health tourism (like destination management).

(Ministry of Local Government, 2007)

This plan implies that a distinction is now being made between medical and wellness services. Although the labelling used in Hungary is generally inconsistent (i.e. 'health', 'medical', 'wellness' and 'spa' tourism are used somewhat randomly and often inter-changeably), this means that there has been a recognition of wellness as a distinctive concept. It also seems that the medical and tourism sectors are starting to work together and a more integrated approach is being adopted (i.e. destination management). The new Széchenyi Development Plan (2010–2020), which replaced the National Development Plan II, seems to focus more on medical thermal and surgical medical tourism and wellness is almost absent from the text. The main objective is to develop the so-called health industry, including mainly curative, preventive and rehabilitation services based on thermal water for locals as well as tourists.

The Hungarian Baths Association (HBA) is also an active stakeholder of the tourism sector. Representatives of the association were members of the National Tourism Board, the advisory body to the minister responsible for tourism. The association is a leading partner in all health-tourism–related issues, for example, in 2001 they developed a trademark system, and are planning to set up a national certificate system for baths. HBA also communicates with national government health agencies [Nemzeti Erőforrás Minisztérium (NEFMI), Health Secretariat] relating to the legal regulation and the financing of spa treatments.

In terms of marketing, the HNTO has been playing a crucial role in promoting medical and wellness tourism for many years. There were years when the promotional campaign was based specifically on medical and wellness tourism services. The HNTO tends to focus on medical and wellness hotels and medical baths in its communication (labelled under the logo of 'Spa & Wellness'). The HNTO does not deal with hospitals or dental clinics offering services for international tourists. For the domestic market, the HNTO separates medical and wellness tourism services. The HNTO had a new strategy (as of January 2011) in which it focussed on 'Natural Waters', i.e. mainly thermal/medical waters. This is highlighted by the campaign in foreign markets under the umbrella of 'winter time is thermal bath time'.

Focussed marketing efforts are continually promoting health tourism. 2011 was the campaign year of Health Tourism run by the HNTO with the slogan 'The

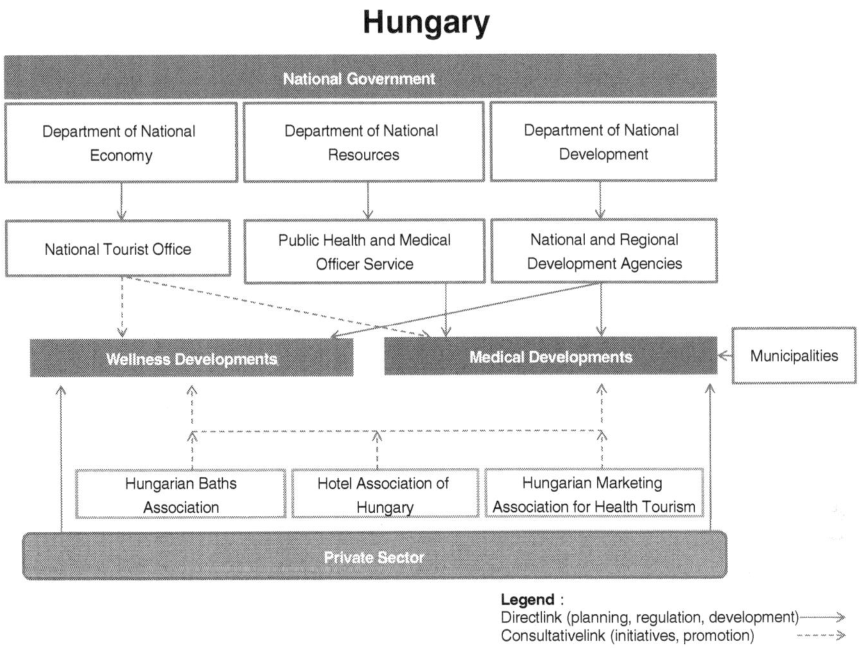

Figure 6.1 Organisational structure of Hungarian health tourism.

Source: Smith *et al.* 2011.

Garden of Wellbeing'. This introduces yet another label which seems (at least on the surface) closely connected to wellness. However, here the term well-being mainly refers to thermal baths and hotels, many of which offer medical tourism. Hungary is also planning to develop the 'Healing Hungary' image as outlined in the New Széchenyi Plan. In the field of medical tourism, they would like to move from a good value/price ratio country to a good quality service provider. In this process, thermal baths will play a key role. According to these guidelines, action plans will be created and tenders will take place in order to support health tourism. The monetary basis for these tenders comes from EU funds. Figure 6.1 provides an outline of the organisation of Hungarian health tourism (Smith *et al.* 2011).

Collaboration initiatives in thermal medical and surgical medical tourism

The connection between thermal medical tourism industries and the government is strong, as most of the thermal/medical baths in Hungary are owned by the state or the local municipality. Medical baths and medical hotels are governed by the National Public Health and Medical Officer Service, which is responsible for the categorisation and classification of medical and wellness hotels and they are working on the new criteria of medical and wellness hotels. Destination Management

Organizations were set up over the past few years, many of which were launched in medical and wellness tourism destinations. The industry expects these new bodies to foster developments and improve cooperation and communication.

Thus far there have been relatively few surgical medical tourism initiatives and the focus has mainly been on thermal medical tourism instead. There are a few examples of cooperation between spa hotels and private clinics in Budapest as well as in the border-land towns, where luxurious hotels with high-quality spas provide a location for surgery and rehabilitation. However, such cooperation seems to be rare, as the rest of the sectors in surgical medical tourism have not yet realised the importance of pre- and post-travel services or the advantages of complex packages (Sziva 2010).

Nevertheless, in 2011, the government of Hungary made a cooperation agreement with the private association of dental touristic service suppliers called Surgical Medical Tourism Agency Ltd (Orvosi Turizmus Iroda Zrt) to develop Hungarian dental tourism further. The development plan focusses on facilitator agencies in ten Western European countries, quality insurance systems and a joint international communication campaign. One billion forints (500 million Euros) were offered by the government in subsidies (Gáti 2011). Although it remains to be seen how the plan will develop, this is at least one example of public and private sector collaboration in surgical medical tourism.

The so-called 'Thermal Clusters' in Hungary are good examples of Public Private Partnership (PPP) cooperation, as they were established to market thermal destinations by municipalities as well as service suppliers connected to thermal tourism (e.g. baths, hotels, tour operators, research institutions, hospitals). In Hungary, five thermal clusters are in operation in the biggest thermal 'hubs' of Hungary: in Transdanubia (in the centre of which are Hévíz and Sárvár, traditional, famous spa destinations), three clusters in the Great Plain (centred around bigger spa destinations like Hajdúszoboszló, Gyula and Szolnok) and one new cluster in the Northern Part of Hungary (Eger and the Matra hill region). These clusters were established because of the motivation of state subsidies given for cooperation and cluster-creation, and focus on thermal tourism. The rest of the clusters only undertake communication activity, and some of them are working only in theory, questioning the effectiveness of forced, top-down cooperation. Only one cluster, the so-called Pannon Thermal Cluster seems to have reached the main objective of innovative cluster development, as good examples of mutual research and product development can be found.

Case study of a health-tourism cluster: Békés

The establishment of the Békés County Health Tourism Cluster in the South East of Hungary was supported by a government tender motivating cooperation in 2009. The main aim of the project was to connect health-tourism actors in the county, to establish a cluster organisation for cooperation, and to develop education and knowledge-sharing with organised programmes (e.g. training, workshops, consulting advice for 18 months with specialised consultants, international study tours) and to support their mutual activity with specially developed positioning and development strategies.

At the end of the project, the cluster had 26 members from different segments: hotels, thermal baths, restaurants, tour operators, Institution for Cooperation, for example, municipalities, national parks and NGOs such as development agencies. In 2011, the cluster incubation project had run for 18 months. During this time, the following results were achieved:

- Two-monthly workshops and conferences on different topics, for example, health and wellness tourism, destination management, marketing.
- Market and benchmark analysis were undertaken to develop the positioning strategy.
- A competitiveness and positioning strategy was written based on the mutual vision of the cluster-members. The main aim was to position the cluster as a unique health-tourism destination based on the healing and relaxing atmosphere and natural healing assets of the rivers in the destination. This unique position was named 'Oasis of the "Körös" valley' (Körös is the name of the river-system of the destination). The strategy was broken down so that smaller strategies were written for different members to help them fit into the entire cluster's position.
- Consulting opportunities were given to all members in the area of marketing, finance and strategy.
- A study tour was taken to Austrian Tyrol and Carinthia, where the members could gain experience from the well-established and successful clusters of Tyrol Wellness, and the water-based Lake Wellness in Carinthia.
- Several ideas were created in order to realise the vision of the positioning strategy, for example, local fruits and drinking water to be provided for the guests at the member service providers, cleaning the riversides, creating supplier networks with bio-food producers of the destination.
- Creating an association to run the cluster after the end of the tender.

From May to December 2010, a research project was conducted on existing demand for health-tourism services in Békés county. In all, 294 customers were interviewed either face-to-face or using self-completion. Random sampling was used and the surveys were undertaken in baths, tourist information centres and accommodation in seven towns within the county. The survey was translated into four languages (English, German, Serbian and Romanian) in addition to Hungarian. The aim of the survey was to identify the motivations of customers and create the basic profiles for segmentation and product development. The major motivation was relaxation (51 per cent) followed by thermal medical treatments (18 per cent), rehabilitation (8 per cent) and rejuvenation (nine per cent). The most important activities during stay are thermal bathing (25 per cent), massage (24 per cent), medical water therapies (i.e. for a certain indication – 13 per cent), and sauna (14 per cent). Visitors were also asked about their lifestyle and three major segments were identified:

- not aware (66 per cent) – they do not pay attention to their state of health;
- health aware (25 per cent) – they are concerned about their lifestyle, but only certain elements (e.g. fitness, nutrition);
- health-centric (9 per cent) – they actively choose a healthy lifestyle.

These results present many challenges for the members of the cluster, as the stated activities of visitors and their lifestyles do not always correspond due to the existing supply. That is to say that even though many visitors (approximately one-third) would like to practice a healthier life, even while on holiday, but the available facilities are too limited. The main products are based either on relaxing in thermal waters or therapeutic medical treatments. What is missing are non-water-based elements such as healthy nutrition, good quality fitness facilities, sports and recreation. It should also be noted that mainly thermal medical treatments are provided; however, the two major hospitals in the county do have the capacity to provide surgical medical tourism (e.g. operations). The same pattern applies here as elsewhere in Hungary, that is, doctors undertake private procedures using public facilities. There are no specific public–private collaborations or specialised packages for tourists. This is exactly why public–private partnerships such as clusters can help to improve existing facilities and develop new products in a coordinated way. The strategy of the cluster is therefore to focus on a wider understanding of health motivation (e.g. including healthy lifestyle) and to develop cooperation and new products for the segments that are not yet provided for adequately (such as 'Health aware' and 'Health-centric').

Clearly, the aim of a cluster development should be to help coordinate management and development of health tourism, for example, through collaboration on joint market research. It should also ultimately help to reconcile public and private sector policy in all areas of health tourism, including thermal medical and surgical medical tourism, but also wellness and lifestyle-based tourism. Unfortunately, although the cluster project worked reasonably well in the short-term, it has been difficult to create co-operative working structures on an ongoing basis and to implement ideas and initiatives. The members are not motivated enough to take an active role in daily cooperation. The main inhibiting factors are distrust, egoistical self-interest, the lack of a culture of cooperation and the difficulties of being small and micro businesses (lack of resources and knowledge). Many of these factors have cultural and historical roots which are typical of former socialist countries, for example, lack of trust, no real history of collaboration and a paternalistic view that 'the state will solve our problems'.

Conclusions

This chapter has shown clearly that the emphasis in Hungarian health tourism is still very much on thermal medical tourism. Hungary is famous for its historic baths (located in Budapest) and thermal spas all around the country; therefore, it is hardly surprising that they should feature so prominently. However, it is also true that the majority of international tourists (outside CEE) do not recognise the benefits of thermal medical tourism, but tend to use the facilities for leisure and recreation, if at all. Although thermal medical baths still attract a large number of domestic tourists, this may change if the social tourism scheme is significantly revised or even abolished in the future.

In terms of policy, it is clear that thermal medical tourism has played a major role in the state's regional and national tourism development strategies for more than half a century. Nevertheless, since the growth of international tourism in the early 1990s, and especially since EU accession in 2004, the emphasis is changing to include surgical medical tourism, although international tourists may already be much more familiar with the advantages of Hungarian dental tourism than thermal medical tourism. However, surgical medical tourism requires public and private sector collaboration, as until recently, private clinics tended to supply most of the surgical medical tourism. Thus far, attempts at collaboration have been mainly limited to state hospitals taking private patients with varying degrees of success.

As can be seen in the latter part of the chapter, attempts at collaboration or clustering tend to be thwarted by historical and cultural factors typical of former Socialist countries. This includes distrust, lack of experience of collaborative working, and the missing skills, knowledge or resources needed to manage clusters on a long-term basis. It should also be stated that public policies in Hungary are currently unclear about the role of PPPs in development strategies which are relatively new in Hungary.

The customer research in the case study of Békés also showed that at least one-third of health tourists are looking for something more than thermal medical tourism in Hungary and would welcome some healthy lifestyle or wellness elements. This tends to reflect international trends and calls for a more holistic approach to health-tourism development in the future and much better coordination of both public and private sector activities.

References

ESKI (2009) *Family Choice Hungary*. [Online]. Available at: http://www.eski.hu/new3/gyogyturizmus/zip_doc_2009/Family_Choice_Hungary2.doc (accessed 22 December 2009).

Gáti, J. (2011) 'Hídépítők, Támogatás a fogturizmusnak', *HVG*, May 14.

Halassy, E. (2007) 'The attitude of the Hungarian population of water-, wellness and medical tourism', *Turizmus Bulletin*, 11(4): 2–12.

HNFR (2009) *The recreation cheque system in Hungary*, Available at: http://www.mnua.hu/pdf/20081023angol.pdf (accessed 25 August 2009).

HNTO (2009) *Health tourism resources in Hungary*, Available at: http://www.hungary.com/main.php?folderID=856&;articleID (accessed 5 December 2009).

HNTO – M.Á.S.T. (2008) *Travelling habits of the Hungarian population*, Budapest: Magyar Turizmus Zrt.

Hungarian Central Statistical Office (HCSO) (2009) *The distribution of the guests regarding the way of booking*, Available at: http://portal.ksh.hu/pls/ksh/docs/hun/xstadat/xstadat_evkozi/tabl4_05_20hb.html (accessed 23 December 2009).

Medical Tourism Association (2009) *Information on European Medical Tourism in different European Countries*. [Online]. Available at: http://www.europeanmedicaltourismcongress.com (accessed 12 February 2010).

Ministry of Local Government (2007) *Országos Egészségturisztikai Fejlesztési Stratégia*, Budapest: Aquaprofit Rt.

Puczkó, L. and Rátz, T. (2011) 'Social tourism in Hungary: from trade unions to cinema tickets', *Current Issues in Tourism*, 14(5): 459–73.

Smith, M., Puczkó L., and Ivett Sziva, I. (2011) *Research Report: Global Spa Summit 2011. Wellness Tourism and Medical Tourism: Where do spa fit?*, New York: GSS.

Sziva, I. (2010) 'Gulliver in the land of giants? The opportunities of the Hungarian initiations in the surgical medical touristic market', in L. Puczkó (ed) *Health, Wellness and Tourism: healthy tourists, healthy business?* Proceedings of the Travel and Tourism Research Association Europe 2010 Annual Conference, Budapest.

VITUKI-MAFI-Aquaprofit (2006) *A fürdőfejlesztésekkel kapcsolatban a hazai termálvízkészlet fenntartható azonosításáról és a használt víz kezeléséről szóló hidrogeológiai kutatás*. Budapest: VITUKI.

Youngman, I. (2009) Medical tourism statistics: why McKinsey has got it wrong. [Online]. Available at: http://www.imtj.com/articles/2009/mckinsey-wrong-medical-travel (accessed 12 February 2010).

7 Health and spa tourism in the Czech and Slovak Republics

Halina Kotikova and Eva Schwartzhoffova

Introduction

Tourism is an important part of the national economy for all European post-communist countries. Most of them actively support the development of tourism, which was deliberately constrained during the communist era. During this period, most of these states took very strict measures to limit not only outbound tourism, but also to some extent inbound tourism. These restrictions were not limited exclusively to visa restrictions, but also included other legislation limiting the opportunities for citizens to leave the country and unfavourable currency exchange rates for visitors to these countries. The Czech and Slovak Republics, as successor states to Czechoslovakia, are now trying to continue in the tradition of tourism which was interrupted during the state communist government period from 1949 to 1989.

The tourism industry is an important part of the national economy of both countries. The economic impact of the development of tourism is reflected in the revenue it brings to state and local budgets, the profits earned from currency exchange and the considerable number of jobs it creates. For this reason, both states make considerable effort to support the development of both traditional and modern forms of tourism. In both, the Czech and Slovak Republics, the spa industry ranks among the traditional forms of tourism which has undergone particularly dramatic developments during the twentieth century. Even today, the emphasis of spa tourism in both countries has been on spas as a component of medical care and thus spas have become a major component of medical tourism. The following chapter focusses on the development of spa tourism in both countries and especially in the period from the separation of the two countries in 1993 to the present.

What is the difference between medical and health spa tourism?

In the current literature, terms such as health tourism, medical tourism and spa tourism are used almost interchangeably (see Chapter 1; see also Hall 2003, 2011; Connell 2006). Tressider (2011: 268) defines medical tourism as 'undertaking a medical intervention away from the home country, where the medical element is the central theme of activity'. The same author places health tourism along with medical tourism, and in the context of this segmentation, spa tourism clearly falls under the heading of health tourism. Similarly, Cook (2008) regards medical tourism as a subset of health tourism, while Smith and Puczkó (2009) divide health tourism into wellness tourism and medical tourism. According to their division, spa tourism sits somewhere on the border between wellness and medical tourism (see Chapter 6).

Spa tourism is defined by Smith and Puczkó (2009: 85) as 'tourism which focused on the relaxation or healing of the body using mainly water-based treatments, such as, mineral or thermal pools, steam rooms and saunas. Emphasis tends to be focused on curing, rehabilitating, or resting the body.' This definition covers many types of spas. In the Czech and Slovak Republics, medical spas are more typical, these are facilities that offer traditional and complementary therapeutic and health protection treatments as well as other spa services and may also include health institutions. According to Horowitz and Rosensweig (2007), the main motives for participating in medical tourism (and we can consider these to be the same motives to apply to spa tourism) are low cost, avoid waiting lists, procedure not available in home country, tourism and vacations and privacy and confidentiality.

For the purposes of this chapter, we will take spa tourism to be a category of health tourism. At the same time, we must start from the fact that in both countries this phenomenon comes in two forms. The first clearly falls under the title of medical tourism as it falls under the competence of the Ministry of Health and is regulated by the modified *Healthcare Act of 1960*. The second expands the possibilities of spa tourism to include stays that are also motivated by health concerns, but are not directly associated with treatment or with health-care institutions.

The development of balneology in the Czech and Slovak republics in the context of European spas

Spa culture in Europe has a long tradition with roots leading all the way back to Roman times. Spas and the development of spa culture are associated not only with medical advancement, but also with culture, natural sciences and technological development. Most European spas were founded and functioned mostly on the principles of hydrotherapy originally using baths and only later adopting drinking cures. While the origins of European spa culture stretches back to the ancient Greeks, spas achieved the pinnacle of their development in classical Rome. The tradition of spas in Central and Western Europe is significantly younger than that in southern Europe and the Mediterranean states.

European spas were originally of two types: (1) mineral springs spas including natural hot springs, which were thought to have healing proprieties, and cold water springs used for drinking and (2) thalassotherapy spas based upon hydrotherapy using sea water, seaweed, seaweed cosmetics and mineral bath sea salts (Tabbachi 2008). The history of balneology in the territory of today's Czech Republic and Slovakia is closely related to the history of spas in Germany, Switzerland, Austria, Hungary and Poland. The latter three countries, like the Czech and Slovak Republics, are located on the territory of the former Austro-Hungarian Empire where the spa experienced its heyday in the nineteenth century. In the territory of today's Czech lands, the most important spa has traditionally been Karlovy Vary (Karlsbad), which was supposedly founded in the fourteenth century by the Czech king Charles IV. In Slovakia, the most significant spa is Piešťany, which became notable for exploiting the therapeutic effects of mud. In the nineteenth century, spas in this area were visited by some of the best known personalities of the time such as Goethe, Chopin and Pushkin. At the time, spa towns were also important social centres with the taking of the spa waters and medical treatments being combined with gambling, sporting events orchestras and chamber music for the leisured classes (Ellis 2008).

The social life at Czech and Slovak spas was vibrant even if gambling never became as widespread as in Germany (Křížek 2002). It is worth mentioning that the first golf course in the territory of the present-day Czech and Slovak Republics was established in Karlovy Vary in 1904, and the golf course in Marianské Lázně was opened by the King of Great Britain, Edward VII, a year later. In the year 1899, the race track in Karlovy Vary was opened. Spas also acquired their own characteristic and unique architectural and landscaping style. A typical architectural element of spas became the colonnade. Leading architects of the period contributed to spa design including such names as Fellner and Hellmer in Karlovy Vary, Wiedermann in Františkovy Lázně or Jurkovič in Luhačovice. This period also saw the construction of high-altitude sanatoria (Vyšné Ružbachy, Lúčky), which today are still referred to as 'Swiss houses' (Attl 2005b).

The spa tradition was maintained after the establishment of an independent Czechoslovakia in 1918. Despite the fact that the interwar period was marked by economic crisis, the travel industry, including spa tourism, nevertheless developed quite extensively. This period also saw the appearance of a new type of spa guest, the patient whose stay is paid for entirely by health insurance. Health-insurance companies also began to build their own spa buildings. Understandably, the level of services for clients whose stays were paid for as they say 'on the treasury' was much more modest. Although there were not many such clients, a spa stay ceased to be a luxury reserved exclusively for the elite. Nonetheless, emphasis continued to be placed on the social aspects of spa stays.

This improvement in spa services in Czechoslovakia was interrupted by the Second World War and the communist takeover in 1948. The nationalisation of private property by the communist regime had dramatic effects on the spa sector. In this period, there was greater emphasis on the medical aspects of spa treatments and a suppression of their entertainment, cultural and social aspects. An entire system for organizing and delivering spa services was created but with only very limited social facilities. Spa treatments for Czechoslovak citizens were fully funded by the state health services. This was made manifest by the insufficient investment made into spa infrastructure and especially into services. While the quality of health-care services improved, accommodation and meal services were considered to be of subordinate importance to medical aspects and the quality of these services suffered significantly. Patients were housed in multiple-occupancy rooms, usually with common bathrooms. Meals had the character of hospital food with a uniform diet assigned for each category of illness. House rules in spa accommodation were strictly enforced and their violation could be grounds for expulsion. Since the whole system of spa treatment was organised within the health-care system, it allowed for the maximum and optimal use of spa facilities. The patient had no practical influence over which spa they would be assigned. The patient's doctor would make a diagnosis and then the patient would be assigned a particular date and location according to a list of approved diagnoses and the availability of free spaces. Therefore, there was no true seasonality to spa services, and guaranteed occupancy meant that there was no incentive for spa operators to improve the quality of their services.

Spas were visited mainly by Czechoslovak citizens and emphasis was placed on their therapeutic significance. Foreign visitors consisted primarily of guests from the Soviet Union and the German Democratic Republic, with a very small number coming from Western Europe and other countries. The medical character of spa care meant that, at that time, spa stays were focussed on direct therapeutic procedures (such as postoperative convalescence), on chronic diseases or on disease prevention, and always on the recommendation of a doctor.

The separation of Czechoslovakia in 1993 and its reflection in the development of the spa industry

The beginning of the 1990s was a pivotal moment in the development of Czech and Slovak society. The Velvet Revolution at the end 1989 was the beginning of a change in the structure of society and of a new stage of democratic governance in Czechoslovakia. Not long thereafter, in the year 1993, the division of Czechoslovakia into the Czech and Slovak Republics took place. While it should be noted this separation took place without the slightest conflict, it is clear that these events had a marked effect on the tourism industries in both countries. When considering statistical information related to spas in the Czech and Slovak republics, it is necessary to note that these data come from the statistics collected by the Ministries of Health in the two countries, and the methodology for reporting the number of clients using spas is not uniform throughout Europe and therefore does not allow valid comparisons of data across state borders but rather points to trends in the spa industry in the particular state. The number of visitors to Czech and Slovak Spas for 2006–2010 is indicated in Table 7.1.

Spa tourism in the Czech Republic after 1993

Spas in the Czech Republic are grounded mainly on natural medicinal resources, and these consist mainly of mineral and thermal waters, peloids (hummus, peat and mud), natural gases and climates. The best known spas are those in Karlovy Vary and Mariánské Lázně. The significance of the spa as an institution is witnessed by the fact that the Western Bohemian spas, along with other Western European spas, are preparing a joint candidacy for entry on the United Nations Educational, Scientific and Cultural Organization (UNESCO) list of World Heritage sites.

The illnesses treated in Czech Spas are primarily diseases of the musculoskeletal system (52 per cent), followed by neurological disorders (18 per cent) and finally

Table 7.1 Visitors to Czech and Slovak spas for 2006–2010

Year	*2006*		*2007*		*2008*		*2009*		*2010*	
	Czech	*Slovak*	*Czech*	*Slovak*	*Czech*	*Slovak*	*Czech*	*Slovak*	*Czech*	*Slovak*
Number of visitors	327,078	253,260	346,556	276,164	383,414	284,806	378,181	241,309	375,866	259,506
Domestic guests	192,275	159,339	212,594	178,895	229,399	192,051	234,259	180,983	237,056	194,705
Foreigners	134,803	93,921	133,962	97,269	154,015	92,755	143,922	60,326	138,810	64,801
number of overnights	5,669,938	2,277,187	5,610,641	2,453,285	5,783,213	2,606,848	5,673,311	2,391,089	5,653,004	2,490,040

Sources: Derived from Czech Ministry of Regional Development and SACR-Slovak Tourist Board, 2011.

circulatory illnesses (12 per cent). Other diagnoses are occasionally represented. The number of patients in spas during the 1970s and 1980s hovered around 280,000 per year. The year 1991 was marked by a dramatic decrease in the number of patients, a drop of 21 per cent compared to the year 1990, and the year with the lowest number of clients in Czech spas was 1993 with only 171,000 clients (a decrease of 64 per cent from 1991 levels). Subsequent years saw a slow but steady increase in the number of patients, and the number of days of stay. This trend began to stagnate only in 2007. In 2010, Czech spas were visited by 376,000 clients, and the number of overnight stays had also grown from 3,900 in 1993 to 5,700 in 2010. The overall composition of the clientele has however changed significantly. The number of patients whose stays are paid for by insurance companies has decreased while the number of self-payers has increased. In 1993, self-payers from the Czech Republic made up less than 7 per cent of the clientele and self-payers from abroad only 17 per cent. In 2010, Czech self-payers made up 39 per cent and foreign self-payers 37 per cent of the total clientele. It follows that spas in the future will need to focus on these target groups of clients. The results of a 2008 survey (Mlejnková 2011) showed that a third of spa clients whose stays are currently paid for by their health-insurance company would stop going if these stays ceased to be funded. While the average length of stay for an insurance-funded patient is 27 days, the average length of stay is 6 days for Czech self-payers and 13 days for foreign self-payers.

The composition of the foreign clientele at Czech spas is also interesting. Since the 1990s the majority of these were clients from Germany and Russia. Germans make up about half of the foreign guests and about 20 per cent come from Russia. Other foreign spa visitors often include guests from Ukraine, Israel and Austria. Slovaks make up only 1.4 per cent of foreign visitors. The Czech Republic has a total of 33 cities with the status of spa towns in 2010 and these had a total of 88 spa facilities with 26,000 beds. While spas are evenly distributed around the Czech Republic, the importance of if individual spas as tourist attractions varies greatly. The most important are Karlovy Vary, Mariánské Lázně and Františkovy Lázně. In 2010, these accounted for 58 per cent of all Czech and 94 per cent of all foreign spa visitors. It follows that other spas have rather a regional character.

The characteristic features of spas in the Czech Republic can be described as

- The use of natural medicinal resources and the medical character of services coupled with highly skilled personnel among which doctors and nurses are the most essential component;
- The complex influence of individual components of the environment (the mutual interaction of natural cultural and aesthetic elements);
- The change in environment (which is considered to help in achieving the overall therapeutic effect of spa treatment);
- The dominance given to the curative function of treatment (healing, follow-up treatment and prevention);
- Long-term exposure. In the Czech Republic the minimal length of stay to achieve therapeutic effect is considered to be 21 days.

(Attl 2005a)

In the Czech Republic, we distinguish between three types of spa stays according to the means of payment. This system is based on the fact that all citizens are by law covered by health insurance. Mandatory health insurance is either deducted as a percentage of one's income or covered by the state in the case of persons who are without income (such as children, students, pensioners or the unemployed).

Spa care covered by health insurance is divided into comprehensive and co-payment spa treatment. Comprehensive spa treatment builds on postoperative care or specialised outpatient care. It focusses on follow-up treatment, prevention of disabilities and invalidity or limiting the level of invalidity. It also covers occupational diseases and other types of health problems associated with particular professions. The patient is eligible for sick pay during the time they are at the spa. The full costs of the spa stay (including accommodation, full board and all prescribed treatments) are covered by the health-insurance company. Up to 2007, this type of treatment was completely free of charge. Since 2007, however, clients must pay a symbolic co-payment of 60 CZK (about US$ 4) for each day of their stay. The length of stay can be 14, 21 or 28 days depending on the particular diagnosis and can be prolonged by 7 days on the recommendation of the spa doctor. This type of stay accounts for 90 per cent of all visits funded by insurance companies. Co-pay spa treatment is provided primarily to patients with chronic illnesses – and on an interval of once every 2 years unless otherwise recommended by an insurance company panel doctor. Accommodation and meals are paid by the client, who is not eligible for sick leave but must draw vacation days during their time in the spa.

In addition to these categories of spa treatment which are funded by health insurance, there also exists the category of so-called self-payers in which all expenses for the spa stay are paid by the client. In this case, the client does not need a medical referral and the length of stay is in no way limited.

Recent years have seen a marked increase in the number of domestic self-payers, the main reason for this is the expanded offering of therapy options, especially the offering of weekend relaxation and rehabilitation stays. Although in recent years there has not been a great increase in the amount of money coming from insurance companies, all spa enterprises have been trying to improve their services not only in the fields of accommodation and food services but also in the field of treatment. In this way, they hope to gain healthy clients for whom drinking medicinal waters, mud baths and massage are considered a normal way of spending their holiday.

Spa treatment is one form of follow-up care. The Czech Republic has a highly developed system of spa medicine. The conditions under which a patient can undergo spa treatment fully or partially paid by health insurance are set by the Ministry of Health in a list of official diagnoses. Spa treatment must be prescribed by an attending doctor (general practitioner or specialist) who sends a request to the patient's insurance company. The request for spa treatment must be confirmed be a panel doctor who decides whether or not to cover spa treatment. Traditional Czech spa services are one of the major pillars of the travel and tourism industry in the Czech Republic. However, relative to comparable competitors abroad,

Czech spa facilities still lag behind in development, particularly in the offering of quality accompanying programmes and services in spa towns. This deficiency is especially noticeable in smaller spas.

Spa tourism in the Slovak Republic after 1993

Guests in Slovak spas are treated by means of climatic, balneological and combined climatic-balneological cures. Natural medicinal resources are to be found in the form of water (mineral, thermal and radon enriched), pelioid (peat, humus and mud) and gases. These resources require that curative spas be located in particular locations. Most Slovak spas operate on the basis of natural resources such as waters with known curative properties which are used in balneotherapy or underground mineral waters for drinking. Currently, Slovakia has around 1,500 natural sources of mineral waters (springs, boreholes, wells). For spas, the most important are natural healing waters and natural mineral waters. Of these 1,500 sources, there are only 110 recognised healing water springs (Eliášová 2005). Currently, there are 25 Slovak spa towns with 31 spa enterprises. This number is slightly lower than it was in the past. Over the centuries, 52 spa places have ceased to exist entirely and some facilities are temporarily out of operation while waiting for reconstruction (Zálešáková 2008). The most recent Spa Act, in force since 2006, guarantees the protection of natural medicinal resources and natural curative spas. This law introduced a division between health-care facilities providing medicinal baths into natural curative spas and spa sanatoria. It also introduced a new system regulating the licensing and operation of these facilities. The uniqueness of each such facility in Slovakia is dependent on the particular mineral content of the medicinal waters available there. Among the best are Piešťany, Trenčianské Teplice, Rájecké Teplice and Sliač. Mountain and alpine climates are also a basis of therapy at seven Slovak spa locations. The High Tatra Mountains are the setting for several so-called climatic spas.

The separation of the Slovak and Czech spa industries effectively took place first in 1969, when the independent Slovak spa association 'Slovenské kúpele a žriedla' was established with its seat in Bratislava. This organisation continued to exist until 1993, when Czechoslovakia disintegrated and the independent Slovak Republic was founded. After the split of Czechoslovakia, providing sufficient spa care for all Slovaks became a problem. Nonetheless, Slovak spas were better equipped and had a greater capacity than those in the Czech Republic to provide postoperative rehabilitation. In the period between 1990–1993, there were 23 spa localities and 38 spa facilities with a total of 11,171 beds, and over 150,000 guests were treated every year (Eliášová 2009). There were 11 state-owned spas in operation which were progressively privatised. The privatisation of these spa enterprises between 1995–1997 ended central control and allowed the entry of private capital into the spa industry. Every spa which was transformed into a joint stock company gained a strategic investor (including foreign investment groups) with majority shares. Other shares were transferred to municipalities or cities where the spas were located, and still others went to the State Health Insurance

Company. Since 1993, legislation and the conditions for obtaining public funding have changed several times, and this has greatly affected the business environment of the industry. Today, spas are no longer exclusively medical facilities designed solely to provide health care from public funds, but have become businesses with their own economic activities. As a result, spa treatment as a form of health care is forced to adapt itself to growing economic pressure which is expressed most noticeably in

- a reduction in public spending on health care;
- reduced outlays for spa treatment on the part of insurance companies;
- attempts on the part of spas to find alternative sources of funding;
- acceptance of private patients;
- price regulation by the Ministry of Health.

For these reasons, the responsibility for dealing with the economic problems of the spa industry falls on the spa enterprises themselves. Spa service providers are mostly publicly traded companies or, in a few cases, facilities belonging to the Interior or Defence Ministries. Two spas are still under state ownership (Slovthermae Dudince and Kováčova). From 1998 to 2004, public spending on spa treatments decreased, and by 2003 total public outlays on had fallen to 50 per cent of the rates of 1997. From the year 2004, funding of spa treatments was transferred exclusively to health-insurance companies which had a dramatic adverse effect on the spa industry. For comparison, the total number of spa vouchers purchased in 2004 was only 30,000, which was only 42 per cent of the number in 2000. This decline in the purchase of spa vouchers on the part of insurance companies has continued to the present, with insurers now allocating only 0.5–1.5 per cent of their budgets to spa treatments (Eliášová 2007).

In its 2006 health-care reform bill, Slovakia introduced co-payments for health care and implemented further restrictive measures reducing payments for spa treatments. Slovaks must now often co-pay for their treatment, but the level of these payments is limited by the state to prevent spas from making illegal profits. Since 2008, the state has divided the financing of spa treatments into three treatment categories and established payment limits for each of them.

The offering of Slovak spa operators represents a range of activities from which it is possible to create a service for everyone. All these services combine high-quality medical facilities with recognised natural medicinal resources in a typical spa environment. In setting their prices for spa procedures, insurance companies have not taken into account the increasing costs of such procedures, forcing spas to develop new profit-making activities. Now Slovak spa service providers are forced to deal not only with the fact that Slovakia, like the rest of the world, is going through an economic crisis but also with increasing competition coming primarily from modern waterparks, thermal baths and wellness hotels. Therefore, spa service providers focus on self-payers, both in the field of traditional medical-spa treatments and in wellness spa services. However, in some areas, the infrastructure of spa towns still lags behind. In the past few years, Slovak spas have invested massively into the renovation and development of their equipment and infrastructure. Many Slovak spas have International Organization for Standardization (ISO) certificates confirming the quality of their services, and the spa in Turčianské Teplice is the first Slovak spa to be awarded the European certificate of quality, Eurospea med (Zálešáková 2007). These certificates have an important positive impact on closing contracts with foreign health-insurance companies.

Clients and services

Currently, self-payers make up more than half of the clientele at Slovak spas. For this reason, most Slovak spas offer potential self-paying clients wellness procedures, the main enticements being medicinal thermal waters, mud treatments and experienced doctors and therapists. Some spas currently offer more than 50 procedures. In addition to these, facilities also offer so-called spa services, meaning baths or 'health through water'. These procedures can make use of either thermal or ordinary water. Unlike water-based spas, wellness facilities are not dependent on the presence of a natural water source and can be built anywhere. One result of the current recession is that the average length of a stay at Slovak spas has been decreasing. Since the mid-1980s, the average length of stay has reduced from 23 to 18 days. Wellness stays usually last 3–4 days and most often take place over an extended weekend with an average length of 3.2 days for foreign clients and 3.1 days for domestic clients (Budínská 2008).

The number of insurance-paid stays at spas in Slovakia according to the National Health Information Centre is around 35,000 per year. Every year the proportion of self-payers increases. The total number of beds is around 10,500, and every year there are approximately 3 million overnight stays registered. Foreign clients are also included in the annual statistics. The foreign portion of the total number of clients at Slovak spas is 35 per cent with most coming from other European Union (EU) states. Some spas have more than 50 per cent foreign visitors, and the total proportion of foreign guests increases every year. Their average duration of stay is 17 days as a result of their preference for traditional medicinal stays (Mušáková 2007). The most numerous group of foreign visitors is Germans, followed by Czechs, Poles and Austrians. Target markets also include the Netherlands and Russia, as well as Israel and Arab nations. The latter group has been quite important to Slovak spas as a substitute for last year's drop in German and Czech visitors. Many spas have contracts with foreign health-insurance companies which pay a portion of their clients' fees.

Waterparks and thermal swimming pools

The integration of purely recreational use of water is the field in which Slovak spas differ most from those in the Czech Republic. While Czech spas have maintained their primarily medical character, Slovakia had become a paradise for thermal swimming pools and waterparks. Although the term spa is used to describe more than 80 businesses in Slovakia, not all of these really have a medical character. This category also includes waterparks and thermal swimming pools, which have a completely different offering of services and are oriented towards an entirely different type of clientele than health spas. The difference lies in the fact that natural medicinal spas make use of state-recognised and proven natural medicinal resources. Thermal swimming pools for the most part do not use waters with recognised curative properties. The difference in the offering is also evident in the composition of the clientele and in the average length of stay. At health spas proper, a majority of clients are accommodated directly in the spa while at waterparks they are typically 1-day visitors. Nonetheless, the total number of tourists coming to Slovakia is increasing annually thanks to tourists who come to Slovakia specifically to visit these thermal swimming pools and waterparks, and these attractions are particularly popular among Czechs. Many of them have the advantage of being able to offer other tourist attractions in the same location. For example, skiing in the High Tatras can be combined with the largest Slovak waterpark, Tatralandia. Currently, there are 25 thermal swimming pools and eight waterparks in Slovakia. The boom in the construction of these facilities started approximately 7 years ago, primarily thanks to financial subsidies their owners received from EU funds. They are supplied with mineral water, which means they can be operated all year round. Although not officially recognised as medicinal, these waters nonetheless are regarded as having medicinal effects, and for many guests they are a cheaper alternative to the official medical spas.

Assistance for the spa industry in the Czech Republic and Slovakia

Spa tourism is a traditional and a highly promising form of tourism in both countries. This is reflected in the support given to spa tourism by both states. Starting in 2001, the Czech government implemented the 'State Program for the Support of Tourism', which was divided into four sub-programmes: (1)Support for Cities and Towns with the Status of Spa Towns; (2) Support for Owners of Spa Infrastructure; (3) Expanding Accommodation Capacity in the Category of Private Accommodation in Cities and Towns with the Status of Spa Towns; and (4) Spa Tourism supported the creation of new spa-tourism products. This programme continued until the year 2006 when it was replaced by travel and tourism projects financed through EU funds. At present, in the difficult economic conditions for spa operators, the acquisition of finances through EU funds and in the form of state aid is an opportunity for further development of their business activities. In both programming periods, 2004–2006 and 2007–2013 project implementation has continued for the support of the tourism industry, and as a result of spa tourism, in both states.

Since 2004 almost all Slovak spa enterprises have submitted projects for EU funding, but only a few of these projects have been successful. In 2010, the EU rewarded €6.5 million in financial support to five projects in three spa locations in Slovakia (Cernáková 2011). In addition to financial assistance for the development of the spa industry, the state also provides important assistance in marketing and promoting spa tourism. In the Czech Republic, the promotion of tourism, especially abroad, is the role of the Czech Tourist Authority – Czech Tourism. This agency invests considerable resources (both state and EU) to promote tourism in the Czech Republic. It manages specialised web sites as well as organises road shows, farm trips and press trips with spa themes and participates in thematically organised trade fairs and exhibitions focussed on spas and spa tourism. The presentation of spas and spa tourism is a part of two projects financed by EU funds – one is focussed on propagating domestic tourism and the other on building awareness of the Czech Republic as a tourist destination abroad. The total support to be invested by the year 2015 is scheduled to be €77.5 million in the Czech Republic. Similarly, the Slovak Tourism Agency is currently implementing an EU-funded programme called Support for the Promotion of Slovakia as a Tourist Destination with the budget of €27.3 million (Cernáková 2011).

The prospects for the development of spa tourism in the Czech Republic and Slovakia

Spa tourism in both the Czech and Slovak republics will be required to react to new situations. These changes relate to the demands of self-payers, who put increasing emphasis on the quality of services in relation to price, and to the apparent fact that the number of visitors whose stays are covered by health insurance will continue to fall.

We expect that in the Czech and Slovak republics the system of payment for spa treatment through health insurance will be maintained. In both countries, however, there is a similar trend to restrict public funding for spa treatment. This trend is caused by the widening deficit in the health-care systems of both countries. Spas have registered a long-term drop in the number of patients whose stays are paid for by insurance companies. The Czech Republic is currently going through a reform of its health-care system. Its goal is to limit outlays. The Ministry of Health is revising its list of diagnoses that call for spa treatment with the aim of removing some diagnoses entirely from the list and moving others from the list calling for comprehensive treatment to the list calling for co-pay treatment instead. These changes in the payment system for treatment are affecting the future orientation of spa enterprises. These enterprises will have to focus their offering on self-payers more than ever. The offering will have to be increasingly targeted on the specific health needs of the clients, and pressure from clients for better quality care and services will grow.

Trends that will continue due to these changes in the system of financing will include a shortening of the average length of stay and a change in the structure of the clientele in terms of their means of payment. A persistent question is whether it is best to continue to insist on a strictly medical character to spa stays. This insistence is very expensive because medicinal spas must meet a number of conditions specified by law. It turns out that clients often prefer a stay of a more recreational character, which they only compliment with some curative treatments at the spa. In this way, the competitiveness of hotels and other accommodation, which also offer balneological services without being part of a spa facility within the health-care system, is increasing.

There are however positive perspectives on the future of Czech and Slovak spas in the fact that ever younger guests are visiting spas and the number of families with children visiting spas is increasing. This raises the possibility that, in the future, the spa will become a place where people go to find culture or culinary experiences and where corporate guests will organise their conferences.

Conclusion

The purpose of this chapter was to illustrate the different paths taken by the two successor states of Czechoslovakia (the Czech and Slovak Republics) in developing their spa industries. Both of these countries have rich spa traditions which go back centuries. Before the communist era, spas in both countries were of world-class quality. However, after the separation of Czechoslovakia they have gone about achieving this goal in notably different ways. In recent years, public financing of spa services has been decreasing in both countries, which has had a negative impact on spa development. A comparison of statistical data points to differences not only in the structure of visitors from abroad, but also in the approach to further spa development as an important part of the tourism industry. The Czech Republic leans towards more traditional all-inclusive spa treatment (complete therapy) in the so-called 'medical spa' approach. In the Slovak Republic, many new thermal swimming pools and waterparks are being established. In addition to their medical function, these new Slovak spas serve as recreational and amusement centres for the general public.

The spa industry in both countries ranks among the sectors of their respective national economies, which are competitive on an international level. Its success also has a multiplier effect on the development of other tourism services and a resulting positive impact on the regions where spas are located. The potential of both countries lies primarily in improving existing services and offering new services. Both states consider spas to be a principal source of tourism. The authors believe that in spite of the problems described, Czech and Slovak spas will remain and become even more significant not only in the Central European, but also in the international context.

References

Attl, P. (2005a) 'K pojetí lázeňství', *Czech Hospitality and Tourism Papers*, 1: 43–67.

Attl, P. (2005b) 'Slovenské lázeňství známé i neznámé', *Communication Online Travel Business*, 11: 42–43.

Budínská, J. (2008) *Kúpelnictvo na Slovensku včera a dnes*. [Online]. Available at: http://www.voyagemagazine.sk/2008/03/15/kupelnictvo-na-slovensku-vč;era-a-dnes.html (accessed 7 June 2011).

Cernáková, T. (2011) 'Projekty financované z forndů EU'. E mail (23 June 2011).

Connell, J. (2006) 'Medical tourism: sea, sun, sand and. surgery', *Tourism Management*, 27: 1093–1100.

Cook, P.S. (2008) *What is health and medical tourism?* [Online]. Available at: http://utas.academia.edu/PetaCook/Papers/225976/What_is_Health_and_Medical_Tourism (accessed 10 May 2011).

Eliášová, D. (2005) 'Ochrana a rozvoj slovenských liečebných kúpeľov', *Ekonomická revue cestovného ruchu*. XXXVIII (1): 24–34, Bánská Bystrica: Univerzita Mateja Bela.

Eliášová, D. (2007) 'Podnikanie kúpeľných podnikov v novom ekonomickom prostredí', in: *Semafor – Ekonomika firiem*, Bratislava: Ekonomická univerzita.

Eliášová, D. (2009) *Slovenské kúpelnictvo ve 20 storočí*. Bratislava: Ekonom.

Ellis, S. (2008) 'Trends in the global spa industry', in: Cohen, M. and Bodeker, G. *Understanding the Global Spa Industry*. Oxford: Elsevier Butterworth-Heinemann. 67–84.

Hall, C.M. (2003) 'Spa and health tourism', in: Hudson, S. *Sport and Adventure Tourism*. Binghamton: Haworth Press.

Hall, C.M. (2011) 'Health and medical tourism: kill or cure for global public health?', *Tourism Review*, 66(1/2): 4–15.

Horowitz, M.D. and Rosensweig, J.A. (2007) 'Medical tourism – health care in the global economy', *Physician Executive*, 33(6): 24–26, 28–30.

Křížek, V. (2002) *Obrazy z dějin lázeňství*, Praha: Libri.

Mlejnková, L. (2011) 'Spotřební chování v lázeňském cestovním ruchu České republiky – consumer behavior in spa tourism in the Czech republic', *Acta Oeconomica Pragensia*. 19(1), 54–72.

Mušáková, M. (2007) 'Slovenské kúpeľníctvo má co ponúknut'. [Online]. Available at: http://www.novaera.sk/clanok/348/slovensk-kpenctvo –m-o-ponknu.html (accessed 13 June 2011).

Smith, M. and Puczkó, L. (eds) (2009) *Health and Wellness Tourism*, Amsterdam: Elsevier Butterworth-Heinemann.

Tabbachi, M. (2008) 'American and European spa', in: Cohen, M. and Bodeker, G. (ed.) *Understanding the Global Spa Industry*. Oxford: Elsevier Butterwoth-Heinemann.

Tressider, R. (2011) 'Health and medical tourism', in: Robinson, P., Heitmann, S. and Dieke, P. (eds) *Research Themes for Tourism*. Wallingford: CAB International.

Zálešáková, J. (2007) 'Kúpele centra pozitívnych podnetov', *Tophotelierstvo*, 1: 20–30, Bratislava: Media/ST.

Zálešáková, J. (2008) *Liečebné kúpele v Slovenskej republike*. [Online]. Available at: http://www.ask.sk/sk/liecebne_kupele.php (accessed 7 June 2011).

8 Macao's cross-border medical tourism

A new way forward?

Cindia Ching-Chi Lam, Hilary du Cros and Louis Vong

Introduction

Macao has only recently been the subject of several studies on cross-border medical tourism. These studies include a preliminary study of Macao's potential for medical tourism (Lam and Lei 2010) and one that examined the issue further in relation to the demand by visiting mainland Chinese tourists (Lam *et al.* 2011). This chapter progresses the topic further by analysing the results of the previous studies in terms of the regional competitiveness of Macao's medical carrying capacity, the attractiveness of its additional tourism attractions to cross-border tourists, and their demand for certain treatments and practices. By placing this data in the context of competitiveness and the competitive advantages of other medical tourism destinations, it will be shown that Macao could develop further and needs more specific policies from government for encouraging development that will be attractive to these Chinese tourists, while also allowing the provision of medical services to local residents.

A number of Asian countries appear to have taken the lead in promoting their medical tourism resources (Henderson 2004; Hall 2011). Connell (2006) noted that the Malaysian government introduced medical tourism as early as in 1998 in order to stimulate its battered economy in the aftermath of the Asian economic crisis. Non-government hospitals, such as Bumrungrad in Bangkok, also turned to medical tourism when the local economy reduced their appeal to the domestic market and were rewarded with a significant amount of international investment funding to expand (Mintier 2009). In the Jeju Province of the Republic of South Korea, the local authorities leveraged their medical products and services to attract both national and international tourists (Kim *et al.* 2009). Although Singapore has long gained global reputation as a top-tier medical tourism centre in the world (World Health Organization 2000), the Singaporean government continues to boost its world-class medical resources in order to meet its ambitious target of attracting one million medical tourists annually from 2012 (Lee 2010).

Macao's health-care system

Macao's health-care system comprises two main components: (a) hospital care and (b) primary health care. As their names imply, hospital care refers to general

Table 8.1 Number of medical services facilities in Macao (1999–2010)

Year	*1999*	*2004*	*2007*	*2008*	*2009*	*2010*
Types of medical services						
Hospital care	2	2	3	3	3	3
Primary health care	384	409	477	492	495	496
Chinese medicine and therapy	160	209	233	226	228	238

Source: Statistics and Census Service Macao (2011).

hospitals that provide specialised medical treatment with in-patient and out-patient facilities for the sick and the injured. On the other hand, primary health care refers to all those health-care establishments, such as public health-care centres and private clinics, that are responsible for non-specialised and basic health-care services. In Macao, there are three general hospitals the Hospital Conde S. Januário, Hospital Kiang Wu and Macau University of Science and Technology Hospital (also known as MUST Hospital). Only Hospital Conde S. Januário is a public hospital. In the other two, patients often have to pay much of their own costs through either insurance or their own funds. Acting as the sole public hospital in Macao, Hospital Conde S. Januário provides free medical services to special patient groups including, but not limited to, pregnant women, the elderly (aged +65), and children aged below ten. Hospital Conde S. Januário is complemented by Hospital Kiang Wu, which can deal with some overflow from the public hospital and helps to prop up Macao's stressed public health-care system. MUST Hospital, on the other hand, also provides services to tourist and expatriates. According to current practices, Hospital Conde S. Januário focuses on providing medical services to local Macao citizens, while Hospital Kiang Wu and MUST Hospital have higher potential to serve Chinese tourists.

Besides these hospital facilities, Macao also has seven public health-care centres – five in Macao Peninsula, one in Taipa and one in Coloane. Together, these health-care centres are joined by the hundreds of private clinics and Chinese medicine therapy treatment centres which collectively form the backbone of Macao's integrated primary health care network (Table 8.1). As of now, Macao has 477 Western private clinics (mainly general practitioners) and public health-care centres as well as 233 facilities providing Chinese medicine (Lam *et al.* 2011). Most of these facilities also attract tourists and expatriates.

Although these figures look remarkable for a small city with a population of only around half-a-million people, Macao actually faces many challenges. From a supply side perspective, there are a number of indicators commonly used to assess a city's medical service standard which suggest that there is an impending need for Macao to expand its sources of medical supply. For instance, the chronic shortage of registered nurses has been an enduring problem facing Macao society. Table 8.2 shows the ratio of doctors to nurses engaged in hospital care during the

Table 8.2 Medical human resources engaged in hospital care

Year	*1999*	*2004*	*2007*	*2008*	*2009*	*2010*
Doctor to nurse ratio	1:1.9	1:1.8	1:1.9	1:2	1:2	1:2.1
Doctors	379	464	547	555	560	564
Dentists	2	11	14	15	14	14
Nurses	716	834	1042	1115	1169	1200

Source: Statistics and Census Service Macao (2011).

Table 8.3 Health indicators of Macao (1999–2010)

Year	*1999*	*2004*	*2007*	*2008*	*2009*	*2010*
Doctors per 1,000 population	2	2.2	2.3	2.3	2.4	2.4
Nurses per 1,000 population	2.1	2.3	2.5	2.6	2.8	2.8
Doctors of Chinese medicine per 1,000 population	n.a.	0.6	0.8	0.8	0.9	0.9
In-patient beds per 1,000 population	2	2.1	1.9	1.9	2	2.1
In-patient bed occupancy rate	69.6	72.8	76.9	78.4	73.8	73.2

Source: Statistics and Census Service Macao (2011).

previous years. Based on international standards, this ratio should exceed 1:2 in order to provide quality medical services to patients (Van 2010). However, as indicated in Table 8.2, the doctor–nurse ratio in Macao has been hovering below or near par for most of the time in the last decade.

Also, other health-care indicators are also revealing signs that Macao's medical manpower and facilities are just barely sufficient, if not already stretched thin (Table 8.3). On top of this, Macao, like many other developed cities or places, is facing a looming challenge of aging population. Statistic Census and Service (DSEC) of Macao forecasted that the elderly population (i.e. aged 65 and above) in Macao will increase from 7 per cent in 2006 to 19 per cent in 2031 (DSEC 2010). Needless to say, this imminent reality will cause acute demand for medical services among Macao population in the years to come. This raises the question whether Macao – given its already stretched medical resources – has the luxury to compete for medical tourism business regionally.

From a tourism perspective, Macao also seems to be falling behind when compared with other regional cities or places that are also focusing on medical tourism for new revenues. In particular, Macao will face uphill battles competing against prominent destinations like Singapore which is determined to position itself as a regional, if not world, market leader in the area (Lee 2010; see Wong and Musa, Chapter 11). Indeed, even when compared with other emerging medical tourism destinations such as Hong Kong and Taiwan, Macao has been perceived as a weak competitor when considering its medical resources. In addressing the chronic shortage of registered health workers in Macao, Van (2010) lamented that Macao seriously lags behind other developed cities or places in terms of doctor–nurse ratio. It has also been a long-time practice for Macao to bring in the needed medical professionals or specialists from outside such as mainland China, Hong Kong and Portugal. Though, some locals who have graduated from accredited foreign medical schools have returned home to render their professional services in Macao. To a certain extent, this has constrained the development of Macao's health-care system given the highly competitive international market for health professionals.

In view of the above, if Macao wishes to compete in medical tourism, one precondition is for the city to resolve its medical labour supply. This requires Macao to overhaul its medical resource policies with the long-term goal of expanding the sources and varieties of medical professionals. Therefore medical education in Macao assumes a critical role in terms of the long-term availability of medical human resources. Put differently, unless Macao is able to strengthen its flimsy foundation of medical resources, it seems that Macao is not in the best position to venture into medical tourism any time soon.

The positioning of Macao in medical tourism

Is Macao really in such an unfavourable position for medical tourism? If the capability to train medical personnel is the *only* factor of consideration, then that may affect its competitiveness. However, when other factors are also considered, a different story is revealed. In discussing its potential and likely competitiveness for providing medical tourism, one factor cannot be disregarded – what are potential customers looking for from medical tourism and is this available in Macao? There are a number of factors involved; the nature of customers' demand, the competitive positioning in respect to nearby competitors, the political positioning, as well as the available supply at the destination (Figure 8.1). These will be discussed to demonstrate the potential of medical tourism in Macao, under the current resources and situation, and how this new form of tourism should be positioned for the city.

What are potential customers looking for from medical tourism?

One crucial factor for the practice of medical tourism is the existence of customers. According to the study of Lam and Lei (2010) on the potential of medical tourism in Macao, definite comparative advantages are found in the city to capture the market of tourists from China. Medical practices in China are characterised by a number of negative features that would drive Chinese tourists to seek medical services outside their home country. This notion was examined in the study by Lam *et al.* (2011) and it was found that the majority of Chinese tourists believed that medical tourism is either travelling to a foreign destination for surgical treatment and procedures or to have preventive health services or body check.

The provision of surgical treatment and procedures can be distinguished as *high-end medical services* when specialised medical services that require specific

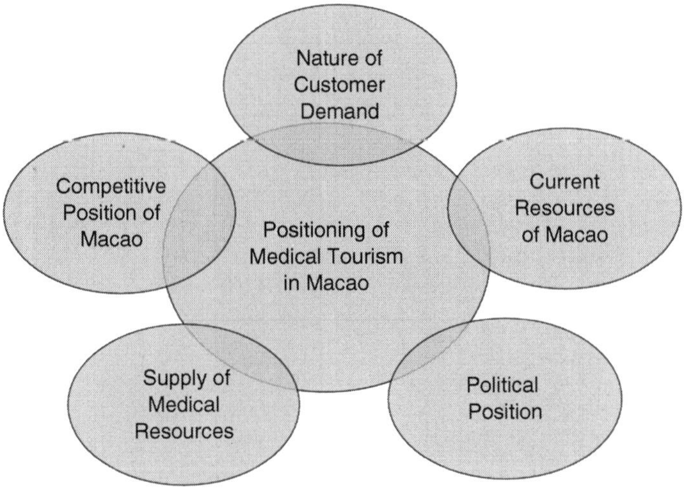

Figure 8.1 Factors in the positioning of medical tourism in Macao.

and rare medical skills are the basis. Globalisation, including the opening of trade in health services and the availability of rapid international transport, has permitted the provision of high-end medical services, when customers are willing to pay high price for specialised services (Hall 2011). The Pavilion at McLean Hospital in Massachusetts, an affiliate of the Harvard Medical School and the Bumrungrad Hospital in Bangkok, the largest private hospital with around 40 per cent of customers as international and expatriates, are apparent models that serve this market.

In contrast, preventive health and body check services can be distinguished as *preventive medical services* that serve preventive medical investigation, consultation and treatments. This requires comparatively less specialised medical skills but has a more extensive potential market. The growth of economies, the increase in wealth of people and higher education has created the need and supports the development for this kind of medical service.

A survey was conducted by the authors in December 2008 on tourists coming from Mainland China (China) to Macao aged 18 or above. The first part of the survey covered the knowledge and perception of medical tourism, as well as the standard of the available health-care system of the samples. The second part covers different aspects of medical tourism. Questions were designed and structured on the basis of previous literature and practical consideration of the local society. The first part of the survey includes four questions of multiple response and dichotomous answer sets. Multiple response questions were made with respect to the perception of medical tourism and the opinion of the health-care system at the hometown of participants. Dichotomous questions were used to identify whether the participants had ever heard about medical tourism and if they or their family members have ever consulted medical treatment outside their hometown while still within their country (see also Lam *et al.* 2011).

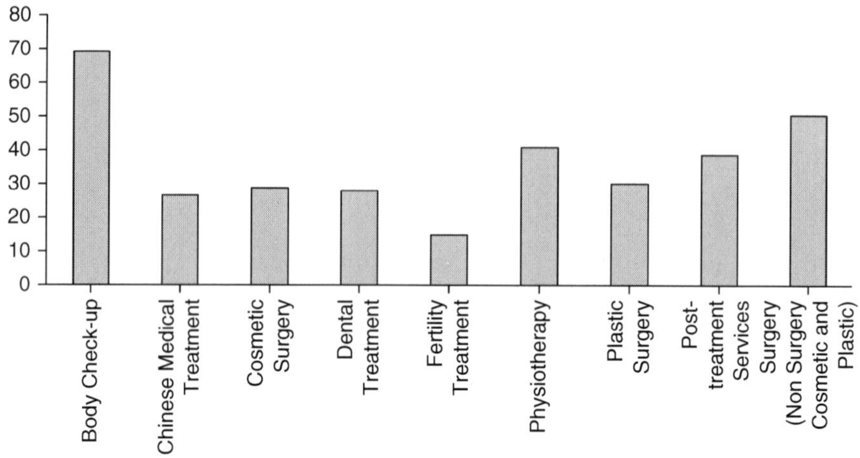

Figure 8.2 Demand for various medical services by Chinese medical tourists (in percentage).

A total of 772 visitors participated in the survey with female visitors (57.4 per cent) slightly outnumbering male (42.6 per cent). The majority of respondents were between 21–50 years old (88 per cent), and 49.2 per cent of the total sample population were single and 48.4 per cent married (48.4 per cent).

The research found just over half (50.9 per cent) rated the quality of health services in their home environment as average. Seventy per cent of visitors had not heard of the term medical tourism while of those who had heard of it the common perception of medical tourism was that it is 'the travelling to a foreign destination for major surgical treatment and procedure' (40.3 per cent), followed by 'taking preventive health or body check' (39 per cent). The most influential factors in affecting the decision to seek medical treatment outside of their home environment were insurance coverage, inadequate local medical support and availability of transport to the destination.

Of the nine different types of medical services that were identified by the authors as common in medical tourism (Figure 8.2), three of these body check up (69.4 per cent), non-cosmetic and plastic surgery (50.4 per cent) and physiotherapy (40.8 per cent) were clearly the most desired in the sample population. The three types of medical services for which there was the least demand were fertility treatment (14.6 per cent), Chinese medical treatment (26.8 per cent) and dental treatment (27.8 per cent).

The most influential factors in the selection of medical tourism services (Figure 8.3) were price (69.4 per cent), cleanliness (54.4 per cent), quality of medical equipment (54.5 per cent) and quality of medical service (51 per cent). Whether or not a facility was publically or private owned was only considered significant by 10.2 per cent of respondents.

Questions were also asked as to the desirability of packaging a medical trip with other activities. Amongst which, tourism is most highly desired (Table 8.4).

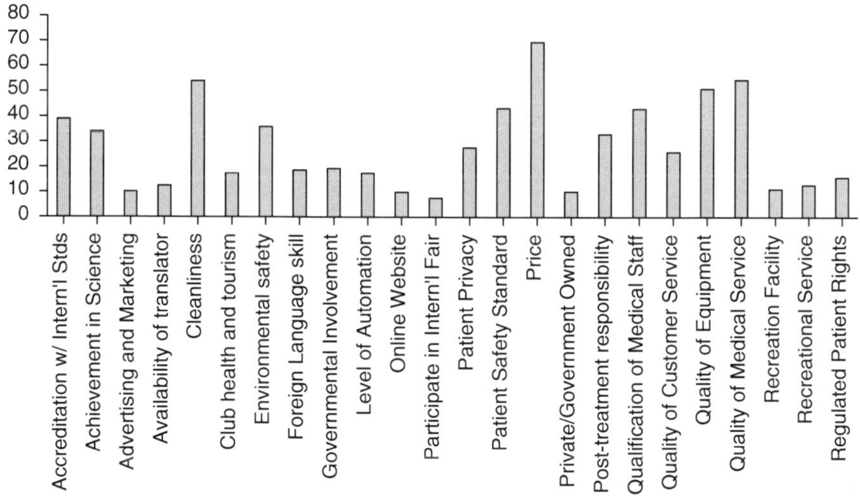

Figure 8.3 Strength of factors (percentage) that determine the decision of Chinese tourists to have outbound medical treatment.

Table 8.4 Preference of tourists (in percentage) to package different options with a medical trip

Package with tourism	57%
Don't want to package	22%
Package with study	12%
Package with business	9%

Only 22 per cent indicated that they did not want a package, with the majority (57 per cent) indicating that they wanted a package with tourism. A number of different tourism activities were also presented to respondents as options that could be included as part of any medical tourism package. Of these scenery and cuisine were chosen by 50.9 and 50.4 per cent of respondents, respectively, with shopping being selected by 48.4 per cent. Perhaps surprisingly for some readers, given the extent of Macao's gaming industry, was that gambling was selected as a package option by only 14 per cent of respondents. However, it is significant to note that in an earlier study Lam and Vong (2009) had found that gambling was not a major motive for tourists to come to Macao.

In summary, Chinese tourists who are the most likely customers of medical tourism in Macao, are mainly seeking preventive medical services at reasonable prices and would like to package these services with tourism activities. To capture this group of potential customers, Macao needs to demonstrate a greater comparative advantage over its competitors. The following section will discuss the competitive advantages of Macao with respect to nearby competitors.

Table 8.5 Comparison on the potential for medical tourism between Macao and major nearby competitors

City/country	*Macao*	*Hong Kong*	*Singapore*	*Taiwan*	*Thailand*
Area (km^2)	29.5[a]	1104[b]	712.4[c]	36,000[d]	513,120[e]
Population (in thousands)	552.3[a]	7097.6[b]	5,076.7[c]	23,162[d]	66,720.2[e]
Location[f]	✓	✓	x	x	x
Infrastructures[g]	✓	✓	✓	✓	✓
Human resources[h]	x	x	✓	✓	✓
Government support[i]	✓	x	✓	✓	✓
Active tourism market?[j]	✓	✓	x	x	x
Tourists from China (annual, million)	13.23[k]	22.7[l]	1.2[m]	1.6[n]	1.1[o]
Medical tourists [p] (annual)	N/A	N/A	665,000	85,000	1,000,000
Differentiation in medical services	Preventive health care comparative prices	Luxury hospitals	High-end medical services	Competitive prices	Plastic/specialist surgery competitive prices

Sources: a Statistics and Census Service Macao (2010); b Census and Statistics Department of Hong Kong (2011); c Department of Statistics Singapore (2011); d Directorate General of Budget, Accounting and Statistics of Taiwan (2011); e Central Intelligence Ageny, 2011; f Location that is easy to reach by Chinese visitors; g Infrastructures of medical tourism readily available; h Human resources of medical tourism readily available; i Government is supportive to medical tourism; j Active tourism market of China; k Statistics and Census Service Macao (2010); l Commerce and Economic Development Bureau (2011); m Singapore Tourism Board (2011); n Directorate General of Budget, Accounting and Statistics of Taiwan (2011); o Department of Tourism, Thailand (2011); p Sui (2011).

Competitive position of Macao in medical tourism

Macao is a city with around 550,000 of population. It is a Special Administrative Region (SAR) of China, connected to the country through the Border Gate. Tourists from China can enter the city by car, bus, ferry, airplane or even on foot. In 2010, Macao has welcomed around 13 million tourists from China. To support the development of Macao as a tourism and leisure destination, China has started the Individual Visit Scheme (IVS) since 2003. Through the IVS, citizens from 47 prefecture-level regions and two municipalities of China could visit Macao on an individual basis. This revived tourism for Macao post-SARS, when around 1.7 million tourists visited the city through the IVS in the first 6 months after implementation (Macau Government Tourist Office 2004). The increase has not halted to grow since then. From 2004 to 2010, there has been an accumulative increase of more than 90 per cent for Chinese tourists to Macao (Statistics and Census Service Macau (DSEC) 2011). Table 8.5 provides a synopsis on the comparative situation of Macao with respect to major nearby competitors in medical tourism, namely Hong Kong, Singapore, Taiwan and Thailand.

Competitiveness of Macao versus Hong Kong

Compared with the major nearby competitors, Hong Kong is the only destination that has similar competitive advantage. Chinese tourists travelling to other destinations have to apply visa through a more complex process and are subjected to more extensive restrictions. Although benefiting from similar competitive advantage on ease of entry, Hong Kong has been suffering from serious local objection to provide medical services to citizens of China. Violent debates have been carried out and first restrictions on the provision of prenatal medical treatment began in 2007, because of how it impacts on the provision of services to local mothers. By July 2011, Mainland Chinese mothers were no longer permitted to book in to deliver in the public hospitals of Hong Kong, as quotas had already been reached long before the end of the year (Gottlieb 2011). Under these controls, Hong Kong could not exceed its current levels of maternity tourism, unless more private maternity facilities are built and staff allocated. However, Hong Kong is still seen as attractive by mainland mothers as it grants their children 'Right of Abode' where Macao does not. This is also useful where a mainland mother is trying to evade the 'One Child Policy' and have a second child in Hong Kong.

Competitiveness of Macao versus Singapore

The government of Singapore is a strong supporter of the development of medical tourism (see Wong and Musa, Chapter 11). Singapore possesses state-of-the-art medical equipment and has internationally recognised doctors. However, in regard to price, her competitive power is minimal when compared to nearby major medical tourism competitors. When comparing the number of the Chinese tourists that visited Macao and Singapore during the current years, substantial differences are observed. For 2010, Macao had 11 times more tourists from China than Singapore, when the geographic area of Macao is only around 4 per cent that of Singapore. Furthermore, Singapore focuses at providing high-end medical services. Nonetheless, the majority of Chinese tourists are seeking preventive health-care services, which suggests that a significant opportunity remains available given the nature of demand indicated in Macao.

Competitiveness of Macao versus Taiwan

Medical tourism is gradually expanding in Taiwan. Similar to Singapore, Taiwan has emphasised their state-of-art medical equipment and well-recognised doctors. Based on the official declaration of their legislative speaker, Wang Jin-pyng, language is the major competitive advantage of Taiwan, when doctors in Taiwan can communicate in both Mandarin and English (Chen 2011). In regard to language, Macao acquires similar competitive advantage. After the return of the sovereignty of Macao to China in 1999 and the signing of the Closer Economic Partnership Agreement (CEPA) between Macao and China in 2003, Mandarin has become one of the core courses since primary education. In addition, being a colony of Portugal for more than a century and still maintaining a close relationship after the return of the city, Macao has a definite advantage with respect to European languages including in spoken English.

Therefore, the area of higher concern should be the potential number of tourists from China that can be expected to visit by Macao and Taiwan. As of 2011, tourists from China can only visit Taiwan through group tours that have pre-defined itineraries and medical treatment generally is not a focus. Commencing from June 2011, up to 500 tourists per day from China can visit Taiwan on an individual basis. This implies that around 182,500 Chinese tourists can visit Taiwan each year on an individual basis. However, this represents only around 1.4 per cent of the total number of Chinese tourists visiting Macao in 2010. Accordingly, Taiwanese authorities have stated that they are also expecting only around 2,000–4,000 medical tourists from China every year (Chen 2011). Under such circumstances, Macao and Taiwan possess comparable competitive advantages in language and are providing similar types of medical services. The competition will not be severe when the number of potential customers is far more than the capacity of supply. Conversely, given the existing business relationship between Macao and Taiwan, a strategic cooperation may bring upon mutual benefits.

Competitiveness of Macao versus Thailand

Under the encouragement of the government Thailand has been receiving mainly overseas private investment, particularly from the Middle East, for the development of medical tourism (Mintier 2009). It is also one of the countries in Asia that appears to have attracted the largest number of medical tourists (see Wong and Musa, Chapter 11). This success is closely related to the policy of attracting internationally trained and recognised doctors and dentists (many of which were born in Thailand) with appealing salary packages. Thailand is well recognised for offering plastic and specialist surgery and body check up services, at prices that remain strongly competitive due to the low cost of non-medical labour and construction of facilities. Overall, the medical tourism market in Thailand has up-to-date equipment, good hospitality and management of human resources that has been established since the 1990s. Recent political troubles aside, Thailand has a strong appeal to regional tourists but not always Chinese.

In 2010, Thailand had only 1.1 million tourists arrive from China. This suggests that though Chinese tourists have the underlying reasons to seek medical services overseas and such medical services are available in Thailand, it is not their preferred destination under the existing environment, possibly because of destination branding (of Thailand in China), geographic or cultural distance. This, in turn, implies that the possibility that Macao and Thailand will grow to be direct competitors of medical tourism is remote.

Conclusion: political position and economic readiness of Macao

According to the President of China, Hu Jin-tao, Macao needs to diversify its economy for both greater stability and to balance development. This is reaffirmed by the Chief Executive of Macau, Chui Sai-on, who has announced that the active diversification of the economy to upgrade and transform traditional industries will be implemented from 2011 (Macau Government Tourist Office 2010). This is also supported by both Macao's academia (Li and Cheng, 2010) and industrial sectors, such as tourism and hospitality.

Macao is the only city in China where gambling is legalised. The success of this is seen in how it has surpassed Las Vegas in 2006 in regard to the profits made from gambling in Macao. By 2010, annual tax on the revenue received from gambling has amounted to MOP 68.8 billion (US$ 8.6 billion) and Macao's foreign exchange reserves have reached MOP 204 billion (US$ 25.5 billion) (Monetary Authority of Macau 2011). There are more than adequate monetary resources for Macao to carry out plans that can help to reach her objectives of diversification.

In the city, the only government hospital is still under considerable pressure and has saturated its capacity. The private hospitals have well-established preventive medical care services, such as dedicated departments have been organised for health checkups and follow-up services that may be available to tourists. Medical equipment, is mostly state-of-the-art though in quantity may not be comparable to countries such as Thailand and Singapore. There is also anecdotal evidence that it is not always accompanied by staff who knows exactly how to use it for diagnostic purposes. Once again, capacity and number of human medical resources remain an issue for Macao. Nevertheless, quite a number of private clinics have been established since 2010 to provide different types of specialised preventive services, including cancer, cardio-system, HIV and sleeping disorders.

By 2010 Macao had welcomed more than 13 million tourists from China as the result of a steady increase since the return of Macao in 1999. Together with the continued support of China through the Individual Visit Scheme, it is hoped that more Chinese tourists will prefer Macao as their tourism destination. To understand the situation further, it is useful to apply the key conclusions from the study to the competitive factors identified in Figure 8.1. Figure 8.4 illustrates the position of medical tourism in Macao, with the current resources and supply and demand situation.

Accordingly, the limitations on the size of Macao's geographic area and the preceding practice in education may place restrictions on how far Macao can compete with nearby places in terms of skill-sets and the quantity of its medical infrastructure. However, the well-established tourism industry of Macao, the welcoming culture of the city and, most critically, the strategic position of the government in its decision to diversify the existing industries with the support of China, have provided definite advantages for Macao to develop medical tourism more fully. To optimise the potential of these advantages the authors suggest focussing on three major areas of development for a strategic plan for medical tourism (Figure 8.5).

To become a medical tourism centre that can compete on the global arena, Macao must possess its own human medical resources. This must be realised through training of locally born staff locally and overseas, which can only be achieved through time and with appropriate funding. However, since Macao needs to focus on the provision

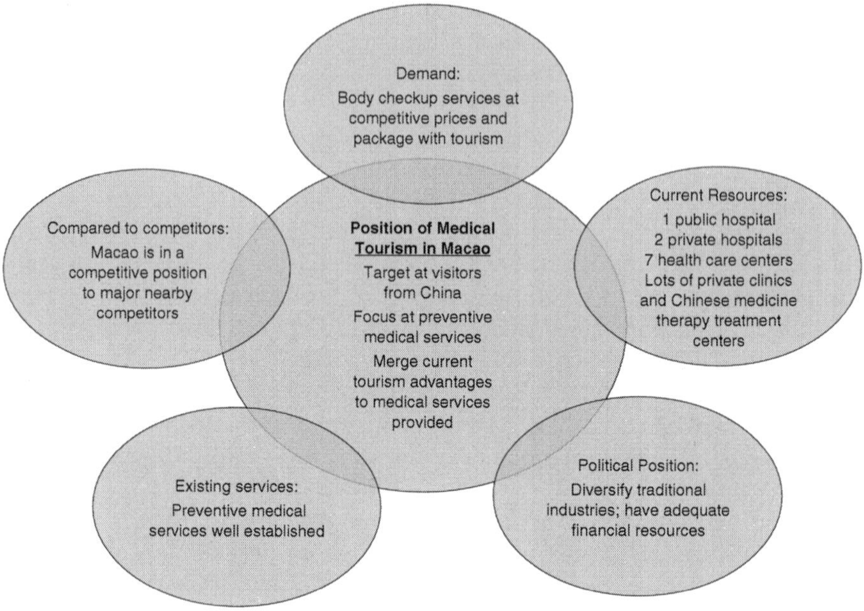

Figure 8.4 Positioning of medical tourism in Macao.

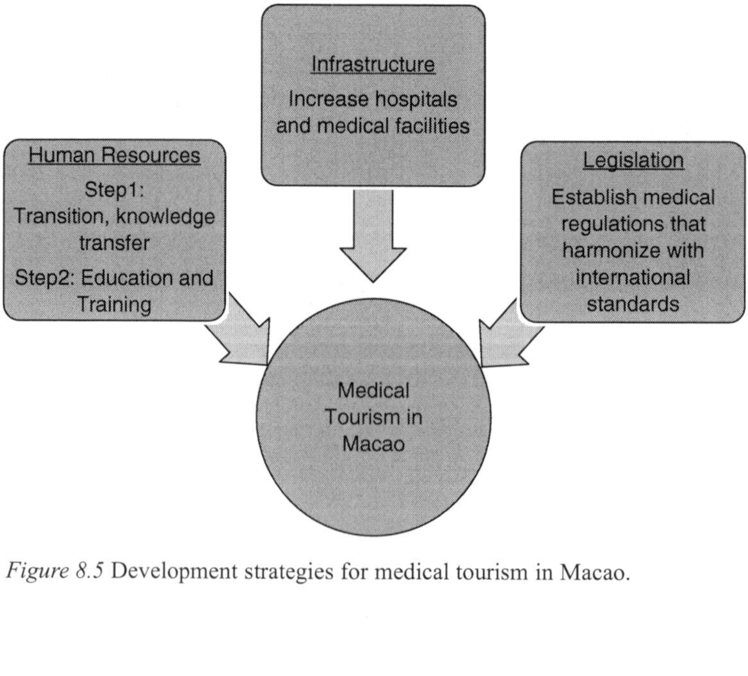

Figure 8.5 Development strategies for medical tourism in Macao.

of preventive medical services, the time required for the training of such resources may be less demanding than resources for high-end medical services. During the transition period, Macao can rely on external resources from other places of the world, until locally born individuals have received training there or elsewhere. It is already a common practice for Macao to recruit doctors from Portugal, Hong Kong and China. Furthermore, incentives should be created to attract well-recognised medical resources from the international and regional market. Similar strategies have already been proved successful in academia, when internationally recognised scholars were invited to Macao and have brought in advanced ideas and practices.

In terms of infrastructure, more hospitals and medical facilities have to be established for both tourists and local residents for the sector to grow without friction. The difficulties at achieving this new infrastructure are less challenging than that of improving the medical services, as financial resources is then the main concern. The current reserves of the government can well support this area. At the same time, as medical issues are involved, a clear and widely accepted set of standards and regulations must be in place to ensure the kind medical services provided that meet the international standards and requirements. This will involve further research by authorities and development policies that integrate international practices with that of the local situation in Macao.

References

Census and Statistics Department (2011) *Hong Kong in Figures 2011*. Hong Kong: Hong Kong Special Administrative Region.

Central Intelligence Agency (2011) 'Thailand', *The World Factbook*. [Online]. Available at: https://www.cia.gov/library/publications/the-world-factbook/geos/th.html (accessed 15 June 2011).

Chen, C.F. (2011). Medical tourism holds promise: legislative speaker. *Focus Taiwan, the Central News Agency*, 24 June. [Online]. Available at: http://focustaiwan.tw/ShowNews/WebNews_Detail.aspx?Type=aLIV&;TNo=&ID=201106240020 (accessed 24 June 2011).

Commerce and Economic Development Bureau (2011) *Tourism performance in 2010*. Hong Kong: The Government of Hong Kong Special Administrative Region. [Online]. Available at: http://www.tourism.gov.hk/english/statistics/statistics_perform.html (accessed 15 June 2011).

Connell, J. (2006) Sea, sun, sand and surgery. *Tourism Management*, 27: 1093–1100.

Department of Statistics Singapore (2011) *Statistics*. Singapore: Government of Singapore. [Online]. Available at: http://www.singstat.gov.sg/stats/latestdata.html (accessed 14 June 2011).

Department of Tourism (2011) *Tourism Statistics*. Thailand: Department of Tourism.

Directorate General of Budget, Accounting and Statistics (2011) *National statistics*. Taiwan: Directorate General of Budget, Accounting and Statistics. [Online]. Available at: http://eng.stat.gov.tw/mp.asp?mp=5 (accessed 15 June 2011).

Gottlieb, B. (2011) 'Mainland Chinese no longer permitted to give birth in Hong Kong', University of Southern California, Annenberg, School of Communication and Journalism. [Online]. Available at: http://ascportfolios.org/chinaandmedia/2011/04/12/mainland-chinese-no-longer-permitted-to-give-birth-in-hong-kong/ (accessed 18 June 2011).

Hall, C.M. (2011) 'Health and medical tourism: kill or cure for global public health?' *Tourism Review*, 66(1/2): 4–15.

Henderson, J. (2004) 'Healthcare tourism in Southeast Asia', *Tourism Review International*, 7(3–4): 111–121.

Kim, Y., Boo, C. and Kim, M. (2009) 'A framework for health tourism: a case study of Jeju province in the republic of Korea (South Korea)', Paper presented at the *International CHRIE Conference*, San Francisco, California. [Online]. Available at: http://scholarworks.umass.edu/cgi/viewcontent.cgi?article=1227&context=refereed (accessed 5 May 2012).

Lam, C.C. and Vong, T.N. (2009) 'Macao: the gambling paradise. Profiling the roles and motives of customers', *Journal of China Tourism Research*, 5(4): 338–400.

Lam, C.C. and Lei, W.S. (2010) 'City brands and special interest tourism: Macau', in N. Morgan, A. Pritchard and R. Pride (eds) *Destination Branding: Creating the Unique Destination Proposition*, 3rd edn, Oxford: Elsevier.

Lam, C.C., du Cros, H. and Vong, T.N. (2011) 'Macao's potential for developing regional Chinese medical tourism', *Tourism Review*, 66(1/2): 68–82.

Lee, C.G. (2010) 'Health care and tourism: evidence from Singapore', *Tourism Management*, 31(4): 486–488.

Li, X. and Cheng, S.W. (2010) 'The way to the diversification of Macau's social economy: a study on Macau's cultural tourism development', *International Journal of Trade, Economics and Finance*, 1(2): 131–135.

Macau Government Tourist Office (2004) More mainlanders can visit individually. [Online]. Available at: http://cn.macautourism.gov.mo/en/ezone/mttdetail.php?lan=cn&;id=1494 (accessed 21 February 2009).

Macau Government Tourist Office (2010) *Macau SAR Celebrates its Tenth Anniversary*. Macau: Macau Government Tourist Office. [Online]. Available at: http://www.macautourism.gov.mo/en/ezone/mttdetail.php?lan=cn&;id=1991 (accessed 4 June 2010).

Mintier, T. (2009) 'Snapshots: interview with Curtis Schroeder', *Bangkok 101*, July, 10.

Monetary Authority of Macau (2011) *Foreign Exchange Reserves and Nominal Effective Exchange Rate Index for the Pataca March 2011*, Press release. Macau: Monetary Authority of Macau.

Singapore Tourism Board (2011) *Annual Tourism Statistics*. Singapore: Singapore Tourism Board. [Online]. Available at: https://app.stb.gov.sg/asp/tou/tou03.asp (accessed 15 June 2012).

Statistics and Census Service Macau (DSEC) (2010) *Statistics*. [Online]. Available at: http://www.dsec.gov.mo/TimeSeriesDatabase.aspx (accessed 22 February 2010).

Statistics and Census Service Macau (DSEC) (2011). *Health Statistics*. [Online]. Available at: http://www.dsec.gov.mo/Statistic.aspx (accessed 25 July 2010)

Sui, C. (2011). Taiwan taps China for lucrative medical tourism market. *BBC News*, 31 March. [Online]. Available at: http://www.bbc.co.uk/news/business-12889648 (accessed 31 March 2011).

Van, I.K. (2010) 'To prepare nurses for health harmony of community', *Macau Journal of Nursing*, 9(1): 39–43.

World Health Organization (2000) *The World Health Report 2000. Health Systems: Improving Performance*. Geneva: World Health Organization.

Part IV

Branding, markets and promotion

9 Branding health and medical tourism services

An analysis of members of public health insurers in Germany

Tanja C. Boga and Klaus Weiermair

Branding health and medical tourism services

Health and business with health-related goods and services can be seen as one of the mega trends in the twenty-first century (Nefiodow 1999). According to PricewaterhouseCoopers (PWC) (2005) HealthCast 2020, the 24 Organisation for Economic Co-operation and Development (OECD) countries will be spending approximately US$ 10 trillion on health in 2020. In tourism, health related services have become a growing market segment and a billion dollar business. For 2010, the Global Spa Summit estimated the global market size of health tourism (medical and wellness tourism) to be US$ 156 billion (Global Spa Summit 2010). This development in health tourism can be attributed mainly to two driving forces: economic-based driving forces, such as exploding costs for medical treatments in industrial nations, and socio-psychological driving forces, such as value changes in aging societies.

The literature on branding in health tourism is still rather limited. This is somehow surprising, considering the economic significance of this market segment (see Chapter 1). On the other hand here branding is faced with extraordinary challenges making it a taxing task. These challenges result in particular from the absence of a physically tangible object as a medium for carrying the brand. Additionally, they have their origin in the mental intangibility of services and in the supplier–customer relationship: In general, it is difficult for consumers to articulate what exactly it is that they are buying. Thus often suppliers and consumers have no common starting point when discussing a service (Bateson 1979). It seems therefore all the more important to discuss more comprehensively branding in the health-tourism literature. Even more so as consumer behavior in health tourism displays specific characteristics such as a high level of perceived risk, which can be addressed by branding, for example, brands help lower the level of perceived risk.

Branding started to expand into the tourism industry only very recently (Wagner and Peters 2009). In the tourism-management literature, a notable stream of research dealing with the general issue of destination branding is now available (e.g. Hosany *et al.* 2006; Tasci and Kozak 2006). As already mentioned, specific research work on branding in health and medical tourism still remains rather scarce. Smith and Puczkó (2008) noticed in this context that often in health and wellness tourism, brands are seen as either only logos or as a name. In general, the number of publications on branding in health tourism in the medical literature appears to be somewhat larger than in the tourism literature. In the tourism literature, branding issues are mainly dealt with in the context of destination branding. Branding is especially difficult with regards to the subsector of medical tourism. In medical tourism, where the focus is curative and the traveler is, by tendency, ill (Hall 2011), the perceived risk tends to be much higher as much more is at stake than in other subsectors of health tourism, for example, wellness tourism, where the focus is on wellbeing in general.

Some medical-tourism destinations which are situated in emerging markets such as Thailand, India or Malaysia feature a destination image which is otherwise well suited for tourism-market segments such as adventure or beach holidays, but might conflict with consumer needs and risk perception in medical tourism. In such cases, it seems especially of great importance to differentiate between destination branding and branding of a specific tourism product such as in medical tourism.

Theoretical background

Defining the term "brand"

According to the American Marketing Association (2011), a brand is a "name, term, design, symbol, or any other feature that identifies one seller's good or service as distinct from those of other sellers." For further defining in marketing what a brand is, one can either apply an attribute-oriented approach or a behavior (e.g. perception)-based approach. In the classical attribute-oriented approach, a thing is a brand if it possesses specific constitutive attributes (Bekmeier-Feuerhahn 1998; Freundt 2006). According to this approach, only manufactured consumer goods with a consistent appearance, quantity, and quality are brandable. With the emerging of services and hybrid products this traditional goods-based approach became more and more difficult. Under the attribute-oriented approach, some of the most well-established and valuable brands could not be considered a brand since they do not possess all of the required attributes. This applies, for example, to service brands such as Lufthansa (German airline), as well as to service brands such as McKinsey (business consultants). Therefore, the behavior-based approach appears to be more appropriate, since there it is the consumer who decides what a brand is or what it is not. The focus is here on the consumer and his empirical reality. Meffert (2000), for example, defines the term brand from a behavior based approach as a distinctive image of a product or service rooted deeply in the psyche of the consumer. Freundt (2006) uses this definition and adds that these images can influence choice and decision making. We therefore define the term brand as follows: a distinctive image of a product, service or any other associations of an entity rooted deeply in the psyche of the consumer which has influence on choice and decision making.

The sum of all stored brand associations constitutes brand knowledge. According to Keller (2008), brand knowledge can be further differentiated into brand awareness and brand image. Here, the term brand awareness refers to the strength of the brand node or its trace in memory. Brand image refers to the perceptions about a brand. Perception is reflected by brand associations stored in consumers' memory. Brand image therefore is the public image of a brand.

The term brand identity can be defined according to Aaker (1996) as a unique set of associations which the brand strategist creates and which implies a promise from the members of the firm to its customers. There are four dimensions from which to view brand identity: brand-as-product (e.g., product scope or product attributes); brand-as-organization (e.g., organizational attributes); brand-as-person (e.g., brand personality); and brand-as-symbol (e.g., brand heritage). Brand personality as part of the perspective brand-as-person can be defined according to Aaker (1997: 347) as "human characteristics associated with a brand." According to Azoulay and Kapferer (2003: 153) it is "the unique set of human personality traits both applicable and relevant to brands." Altogether, brand identity stands for the essence of a brand from an internal point of view; it is usually termed self-perception or self-image.

Brand associations as core concepts in branding can be established at various association levels, for example, at the attribute level or the consequence level (Kotler *et al.* 2007). These brand associations can be represented as a means-end chain (mec) structure (Aaker 1991). One of the first articles in which the attempt was made to use mec-structures in brand management was by Reynolds *et al.* (1995). They were able to show that mecs contribute to the explanation of brand persuasion. A mec-structure can be depicted as a hierarchical chain with three first-order and six second-order association levels (Gutman 1982; Reynolds and Gutman 1988; Walker and Olson 1991; Ter Hofstede *et al.* 1998). The three first-order association levels are product attributes, consequences, and personal values. The six second-order association levels are concrete and abstract attributes, functional and psychosocial consequences, and instrumental and terminal values. The association level of personal values is the association level closest to the personality (or self) of consumers (Figure 9.1). The association level of attributes is closest to the product itself (Walker and Olson 1991). According to mec-theory, brand associations which are established at levels close to the personality of consumers are deeply rooted and lasting and also of great importance for preference judgments (Reynolds and Gutman 1988). This applies especially to associations at the level of personal values (Kotler *et al.* 2007), a point also shared by Weis and Huber (2000). They claim that if one were to establish a psychological connection between consumers and a brand, it is especially important to know goals and personal values of consumers.

Branding effects

In general, one can differentiate between economic and behavioral effects of branding. It can be said that economic effects are the result of behavioral effects which brands have on consumers. Here we will mainly deal with behavioral effects of branding. Economic effects will be also discussed, but only very briefly. For suppliers, economic effects of branding result from the fact that brands are a

PRODUCT		← →		CONSUMER	
Attributes		**Consequences**		**Values**	
Concrete Attributes	Abstract Attributes	Functional Consequences	Psychosocial Consequences	Instrumental Values	Terminal Values

Figure 9.1 Depiction of mec-structure.

source of competitive advantage and financial return (Keller 2008). These economic effects manifest themselves in an increase of economic target values such as profits, market share or gross margin. For customers, the main economic effect of branding can be seen in the fact that brands reduce search cost (Keller 2008).

Behavioral effects of branding on consumers manifest themselves in something which can be called behavioral target values, such as a decrease of intangibility and perceived risk. As Keller (2008) states, brands can help consumers to identify the source of a product. In doing so, brands can also help consumers in better understanding what a product stands for, meaning that brands can help decrease perceived mental intangibility. In the context of tourism, Clarke (2000) refers to the reduction of the impact of intangibility as one of the benefits of branding. Especially in service industries, where physical intangibility is a constitutive service attribute, brands are important symbolic devices, respectively proxies for the product itself. Another important effect of brands on consumer behavior is that they are risk reducing (Keller 2008). According to Matzler *et al.* (2008) consumers try to minimize perceived risk through the use of various cues, for example, brands, especially when perceived risk in a buying decision is high. And lastly, brands can function as a signal of quality. In general, the overall aim with regards to the behavioral effects of branding on consumers is to influence their behavioral intention in a positive way, as well as to establish brand loyalty. This applies for new customers as well as existing customers.

These behavioral target values are mainly directed to consumer as a target groups. Besides consumers, there are other relevant external target groups (e.g. competitors or the public in general) for which behavioral effects of branding have to be considered. But not only external groups are target groups for branding. The behavioral effects of branding are also important when dealing with internal target groups such as employees. Especially with regards to the effects of a brand on intangibility, employees can be seen as a key target group.

Brand development

Brand images (public image of a brand) as well as brand identities (self-image of a brand) consisting of unique brand associations are established in learning processes. Learning can be defined as the non-observable process of information processing which induces behavior modification (Kroeber-Riel and Weinberg 2003). The storage of knowledge in learning processes is influenced by direct (personal) or indirect (third party or media) experiences with the brand. Every learning process contains constructive elements, that is, all content is individually internalized (Schunk 1996).

In the Customer-Based Brand Equity (CBBE) model Keller (2008) presents a blueprint for building a strong brand. However, there is no common definition of what a strong brand is. In our opinion and in accordance with Keller (2008), a strong brand features three aspects: (1) a rich brand image consisting of a bundle of associations; (2) many of these associations are shared by consumers; and (3) a strong brand awareness so that consumers are able to identify the brand under different situations or conditions. The CBBE model provides a guideline on how, with a sequence of four steps, a strong brand can be established. The structure is contingent; meaning each objective of the previous step has to be fulfilled before the next step can be approached. In the first step, the supplier has to ensure that consumers are able to identify themselves with the brand and then link the brand associations in their mind with a specific anchor, ideally with a specific consumer need. After this has been achieved, it is important that in a second step, the totality of brand meaning is established. Therefore a host of tangible and intangible brand associations with specific properties have to be implemented in the mind of the consumer. Once brand associations have been established, it is equally important to elicit a proper consumer response leading to a positive buying decision. And finally, the first purchase should not be the last: the brand response needs to be converted into an active and loyal relationship between customers and the brand.

"Brandability" of health and medical tourism services

Defining health and medical tourism

Historically, the term health tourism has been more associated with Europe than with America (Hall 2011). Therefore, defining health tourism generally is a challenge. Goeldner (1989) and Kaspar (1996) defined health tourism as featuring two determining elements: (1) staying away from home and (2) health as the most important motive. In addition, Goeldner (1989) adds a third determining element, for example, done in a leisure setting. Kaspar (1996) differentiates the second element further by defining health tourism as traveling for the maintenance, enhancement or restoration of wellbeing in body, mind, and soul. A similar definition can be found in Carrera and Bridges (2006). According to Goodrich and Goodrich (1987), the leisure setting element can be further extended by setting or destination context which provide facilities and health-care services explicitly and in addition to their regular tourist amenities. Consistent with Romeiß-Stracke (2001) we propose to establish health tourism as a higher-order concept. Medical tourism is therefore a subsector of health tourism. In medical tourism, the focus is curative and the patient is, by tendency, ill (Hall 2011).

In public perception, health tourism and medical tourism are often seen as two different concepts. According to our definition, this is not the case. In order to explicitly include medical tourism as a subsector of health tourism, we use the term health and medical tourism.

Intangibility of health and medical tourism services and branding

The literature on branding health and medical tourism services remains rather scarce. At the same time, it is precisely the specific attributes of health and medical tourism services, first and foremost their intangibility, which make branding both a challenge and, from a commercial perspective, a necessity.

Health and medical tourism services are relatively intangible in nature (Bowen and Bowers 1986; Zeithaml 1991; Berry and Bendapudi 2007). According to Bielen and Sempels (2003), intangibility as a determining service attribute can be defined as a two-dimensional construct. In this regard, the dimension physical intangibility refers to physical non-conceivability while the dimension mental intangibility refers to mental non-comprehensibility. For some time, a development has been observed in which service offerings in tourism in general and especially service offerings in health tourism have become more and more intangible (Pikkemaat and Weiermair 2004). This can be seen mainly as a result of two factors: On the one hand, there is the increasing emotionality in the staging of services supplemented by new and exotic forms of treatments [e.g. ayurveda, ai chi, sound therapy (Kirschner 2009)], and on the other hand, there is the technological development of hardware used in diagnostics (e.g. digital radiology) and treatments (e.g. hydro jet) (Boga and Weiermair 2011).

Intangibility leads to specific challenges. Physical intangibility results in the lack of a physical medium for carrying the brand. There are of course physical goods involved in the creation of the service experience in health and medical tourism, but the service as such is physically intangible. Therefore, a suitable medium has to be selected which is able to carry the tangible brand since the service as such is not able to do so. Increasing mental intangibility as described above leads to the fact that it becomes more and more difficult for consumer to articulate what they are buying, and therefore, often the supplier and customer have no common starting point when discussing a service (Bateson 1979). The buying decision for such products is, above all, associated with uncertainty and a high level of perceived risk (Laroche *et al.* 2004; Laroche *et al.* 2005). Perceived risk refers to the nature and amount of risk which a particular purchase decision holds for a consumer or which he perceives (Cox and Rich 1964). To make things even worse, health-related services affect the consumer directly and personally; they are whether they want or not involved. Day (1970: 45) defines involvement as "the general level of interest in the object or the centrality of the object to the person´s ego structure." Therefore, in general, the involvement in health and medical tourism is high, which again leads to higher perceived risk (Goutaland 1999).

Branding can influence or mitigate these negative effects that intangibility can have on consumer behavior. A strong brand is able to minimize intangibility and perceived risk. Especially in health and medical tourism a strong brand therefore appears to be of great importance. A strong brand consists of a rich brand image and of a bundle of associations. Brand associations can be installed on various association levels. Foster (2008) developed in an article on spa branding a shell model with different aspects of branding different association levels which include also mec-structures: attributes, consequences, values, personality, brand essence. Of particular interest is the association level of personal values and its covariability with regards to mitigating the negative effects intangibility upon consumer behavior. Boga (2011) could show that, with increasing importance of personal values in the context of the buying behavior for health tourism, perceived mental intangibility decreases. Accordingly, it seems highly appropriate in health and medical tourism to augment a brand with relevant personal values.

Empirical results from the Alpshealthcomp project

Project and survey design

The European project Alpshealthcomp has been carried out combining seven research partners from Austria, Italy, and Germany. The primary objective was to analyze as to how the competitiveness of Alpine Space as a sustainable health destination could be strengthened. Alpine Space has a long tradition in health-related tourism (e.g. Alpine summer tourism) and health-tourism facilities (e.g. spa resorts respectively "Kurbäder"). The main research question in this project was as to how this competence could be presented and communicated in a coherent way, for example, by branding. Therefore, the aim of a particular empirical survey carried out in this context was to analyze the potential foundations for a strong brand in Alpine health tourism. The results should provide a basis for marketers with regards to the enhancement of existing or the development of new brands.

In this survey, we were not analyzing existing brands with regards to brand associations (e.g. Zaltman and Coulter 1995; Aaker 1997; Torres and Bijmolt 2009). But rather we were analyzing a product type with regards to its generic ability to carry brand associations creating strong and lasting relationships between consumers and the brand. It is often assumed that these brand associations are established only at the level of attributes (e.g. Torres and Bijmolt 2009). In contrast, we used a broader product concept in which a product not only consists of its attributes but has also consequences and values which all are possible carriers of brand associations. Brand associations established close to the personality of the consumer are deeply rooted, lasting and of great importance for the preference decision (Reynolds and Gutman 1988). They can be seen as a prerequisite for the development of a strong brand. We used mec-structures in order to measure association structures. Of all three mec-association levels, the level of values is closest to the personality of consumers. Brand associations are therefore to be established preferentially at this level. But if brand associations should be established at the level of values, an identifiable and describable common value structure for service offerings in Alpine health tourism must be observable.

The survey was conducted in co operation with two of the largest public health insurances in Germany. The focus was on general service offerings in Alpine health tourism and not a specific brand. Therefore we did not employ a method for ex-post measurement of brand associations such as the Zaltman's Metaphor Elicitation Technique (ZMET) (Zaltman and Coulter 1995). Instead we analyzed

Table 9.1 Characteristics of the sample

Variables	*(%)*
Sex	
Male	18.3
Female	81.7
Age in years	
< 20	1.6
20–29	16.7
30–39	21.8
40–49	32.0
50–59	19.6
60–69	7.3
70+	1.0
Education	
CSE without completed vocational training	4.1
CSE with completed vocational training	16.3
O-Levels/Secondary school without A-Levels	47.9
A-Levels/University entrance diploma	16.9
University of Applied Sciences/University	14.9
Net household income per month in €	
< 1,000	15.9
1,000–1,499	25.7
1,500–2,499	30.5
2,500–or more	27.9

ex-ante using mec-analysis to find out whether service offerings in Alpine health tourism are "brandable" at all, meaning whether an identifiable and describable common value structure for service offerings can be observed, which then could be used to augment a brand. Data collection was conducted via an online survey through web-based hard laddering (Walker and Olson 1991; Grunert and Grunert 1995). For each participant, four mec-ladders were obtained which when aggregated reflect for each participant the mec-structure for service offerings in Alpine health tourism. The mec-items were derived using the appropriate literature (Rokeach 1973; Hiesel 1975; Winkler and Grimm 2006) and from the results of a consumer survey (n = 1,607) concerning expectations for service offerings in Alpine health and wellness tourism in Germany (Bausch *et al.* 2007). The population of this survey consists of members of two of the largest public health insurers in Germany, who had access to the internet and the insurance website over the sample period. The sampling (n = 491) was done through an online *ad hoc* procedure (for characteristics of the sample see Table 9.1). Noticeable here is the high percentage of female participants. This corresponds with other research on the role of women as chief health-care decision makers for their household or on women's intensive use of the Internet for health-information gathering (Macias *et al.* 2004).

Table 9.2 Principal component analysis for the association level of personal values

Variables	*Components*[a]		*Components*[b]	
	1	*2*	*1*	*2*
V1: "I want to live a healthy life."		0.635		0.640
V2: "I want to enjoy pleasure."	0.581		0.467	
V3: "I want to experience adventures and have fun."	0.721		0.634	
V4: "I aim for security through precaution and prevention."		0.690		0.668
V5: "I wish for balance and internal harmony."		0.593		0.574
V6: "I want to be myself and enjoy life."	0.745		0.765	
V7: "I want to carry my life in my own hands."	0.660		0.707	
V8: "I want to develop personally."	0.655		0.740	0.472
V9: "I want to belong and feel accepted."	0.510		0.619	

Notes

a Pattern matrix.

b Structure matrix.

Results

For each participant, the four generated mec-ladders were aggregated with Predictive Analytics SoftWare (PASW) Statistics 17.0. Functional and psychosocial consequence-items and instrumental and terminal value-items in each mec-ladder were originally binary. As a result of the aggregation of the four mec-ladders, each item has a five-item frequency scale (from 0 = "not selected" to 4 = "four times selected") which can be interpreted as a ratio scale with a non-arbitrary zero value. Concrete and abstract attributes have an ordinal scale (from 1 = "least important" to 4 = "most important" respectively 0 = "not selected") due to the fact that for each of the four mec-ladders there was only one attribute to choose from (without returning) and to sort according to preference.

Subsequently, principal component analysis for the association level of values was conducted. An oblique rotation (promax) was chosen, assuming a correlative nature of the components based on the literature. The Kaiser Meyer-Olkin (KMO)-coefficient (0.775) displays substantial correlations in the sample and average suitability of the data for factor analysis. Based on logical considerations and the eigenvalue, two components (Bühner 2006) were extracted. Component 1 accounts for 31.6 percent and component 2 accounts for 13.6 percent of the total variance in the sample. In Table 9.2, the pattern matrix and the structure matrix are reported. According to Nunnally (1978) loadings at < 0.400 are not considered in the components and are therefore not displayed.

Instrumental (component 1) and terminal value-items (component 2) are represented by one component each. Instrumental values or modes of conduct refer to concrete patterns of behavior (Golonka 2009). Instrumental values can be further differentiated as moral values (interpersonal values) and competence values (intra-personal values). Here instrumental values were competence values. Terminal values or end states of existence refer to desirable final states. Terminal values can be further differentiated as personal and social final states. Terminal values here were personal final states.

Managerial implications

Principal component analysis has shown that for service offerings in Alpine health tourism an identifiable and describable common value structure exists. Two dimensions were identified: terminal values (component 2) and instrumental values (component 1). Component 2 addresses the values "health," "safety," and "harmony." Component 1 addresses the values "personal development," "independence," "being myself and enjoying life," "belong and feel accepted," "enjoying pleasure," and "experiencing adventures and having fun." If consumer and brand share the same values, consumers can develop close connections and identify with the brand; trust and commitment can grow and a strong and lasting relationship between consumers and brands can develop. To create a brand which induces trust and commitment and has unique brand associations, and thus a strong brand (Koll and von Wallpach 2009), marketers should therefore establish brand associations close to the consumers' personality, or at the association level of personal value. This value structure can be addressed in brand communication and could, for example, complement the concept of brand personality (Boga and Weiermair 2011). Personality traits in Aaker (1997) Brand Personality Scale reflect general characteristics of brand personality such as reliable, intelligent or charming whereas the identified values structure could represent specific characteristics complementing a brand personality according to the product type. By using these values to complement brand personality aligned to the individual product and company, the congruity between consumers and brand will grow and simultaneously the preference for the brand will grow (Aaker 1997).

However, these results should not be interpreted in such a way that brand associations should only be established at the association level of values. Brands which address various association levels are stronger then brands which only concentrate on one association level (Kotler *et al.* 2007). Brand personality and the values a brand shares with consumers can function as a stable core around which other, possibly less stable associations (e.g. attributes such as highest quality, lowest price), can be placed (Boga and Weiermair 2011). If such a strong core exists, a brand would "survive" failure of less stable associations due to, for example, variability of service quality or competitive environment. Also, fundamental revitalization processes would be only necessary if important consumer values change. Lastly, since personal values apply for higher aggregated social entities, a brand which has been established on this association level does not have to be highly differentiated in order to address various target groups in parallel. All these aspects have positive impact on the cost of brand management.

Brand personality and the associated personal values in the branding model in Figure 9.2 can be communicated through various potential sources like employees,

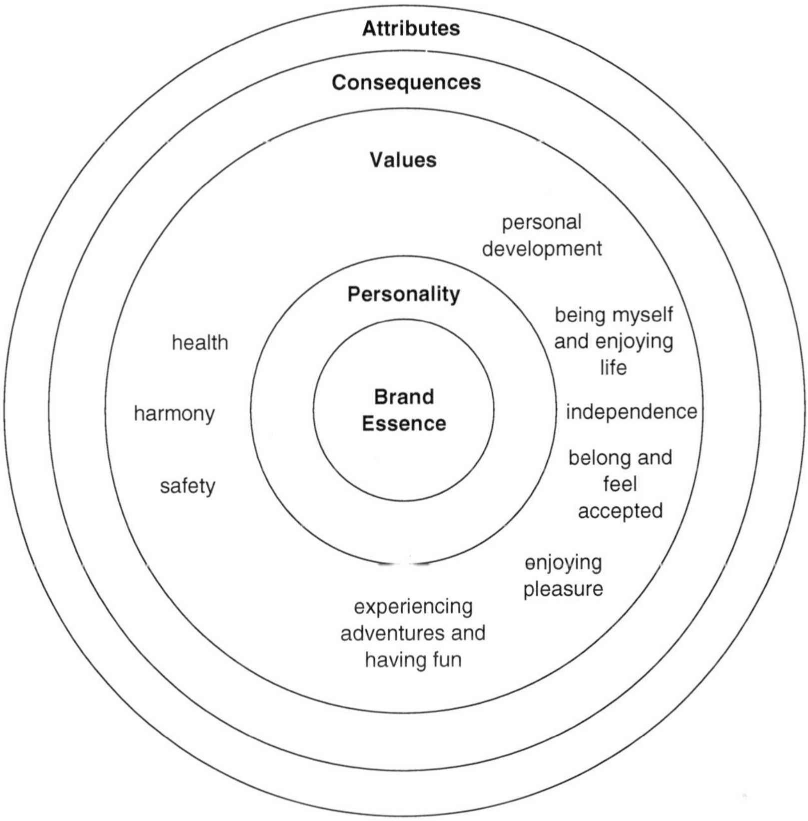

Figure 9.2 Branding model for health and medical tourism.

CEOs, average users, product attributes, own experience from usage, brand name, brand logo, type of advertising, price, country of origin and company values (McCracken 1989; Batra *et al.* 1993; Aaker 1997; Maehle 2007). A good source for terminal personal values such as "health," "safety," and "harmony" would be, for example, the company's moral values. In practice, this could be achieved by communicating them in written form, for example, in the mission statement and on the homepage or any other company-related carrier (Boga and Weiermair 2011). Instrumental values such as "personal development," "independence," and "enjoying pleasure" refer to instrumental aspects of brand personality and competence and excitement issues; good sources could be, according to Maehle (2007), company's employees, CEOs and, in the case of excitement, endorsers. In practice, this could be achieved by having sophisticated and independent employees staging and communicating "personal development" and "independence" (Boga and Weiermair 2011). Behavioral branding focuses on staging and communications of such values. Behavioral branding incorporates, as Henkel *et al.* (2007: 311) define, "any type of verbal and non-verbal employee behavior that directly or indirectly determines brand experience and brand value." In tourism, the concept of addressing employees in internal marketing since they have a large influence on visitor's experiences is not new (e.g. Choo and Park 2009). But the focus is often only on socially conforming behavior such as friendliness or on hospitality. In behavioral branding, socially conforming behavior is considered rather self-evident; instead behavioral branding is mainly about more complex employee behavior. Here employees need to thoroughly know the goals and brand values of their company, and they need specific brand-related skills. Therefore, these employees have to be well qualified and motivated. Nevertheless, it is valuable as brand-consistent employee behavior accounts for a critical success factor (Henkel *et al.* 2007). Lastly, the value "pleasure" can be staged and communicated through advertising style. In practice, this could be achieved by the use of high-quality design and material (e.g. paper, color) and high-quality content (pictures and descriptions) (Boga and Weiermair 2011).

As Pitts and Woodside (1986) have already pointed out, values can play an important role in brand advertising in tourism. We developed in Figure 9.2 a branding model for health and medical tourism based on personal values and a broader perspective on branding integrating multiple association layers around the essence of a brand. A brand based on this value structure, sharing the same values as its customers, would consequently have all the potential of becoming a strong brand with loyal customers (Boga and Weiermair 2011). While implementing and preserving a strong brand, one critical factor of success can be brand behavior, especially where the amount of customer/employees "touch points" is as high as it is in health tourism. Hence this branding model could function, for example, as a basis for developing behavioral branding in health tourism.

References

Aaker, D.A. (1991) *Managing Brand Equity*, New York: Jossey-Bass.

Aaker, D.A. (1996) *Building Strong Brands*, New York: Jossey-Bass.

Aaker, J.L. (1997) "Dimensions of brand personality," *Journal of Marketing Research*, 34(3): 347–56.

American Marketing Association (2011) *AMA Dictionary*, [Online]. Available at: http://www.marketingpower.com/_layouts/Dictionary.aspx?dLetter=B (accessed 31 July 2011).

Azoulay, A. and Kapferer, J.-N. (2003) "Do brand personality scales really measure brand personality?," *Journal of Brand Management*, 11(2): 143–55.

Bateson, J.E.G. (1979) "Why we need services marketing," in O.C. Ferrell, S.W. Brown and C.W. Lamb Jr. (eds) *Conceptual and Theoretical Development in Marketing*, Proceeding Series, Chicago, IL: American Marketing Association.

Batra, R., Lehmann, D.R. and Singh, D. (1993) "The brand personality component of brand goodwill: some antecedents and consequences," in D.A. Aaker and A.L. Biel (eds) *Brand Equity and Advertising*, Hillsdale, NJ: Psychology Press.

Bausch, T., Hanslbauer, T. and Nungesser, S. (2007) *HM ALPSHEALTHCOMP Report 1: Perception of the Alpine Region as Health and Wellness Destination*, Munich: Hochschule München, Fakultät für Tourismus.

Bekmeier-Feuerhahn, S. (1998) *Marktorientierte Markenbewertung*, Wiesbaden: Dt. Univ.-Verl.

Berry, L. and Bendapudi, N. (2007) "Healthcare: a fertile field for service research," *Journal of Service Research*, 10(2): 111–22.

Bielen, F. and Sempels, C. (2003) *The dimensionality of the concept of intangibility: a critical analysis*. [Online]. Available at: www.uclouvain.be/cps/ucl/doc/iag/documents/WP_106_Sempels.pdf (accessed 31 July 2011).

Boga, T.C. (2011) "Wahl und Kaufentscheidungen für innovative und intangible Dienstleistungen: Dargestellt am Beispiel von neuen touristischen Dienstleistungen für Alpine Gesundheit und Wellness," Doctoral thesis, University of Innsbruck, Austria.

Boga, T.C. and Weiermair, K. (2011) "Branding new services in health tourism," *Tourism Review*, 66(1/2): 90–106.

Bowen, J. and Bowers, M.R. (1986) "A marketing contingency approach to service organizations," in Venkatesan, M. et al. (eds), *Creativity in Services Marketing*, Chicago, IL: American Marketing Association.

Bühner, M. (2006) *Einführung in die Test- und Fragebogenkonstruktion*, München: Pearson Studium.

Carrera, P.M. and Bridges, J.F.P. (2006) "Globalization and healthcare: understanding health and medical tourism," *Expert Review of Pharmacoeconomics & Outcomes Research*, 6(4): 447–54.

Choo, H. and Park, S.-Y. (2009), "The influence of the resident's identification with a tourist destination brand on their behavior," Available at: http://scholarworks.umass.edu/refereed/Sessions/Wednesday/5 (accessed 31 July 2011)

Clarke, J. (2000) "Tourism brands: an exploratory study of the brands box model," *Journal of Vacation Marketing*, 6(4): 329–45.

Cox, D.F. and Rich, S.V. (1964) "Perceived risk and consumer decision making—the case of telephone shopping," in Cox, D.F. (ed.) *Risk Taking and Information Handling in Consumer Behavior*, Boston, MA: Harvard Business School.

Day, G.S. (1970) *Buyer Attitudes and Brand Choice*, New York: Free Press.

Foster, S. (2008) "Branding and spas," in M. Cohen and G. Bodeker (eds) *Understanding the Global Spa Industry—Spa Management*, Oxford: Elsevier.

Freundt, T.C. (2006) *Emotionalisierung von Marken*, Wiesbaden: Deutscher Universitätsverlag.

Global Spa Summit (2010) *Spas and the Global Wellness Market: Synergies and Opportunities*, prepared by SRI International, May 2010.

Goeldner, C. (1989) "39th Congress AIEST: English workshop summary," *Revue de Tourisme*, 44(4): 6–7.

Golonka, J. (2009) *Werbung und Werte*, Wiesbaden: VS Verlag für Sozialwissenschaften.

Goodrich, J.N. and Goodrich, G.E. (1987) "Health-care tourism—an explanatory study," *Tourism Management*, 8: 217–22.

Goutaland, C. (1999) "Product and service intangibility: a study of its dimensions and consequences on product/service evaluation," Master's thesis at the Faculty of Commerce and Administration, Concordia University, Canada.

Grunert, K.G. and Grunert, S.C. (1995) "Measuring subjective meaning structures by the laddering method: theoretical considerations and methodological problems," *International Journal of Research in Marketing*, 12: 209–25.

Gutman, J. (1982) "A means-end chain model based on consumer categorization processes," *Journal of Marketing*, 46: 60–72.

Hall, C.M. (2011) "Health and medical tourism: kill or cure for global public health?," *Tourism Review*, 66(1/2): 4–15.

Henkel, S., Tomczak, T., Heitmann, M. and Herrmann, A. (2007) "Managing brand consistent employee behavior: relevance and managerial control of behavioural branding," *Journal of Product & Brand Management*, 16: 310–20.

Hiesel, E. (1975) *Wertorientierungen als Gegenstand einer Testentwicklung*, Köln: Peter Hanstein Verlag.

Hosany, S., Ekinci, Y. and Uysal, M. (2006) "Destination image and destination personality: an application of branding theories to tourism places," *Journal of Business Research*, 59: 638–42.

Kaspar, C. (1996) "Gesundheitstourismus im Trend," *Jahrbuch der Schweizer Tourismuswirtschaft* 1995/96, 53–61.

Keller, K.L. (2008) *Strategic Brand Management*, Upper Saddle River, NJ: Prentice Hall.

Kirschner, C. (2009) *Glossary Cure, Spa, Rehabilitation*, Stuttgart: E. Schweizerbartsche Verlagsbuchhandlung.

Koll, O. and von Wallpach, S. (2009) "One brand perception? Or many? The heterogeneity of intra-brand knowledge," *Journal of Product and Brand Management*, 18(5): 338–45.

Kotler, P., Keller, K.L. and Bliemel, F. (2007) *Marketing-Management*, München: Pearson Studium.

Kroeber-Riel, W. and Weinberg, P. (2003) *Konsumentenverhalten, 8th edn.*, München: Verlag Vahlen.

Laroche, M., McDougall, G.H.G., Bergeron, J. and Yang, Z. (2004) "Exploring how intangibility affects perceived risk," *Journal of Service Research*, 6(4): 373–89.

Laroche, M., Yang, Z., McDougall, G.H.G. and Bergeron, J. (2005) "Internet versus bricks-and-mortar retailers: an investigation into intangibility and its consequences," *Journal of Retailing*, 81(4): 251–67.

McCracken, G. (1989) "Who is the celebrity endorser? Cultural foundations of the endorsement process," *Journal of Consumer Research*, 16(3): 310–21.

Macias, W., Stavchansky Lewis, L. and Shankar, V. (2004) "Dr. mom and Dr. web: a qualitative analysis of women's use of health information on the web," *Journal of Interactive Advertising*, 4(2): 9–19.

Maehle, N. (2007) "Brand personality enhancement. An experimental study of alternative strategies," paper presented at 16th EDAMBA Summer Academy, July 2007, Soreze, France. [Online]. Available at: http://www.edamba.eu/userfiles/Natalia%20Maehle.doc (accessed 31 July 2011).

Matzler, K., Grabner-Kräuter, S. and Bidmon, S. (2008) "Risk aversion and brand loyalty: the mediating role of brand trust and brand affect," *Journal of Product & Brand Management*, 17(3): 154–62.

Meffert, H. (2000) *Marketing: Grundlagen marktorientierter Unternehmensführung*, Wiesbaden: Gabler Verlag.

Nefiodow, L.A. (1999) *Der sechste Kondratieff. Wege zur Produktivität und Vollbeschäftigung im Zeitalter der Information, 3rd edn.*, Sankt Augustin: Rhein-Sieg-Verlag.

Nunnally, J.C. (1978) *Psychometric Theory*, New York: McGraw-Hill.

Pikkemaat, B. and Weiermair, K. (2004) "Einleitung—Zur Bedeutung der Qualität im Tourismus," in K. Weiermair and B. Pikkemaat (eds) *Qualitätszeichen im Tourismus*, Berlin: Schmidt Erich Verlag.

Pitts, R.E. and Woodside, A.G. (1986) "Personal values and travel decision," *Journal of Travel Research*, 25(1): 20–25.

PricewaterhouseCoopers (2005) *Health Cast 2020: Gesundheit zukunftsfähig gestalten*, PricewaterhouseCoopers' Health Research Institute.

Reynolds, T.J. and Gutman, J. (1988) "Laddering theory, method, analysis and interpretation," *Journal of Advertising Research*, 28: 11–31.

Reynolds, T.J., Gengler, C.E. and Howard, D.J. (1995) "A means-end analysis of brand persuasion through advertising," *International Journal of Research in Marketing*, 12: 257–66.

Rokeach, M. (1973) *The Nature of Human Values*, New York: The Free Press.

Romeiß-Stracke, F. (2001) *Markt der Zukunft: Neue Produkte und Dienstleistungen im Gesundheitstourismus*, Bad Kissingen.

Schunk, D.H. (1996) *Learning Theories*, Englewood Cliffs, NJ: Prentice Hall.

Smith, M. and Puczkó, L. (2008) *Health and Wellness Tourism*, Oxford: Elsevier.

Tasci, A.D.A. and Kozak, M. (2006) "Destination brands vs destination image: do we know what we mean?," *Journal of Vacation Marketing*, 12(4): 299–317.

Ter Hofstede, F., Audenaert, A., Steenkamp, J.-B.E.M. and Wedel, M. (1998) "An investigation into the association pattern technique as a quantitative approach to measuring means-end chains," *International Journal of Research in Marketing*, 15: 37–50.

Torres, A. and Bijmolt, T.H.A. (2009) "Assessing brand image through communalities and asymmetries in brand-to-attribute and attribute-to-brand associations," *European Journal of Operational Research*, 195: 628–40.

Wagner, O. and Peters, M. (2009) "Can association methods reveal the effects of internal branding on tourism stakeholders?," *Journal of Place Management and Development*, 2(1): 52–69.

Walker, B.A. and Olson, J.C. (1991) "Means-end chains: connecting products with self," *Journal of Business Research*, 22: 111–18.

Weis, M. and Huber, F. (2000) *Der Wert der Markenpersönlichkeit. Das Phänomen der strategischen Positionierung von Marken*, Wiesbaden: Deutscher Universitäts-Verlag.

Winkler, K. and Grimm, B. (2006) *Reiseanalyse RA 2006. Modulbericht: Gesundheit, Wellness & Kur im Urlaub*, Kiel: F.U.R.

Zaltman, G. and Coulter, R.H. (1995) "Seeing the voice of the customer: metaphor-based advertising research," *Journal of Advertising Research*, 35(4): 35–51.

Zeithaml, V.A. (1991) "How consumer evaluation processes differ between goods and services," in C.H. Lovelock (ed.) *Services Marketing*, Englewood Cliffs, NJ: Prentice Hall.

10 An investigation of Korean health tourists' behavior

Benefit sought, brand equity, and intention to visit

Young Hoon Kim, Changsan Boo and Mincheol Kim

Introduction

As a result of the globalization of tourism and health-care systems, health tourism is now one of the fastest growing areas in tourism. With a high demand by health and medical tourists, a significant attention has been paid to the health tourism (Goodrich and Goodrich 1987; Gilbert and Weerdt 1991; Hall 1992, 2011; Pollock and Williams 2000; Mueller and Kaufmann 2001; Hunter-Jones 2005; Snyder *et al.* 2010). As of 2005, the value of this industry market was up to US$513 billion, together with an estimated 617 million people in the world traveling for medical tourism reasons (Herrick 2007). It was also estimated that Malaysia, Thailand, India, and Singapore alone would generate more than US$4.4 billion through this industry market by 2012 (Singh 2008). This high demand and the lack of supply that has accelerated health tourism can partly be explained by factors such as a long waiting period for treatment, increased interests in health and beauty care, growth in the size of aged populations, and the attractiveness of less expensive medical services that have leisure and recreation components. Health tourism has also linked hot springs, spa, seawater treatment, and medical examination and surgery to tourism (Hall 2011). It may therefore be argued that the development of health tourism, a high profit-added industry, has satisfied the needs of health tourists who are seeking better opportunities: low-cost and high-quality treatment, as well as generating tremendous value to the destinations via products and services as a means of increasing income, generating foreign exchange earnings, and developing tourism.

Many countries, such as Thailand, India and Singapore, have developed strong health-tourism sectors (Kim *et al.* 2011; see also Wong and Musa, Chapter 11). For example, Singapore has developed a "one-stop" service by providing health-travel packages linked with medical systems, Singapore Tourism Board, and travel agencies. Hong Kong, Hungary, India, Thailand, Singapore, and Malaysia have already emerged as major health-tourism destinations and some other countries (e.g. Argentina, Brazil and Mexico) are in the process of developing themselves as destinations (Singh 2008; see also Wong and Musa, Chapter 11). This has occurred not only on account of advanced technology and information but also because of the many merits for destinations (e.g. income) and the attractiveness of health tourism in terms of maximization of the value of investment (e.g. return on investment).

Given its popularity and demand of health tourism in the world, it is therefore surprising that relatively little research has been conducted on health tourist's behavior (see Connell 2006 and Hall 2011 for reviews of the expanding literature).

The purpose of this chapter is to report on a study that seeks to investigate and explain a health tourist's behavior using benefit sought, brand equity, and intention to visit a destination. Using a proposed model and its hypotheses this research will verify the model and show each factor's relationships. Finally, the findings will assist in understanding of health tourists' behavior and provide implications.

Literature review

Development of health tourism

The development of health tourism requires not only a health-care facility or destination (Carrera and Bridges 2006) but also the availability of health-related human resources, technologies, products and services (Laws 1996; Kim *et al.* 2011; see also Chapter 9 for a discussion of this issue in the Macao context). The expansion of the health-tourism market has enabled many countries to design and develop their own health-tourism sectors using existing infrastructure and resources. In addition, as a result of competition, many countries have created lower cost and higher quality health services in order to attract health tourists in a competitive market.

According to Heung *et al.* (2011), economy (costs), infrastructure/superstructure, government attitude, policies and regulations, promotion, expertise/human resource availability, investment potential, language and communication, and facilities and attractions are important assessment criteria for health-tourism development (Keyser 2002; Connell 2006; Bookman and Bookman 2007). Kim *et al.* (2011) explained the development of health tourism in relation to four resources: nature, knowledge, artificial, and expenses, and suggested that destinations should produce innovative and specialized products that can attract international demand and differentiate their products and services from other destinations.

Smith and Forgione (2007) constructed a two-stage model for medical-tourism product selection: the first stage being the evaluation of the foreign country and the second stage the selection of the health-care facility. In the first stage, it was found that country-specific characteristics influence the country of choice which includes economic condition, political climate, and regulatory policies. In the second stage, it was indicated that costs, hospital accreditation, quality of care, and physician training had an impact on the selection of health-care facility. Caballero-Danell and Mugomba (2007) employed 11 factors to explain the components of medical tourism market: product, social issues, the legal framework, consumer benefits, target market, branding, infrastructure, distribution channels, operators, intermediaries, and communication and promotion. Among those factors, *benefit sought* (Haley 1968; Goodrich 1977; Woodside and Jacobs 1985; Gitelson and Kerstetter 1990; Jang *et al.* 2002; Pierskalla *et al.* 2004) and *brand equity* (Aaker 1991, 1996; Yoo and Donthu, 2001, 2002; Kim and Kim 2005) have been often highlighted and examined in many previous studies to measure consumer's intention to purchase products or visit destinations.

Item generation for hypotheses

Benefit sought

The benefit sought can be explained in terms of the necessity and desire of a consumer's subjective feeling as a part of knowledge of product attributes and/or as a subjective reward that a consumer wants from use of products (Haley 1968). The benefit-sought approach is used for market segmentation and provides significant assistance for advertising or the selection of media in marketing. As the benefit sought is a direct reason for selecting products and services, market segmentation via benefit sought has been recognized as a valuable means to approach target markets (Calantone and Johar, 1984; Shoemaker, 1994; Kozak, 2002). Market segmentation using benefit sought has been used to examine and investigate the critical criteria of the existing market segmentation by demographic variables, purchase volume, and brand loyalty.

Goodrich (1977) assessed various benefits: beauty of the scenery, hospitality of local residents, rest, proper accommodations, cultural interest, foods, water sports, shopping facilities, entertainment facilities, golf and tennis opportunities and others. Calantone and Johar (1984) suggested that the benefit being sought by tourists can be changed based on seasonal factors. Woodside and Jacobs (1985) investigated tourist's benefit sought behavior in Canadian, American, and Japanese tourists who visited the State of Hawaii, and the results indicated that Canadian tourists seek comfortable rest and recreation, American tourists seek exotic cultural experience, and Japanese tourists seek to get together with family. Gitelson and Kerstetter (1990) found that there are different benefits sought by visiting region, visiting time, stay period, previous visiting experience and the number of visiting. Jang *et al.* (2002) has performed market segmentation of Japanese tourists visiting the United States and Canada by examining their benefit sought. They found eight factors: nature and environment, knowledge and entertainment, history and culture, field activities, family and rest, escape from usual life, a value, a lifestyle and others, and segmented into three groups: newness/nature-seeking type, escape from usual life/rest-seeking type, family/field activities-seeking type.

Brand and brand equity

Benefit sought has been widely used in studies of brand equity. Brand equity is composed of brand recognition (awareness), perceived brand quality, brand image (association), and brand loyalty (Aaker 1991, 1996; Barwise 1993; Keller 1993; Yoo and Donthu 2001, 2002; Kim and Kim 2005; Konečnik 2006) with these dimensions being used to measure and explore various aspects of consumer behavior.

Keller (1993) found that brand image (associations), as one component of brand equity, depicts functional and experiential benefits of consuming the product. A number of theoretical and empirical studies have also suggested that consumer's benefit, such as functional benefit and emotional benefit, would explain the perceived brand equity and consumer's choice to purchase products (Zeithaml 1988; Sheth *et al.* 1991; Long, 2000).

Perceived brand quality is a key element of brand equity and it can affect a consumer's purchase intention (Aaker 1996). Zeithaml (1988) stated that perceived brand quality is considered as a consumer's judgment over products. The perceived brand quality of a travel destination is the potential tourists' preference which encourages them to visit a destination with a subjective judgment on general quality or superiority.

Brand recognition (awareness) is "the ability for a buyer to recognize or recall that a brand is a member of a certain product category" (Aaker 1991: 61). Brand recognition in tourism can be explained as cognitive self-awareness of a travel destination in both recognition and recall. Finally, a brand image (association) has been defined as "a set of [brand] associations, usually in some meaningful way" (Aaker 1991: 109). As the brand image (association) of a travel destination is a collection of associations that visitors have about the travel destination, it can be understood as a concept explaining various functional attributes of the travel destination such as travel activities and the feelings of visitors.

It has been suggested that brand loyalty, among various elements of the brand equity has attitudinal or behavioral aspects, unlike other elements, which are more likely to be influenced from brand-equity components of cognitive dimensions. These include brand recognition (awareness), perceived brand quality and brand image, as well as brand loyalty being a key factor of brand equity as an attachment level for a specific brand (Aaker 1991). Therefore, brand loyalty, one of the brand-equity components, was positioned in this study as the stage of *behavior* which has been mostly used to measure consumer's intention: purchase loyalty and attitudinal loyalty (Chaudhuri and Holbrook 2001).

Behavioral intention

According to Schiffman and Kanuk (1987), the intention to act is the best predictor of behavior (action to behave). If an understanding of consumer behavior is the main goal of marketing research, the intention to act (purchase) should be measured to examine a consumer's behavior. Loyalty is closely associated with learning, habit, and a consumer's favorable attitude toward a specific brand as expressed by the purchasing patterns of that brand (Anderson and Srinivasan 2003). Accordingly, in this study the brand loyalty toward a travel destination is considered with respect to ongoing purchasing intentions: tourists are more likely to continue to use particular travel products. Finally, the relationships of variables, benefit sought and brand equity (brand quality, recognition, and image), were measured to predict a health tourist's intention to visit. The following hypotheses were tested and examined in the current study.

- H1: Brand equity can be predicted by the benefit sought.
- H2: Behavioral intention can be predicted by the brand equity.

The current study presents a proposed model to delineate the relationship among variables identified in a review of previous literature (Figure 10.1). The application of the proposed model is discussed below.

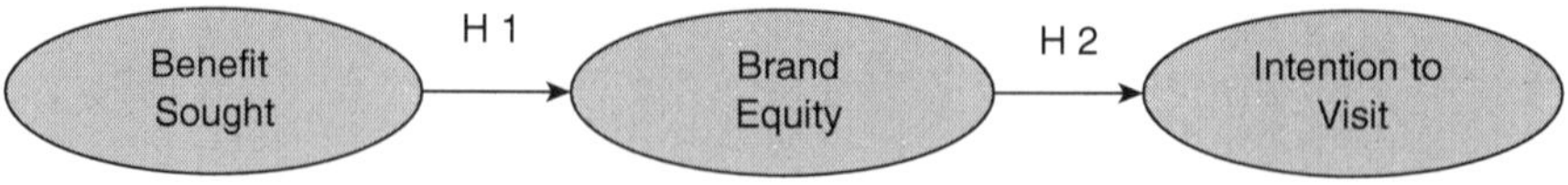

Figure 10.1 Proposed model for this study.

Methodology

Instrument development

After a review of previous studies a questionnaire was designed to measure tourist's benefit sought, brand equity, and intention to visit. A pre-test was administered to five experts in the field of management, tourism management, and hospitality management. Their feedback and suggestions were incorporated into the final instrument. A total of 20 items were used to measure benefit sought. A five-point Likert-type scale was used scaling from (1) "strongly disagree" to (5) "strongly agree." Nine items were employed to measure brand equity: four for brand quality, three for brand recognition, and two for brand image. Finally, to measure the behavioral intention to visit four items, two of brand loyalty and two of intention to visit, were measured.

Survey site

The Republic of Korea (ROK) has many potential advantages with respect to health tourism including competitive price and product, easy accessibility, and high-quality medical service. For example, medical practice in cosmetic surgery has a high international reputation (Medical Tourism Magazine 2008). National and local governments have been trying to develop a strategy to link health-care service to tourism. The national government has also been trying to foster Jeju province as a center of health tourism in Northeast Asia through the development of a Jeju-Style Health Tourism Model. The purpose of this project is to leverage the relationship between the medial and tourism industries in order to provide more jobs, technological development, and attract foreign capital.

Sample, data collection, and analysis

The sample was collected at the Jeju International Airport, Jeju city. Departing tourists, who are over 21 years old, were randomly intercepted. Data collection was conducted over a 2-week period. Graduate students majoring in hospitality management and business administration were employed as field workers. Training sessions and seminars for field workers were provided before data collection. To increase the participation rate, incentives were handed out to the participants at the end of survey. Questionnaires were double-checked right after the participants had handed over the questionnaires to the field workers.

For the empirical analysis, structural equation modeling (SEM) was employed to test the hypotheses. Only valid samples were used to perform the further analysis. The statistical analysis was conducted with SPSS 17.0. and AMOS 7.0. A two-step approach was adopted for this study (Anderson and Gerbing 1988) (1) the model fit was examined through confirmatory factor analysis (CFA) and (2) the significance of the coefficient was tested. In order to investigate the distribution sample and its group property, variables were measured before statistical analysis. The frequency and the descriptive analysis were carried out for the socio-demographic data. Then, Factor analysis, Cronbach's alpha, and its coefficient were measured to summarize and find out the relations of attributes for the benefit sought items. The CFA of items was conducted to secure and examine the reliability and feasibility of data. Finally, the research hypotheses were tested.

Results

A total of 550 questionnaires were distributed and 537 questionnaires were collected with 504 questionnaires being used for the further analysis. The socio-demographic characteristics of respondents are presented in Table 10.1. Over half (55.2 percent) of the respondents were male and 44.8 percent were female. Most participants were married (78.6 percent) and only 21.4 percent of the participants were classified as "single." In terms of age, the largest age group of the respondents was 40–49 years (32.1 percent), followed by 30–39 years old (31.0 percent), 50–59 years old (20.4 percent), 20–29 years old (10.9 percent), and older than 60 years old (5.6 percent). In regards to education level, about 64 percent of the respondents had college and university graduate education.

More than one-third of participants (74.1 percent) responded that their occupations are related to office work. Only 4.8 percent of respondents in this study reported that their monthly household income is less than US$1,500.00. Approximately two-thirds of respondents (64 percent) stated that their monthly household income is more than US$3,000.00.

The CFA was conducted to establish reliability and validity on the all variables: benefit sought (Table 10.2), brand equity (Table 10.3), and behavioral intention (Table 10.4). As the process of CFA on benefit sought, Cronbach's alpha was calculated to analyze the internal consistency of the construct and its reliability. The recommended Cronbach's alpha coefficient reliability of 0.60 (Hair *et al.* 1998) was used to test the reliabilities of each factor. The reliability test for benefit sought was satisfied as results varied from 0.66 (nature sought) to 0.77 (service sought). For the CFA on brand equity, the reliability test was satisfied as it varied from 0.65 (brand recognition) to 0.78 (brand quality). The reliability test on behavioral intention was satisfied with 0.86. The results indicated that the CFA on all three dimensions was conducted with a high degree of reliability.

The structural model fit was also very good with $\chi^2 = 792.55$, $df = 428$, $p = 0.00$, root mean square error of approximation (RMSEA) = 0.04, root mean square residual (RMR) = 0.04, goodness-of-fit index (GFI) = 0.91, comparative fit index (CFI) = 0.92, adjusted goodness-of-fit index (AGFI) = 0.89, again indicating a strong predictive validity. Table 10.5 shows the standardized path coefficients with associated *t*-values for all relationships in the structural model. The

Table 10.1 Socio-demographic profile

Variables	*Frequency*	*Valid (%)*	*Variables*	*Frequency*	*Valid (%)*
Gender			*Occupation*		
Male	278	55.2	Government employee	53	10.5
Female	226	44.8	Administrator	124	24.6
Total	504	100	Specialist/engineer	95	18.8
Age			Agriculture/fishery/ stockbreeding	9	1.8
20–29	55	10.9	Business owner (service)	102	20.2
30–39	156	31.0	Housewife	67	13.3
40–49	162	32.1	Student	19	3.8
50–59	103	20.4	Other	35	6.9
Older than 60	28	5.6	Total	504	100
Total	504	100	Monthly Income (US$)		
Marital status			Less than 1,500.00	115	4.8
Single	108	21.4	1,500.01–2,000.00	42	7.9
Married	396	78.6	2,000.01–2,500.00	42	9.5
Total	504	100	2,500.01–3,000.00	17	13.7
Education			3,000.01–4,000.00	15	20.2
High school	105	20.8	4,000.01–5,000.00	20	21.0
College or university	322	63.9	More than 5,000.01	65	22.8
Graduate school	77	15.3	Total	504	100
Total	504	100			

purpose of this study was to examine the relationships of benefit sought on brand equity (H1) and behavioral intention on brand equity (H2). The results of hypotheses are depicted in Table 10.5. In addition, the constructs of all structural paths were described in Figure 10.2. The results of hypotheses indicated that benefit sought of health tourist positively affected behavioral intention through brand equity.

Conclusions and future research

The current study tested the appropriateness of relationships among three variables: benefit sought, brand equity, and behavioral intention explaining health tourists' behavior. After statistical analysis, all hypotheses were examined and the results provided valuable implications for health tourism. The structure equation modeling enabled us to see the overview of health tourists' behavior which is one of the most critical processes to understand health tourism overall. The most significant contribution of this study is to understand health tourists' behavior with empirical results by developing and examining the model based on literature review on the previous studies.

The results of SEM show that health tourists' intention can be explained and predicted by brand equity. Their future intention to visit is directly predicted by

Table 10.2 The results of confirmatory factor analysis (CFA) on benefit sought

Factors	*Items*	*Estimate*	*S. E.*	*CR*	*P*	*Cronbach's alpha*
Service sought	I seek for a kind and qualitative service	1	–	–	–	0.771
	I seek for cleanness (i.e. sanitation)	1.016	0.084	12.046	***	
	I seek for a value as much as I paid	0.849	0.081	10.515	***	
	I seek for good recreation and lodging facilities	0.992	0.082	12.03	***	
Health sought	I seek for traditional medicine and treatment	1	–	–	–	0.740
	I seek for medical treatment	1.363	0.117	11.618	***	
	I always seek for health prevention and health management	1.355	0.113	11.94	***	
Relaxation sought	I seek to have a recreation and take a rest	1	–	–	–	0.735
	I seek for a time to rediscover myself	0.974	0.088	11.063	***	
	I seek for a time to relieve stress and tension	1.16	0.1	11.062	***	
Experience sought	I seek for interesting things to see and experience	1	–	–	–	0.691
	I seek for a variety of and delicious foods	1.079	0.11	9.789	***	
	I seek for leisure sport activities	0.911	0.105	8.662	***	
	I seek for diverse cultural experiences	1.2	0.115	10.479	***	
Nature sought	I seek to take a walk	1	-	–	–	0.664
	I seek to experience nature closely	1.026	0.094	10.882	***	
	I seek to escape from my everyday life	0.625	0.078	8.048	***	
Beauty sought	I seek for beauty treatment	1	–	–	–	0.696
	I seek for shopping	1.2	0.115	10.479	***	
	I seek for a diet therapy	2.24	0.26	8.604	***	

Model fit statistics: $\chi^2 = 303.59$, $df = 155$, p-value = 0.000, RMSEA = 0.04, RMR = 0.03, GFI = 0.94, AGFI = 0.92, CFI = 0.95, *** $p < 0.01$.

Table 10.3 The results of confirmatory factor analysis (CFA) on brand equity

Factors	*Items*	*Estimate*	*S. E.*	*CR*	*P*	*Cronbach's alpha*
Quality	Jeju has a good quality of tourism infrastructure	1	–	–	–	0.782
	Jeju has a good quality of service	1.034	0.077	13.463	***	
	Jeju has a good quality of food and beverage	0.863	0.071	12.134	***	
	Jeju has a good quality of accommodation	0.81	0.068	11.902	***	
Recognition	It is easy to compare and distinguish other tourist destinations from Jeju	1	–	–	–	0.647
	It is easy to remind of Jeju as a tourist destination	0.822	0.083	9.881	***	
	Jeju is well-known destination	0.502	0.072	7.107	***	
Image	Jeju has a variety of tourism resources	1	–	–	–	0.680
	Jeju has a beautiful image of natural environment	1.073	0.151	7.107	***	

Note: Model fit statistics: $\chi^2 = 68.77$, $df = 23$, p-value = 0.000, RMSEA = 0.06, RMR = 0.02, GFI = 0.97, AGFI = 0.94, CFI = 0.96, *** $p < 0.01$.

Table 10.4 The results of confirmatory factor analysis (CFA) on behavioral intention

Factors	*Items*	*Estimate*	*S. E.*	*CR*	*P*	*Cronbach's alpha*
Behavioral intention	Jeju would be the first selection for health tourist resort	1	–	–	–	0.864
	I have an intention to visit Jeju for health tourism in the near future	1.016	0.061	16.526	***	
	Jeju would provide more benefits than other health tourism destinations	1.234	0.070	17.654	***	
	I am willing to visit Jeju to enjoy and experience health tourism in the near future	1.088	0.070	15.613	***	

Note: Model fit statistics: $\chi^2 = 6.31$, $df = 4$, p-value = 0.04, RMSEA = 0.06, RMR = 0.01, GFI = 0.99, AGFI = 0.97, CFI = 0.99, ***$p < 0.01$.

brand image (β = 0.0336), recognition (β = 0.321), and quality (β = 0.267), respectively. From a managerial perspective, this finding emphasizes that health-tourist visitation can be grown by increasing the value of destination's brand equity in three dimensions (i.e. quality, recognition, and image). It is especially significant that a destination's perceived image is more important than its recognition and/or quality to attract more health tourists.

Table 10.5 The results of hypotheses

Hypothesized paths		*Coefficient*	*t-values*	*Remarks*
H1_1	Service Sought → Quality	−0.051	0.516	Rejected
H1_2	Health Sought → Quality	0.135	1.506	Rejected
H1_3	Relaxation Sought → Quality	0.097	1.345	Rejected
H1_4	Experience Sought → Quality	0.072	0.627	Rejected
H1_5	Nature Sought → Quality	**0.140**	**1.815***	**Supported**
H1_6	Beauty Sought → Quality	0.098	0.942	Rejected
H1_7	Service Sought → Recognition	0.100	0.908	Rejected
H1_8	Health Sought → Recognition	**0.310**	**3.038*****	**Supported**
H1_9	Relaxation Sought → Recognition	**0.155**	**1.921***	**Supported**
H1_10	Experience Sought → Recognition	−0.005	−0.039	Rejected
H1_11	Nature Sought → Recognition	0.106	1.244	Rejected
H1_12	Beauty Sought → Recognition	−0.053	−0.459	Rejected
H1_13	Service Sought → Image	**0.194**	**2.300****	**Supported**
H1_14	Health Sought → Image	0.081	1.080	Rejected
H1_15	Relaxation Sought → Image	**0.111**	**1.807***	**Supported**
H1_16	Experience Sought → Image	0.004	0.038	Rejected
H1_17	Nature Sought → Image	**0.138**	**2.112****	**Supported**
H1_18	Beauty Sought → Image	−0.006	−0.069	Rejected
H2_1	Quality → Behavioral intention	**0.267**	**4.429*****	**Supported**
H2_2	Recognition → Behavioral intention	**0.321**	**5.366*****	**Supported**
H2_3	Image → Behavioral intention	**0.336**	**4.046*****	**Supported**

Note: *Significant at $p < 0.1$, **significant at $p < 0.05$, ***significant at $p < 0.01$.

In terms of the relationship between benefit sought and brand equity, there were significant and positive relationships in several paths of the proposed model. Since brand quality is predicted by the nature sought, a destination's perceived quality can be increased by developing more natural resources (e.g. spa). On the other hand, brand recognition can be predicted by the health and relaxation sought. To be recognized by health tourists, the destination should be known for its medical and wellness tourism. Kim *et al.* (2011: 79) also emphasized that "health tourism based on knowledge should be considered one of most important resources." Finally, a destination's image can be predicted by service, relaxation, and nature sought. It implies that a natural wellness program with improved qualitative service can improve a destination's image which, in turn, is directly associated with health tourists' intention to visit in the future.

In conclusion, the model was well constructed with all hypotheses based on previous studies which would explain health tourists' behavior. The appropriate development of destination with brand equity can help create increased visitation from health tourists as well as improve their perception of a destination. From a long-term perspective, the effects of greater brand equity may not

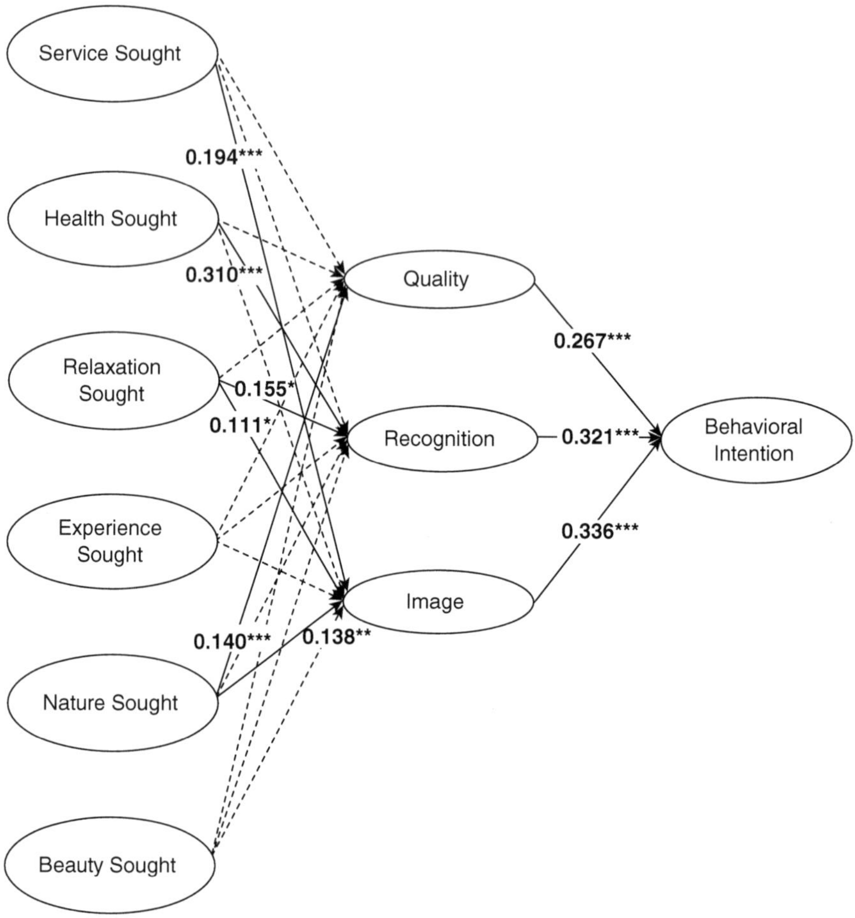

Figure 10.2 Structural equation model (SEM). Model fit statistics: $\chi^2 = 792.55$, $df = 428$, p-value = 0.00, RMSEA = 0.04, RMR = 0.04, GFI = 0.91, CFI = 0.92, AGFI = 0.89. *Significant at $p < 0.1$, **significant at $p < 0.05$, ***significant at $p < 0.01$.

be limited only to health tourism but also generates significant affects on the destination (e.g. brand image). In the short-term, the approach will provide more jobs, direct sales, and community involvement.

There are some limitations that may affect the current study or should be considered in the future. First, the model of this study may have not been designed to cover all possible variables. Although the modified scale and factors were adopted from the literature review, a further modification of model may be necessary to measure health tourists' behavior in detail. Second, the measure of actual behavior or greater collection of data directly from health tourists may provide better and more accurate information about health tourists.

References

Aaker, D.A. (1991) *Managing Brand Equity: Capitalizing on the value of a brand name*, New York: The Free Press.

Aaker, D.A. (1996) "Measuring brand equity across products & markets," *California Management Review*, 38(3): 102–20.

Anderson, J.C. and Gerbing, D.W. (1988) "Structural equation modeling in practice: a review and recommended two-step approach," *Psychological Bulletin*, 103: 411–23.

Anderson, R.E. and Srinivasan, S.S. (2003) "E-satisfaction and e-loyalty: a contingency framework," *Psychology and Marketing*, 20(2): 123–38.

Barwise, P. (1993) "Brand equity: snark or boojum?," *International Journal of Research in Marketing*, 10(1): 93–104.

Bookman, M.Z. and Bookman, K.R. (2007) *Medical Tourism in Developing Countries*. New York: Palgrave Macmillan.

Caballero-Danell, S. and Mugomba, C. (2007) "Medical tourism and its entrepreneurial opportunities: a conceptual framework for entry into the industry," Master's Thesis, Goteborg University. [Online]. Available at: http://gupea.ub.gu.se/bitstream/2077/4671/1/2006_91.pdf (accessed 10 July 2011).

Calantone, R.J. and Johar, J.S. (1984) "Seasonal segmentation of the tourism market using a benefit segmentation framework," *Journal of Travel Research*, 23(Fall): 14–23.

Carrera, P.M. and Bridges, J.F. (2006) "Globalization and healthcare: understanding health and medical tourism," *Expert Review of Pharmacoeconomics and Outcomes Research*, 6(4): 447–54.

Chaudhuri, A. and Holbrook, M.B. (2001) "The chain of effects from brand trust and brand affect to brand performance: the role of brand loyalty," *Journal of Marketing*, 65(2): 81–93.

Connell, J. (2006) "Medical tourism: sea, sun, sand and surgery," *Tourism Management*, 27(6): 1093–100.

Galloway, C. (2008) "Medical tourism in Asia," *Urban Land*, 67(2): 84–88.

Gilbert, D.C. and Van De Weerdt, M. (1991) "The health care tourist product in Western Europe," *Revue de Tourism*, 46(2): 5–10.

Gitelson, R.J. and Kerstetter, D.L. (1990) "The relationship between sociodemographic variables, benefits sought and subsequent vacation behaviour: a case study," *Journal of Travel Research*, 30(2): 24–29.

Goodrich, J.N. (1977) "Benefit bundle analysis: an empirical analysis of international travelers," *Journal of Travel Research*, 16(2): 6–9.

Goodrich, J.N. and Goodrich, G.E. (1987) "Health-care tourism—an exploratory study," *Tourism Management*, 8(3): 217–22.

Hair, J.F. Jr. , Anderson, R.E., Tatham, R.L. and Black, W.C. (1998). *Multivariate Data Analysis*, 5th ed. Upper Saddle River, NJ: Prentice-Hall.

Haley, R.I. (1968) "Benefit segmentation: a decision-oriented research tool," *Journal of Marketing*, 32(July): 30–35.

Hall, C.M. (1992) "Adventure, sport, and health tourism," in B. Weiler and C.M. Hall (eds) *Special-Interest Tourism*. London: Belhaven Press.

Hall, C.M. (2011) "Health and medical tourism: a kill or cure for global public health?," *Tourism Review*, 66(1/2): 4–15.

Herrick, D.M. (2007) *Medical Tourism: Global Competition in Health Care*. [Online]. Available at: http://w.medretreat.com/templates/UserFiles/Documents/Medical%20 Tourism%20-%20NCPA%20Report.pdf (accessed 5 February 2010).

Heung, V.C.S., Kucukusta, D. and Song, H. (2011) "Medical tourism development in Hong Kong: an assessment of the barriers," *Tourism Management*, 32(5): 995–1005.

Hunter-Jones, P. (2005) "Cancer and tourism," *Annals of Tourism Research*, 32(1): 70–92.
Jang, S.C., Morrison, M.A. and O`Leary, J.T. (2002) "Benefit segmentation of Japanese pleasure travelers to the USA and Canada: selecting target markets based on the profitability and risk of individual market segments," *Tourism Management*, 23(4), 367–78.
Keller, K.L. (1993) "Conceptualizing, measuring, and managing customer-based equity," *Journal of Marketing*, 57(1): 1–22.
Keyser, H. (2002) *Tourism development*. Cape Town: Oxford University Press.
Kim, H.B. and Kim, W.G. (2005) "The relationship between equity and firms' performance in luxury hotels and chain restaurants," *Tourism Management*, 26(4): 549–60.
Kim, Y.H., Boo, C., Demirer, I. and Kim, M. (2011) "A case study of health tourism in the Jeju Province, South Korea," *FIU Hospitality Review*, 29(1): 64–84.
Konečnik, M. (2006) "Croatian-based brand equity for Slovenia as a tourism destination," *Economic and Business Review*, 8(1): 83–108.
Kozak, M. (2002) "Comparative analysis of tourist motivations by nationality and destinations," *Tourism Management*, 23(3): 221–32.
Laws, E. (1996). Health tourism: a business opportunity approach. In S. Clift and S.J. Page (eds.), *Health and the International Tourist*. London: Routledge.
Long, M.M. (2000) "Consumption values and relationships: segmenting the market for frequency programs," *Journal of Consumer Marketing*, 17(3): 214–32.
Medical Tourism Magazine (2008) Medical tourism. [Online]. Available at: http://www.medicaltourismmag.com/download/issue6.pdf (accessed 11 February 2011)
Mueller, H. and Kaufmann, E.L. (2001) "Wellness tourism: market analysis of a special health tourism segment and implications for the hotel industry," *Journal of Vacation Marketing*, 7(1): 5–18.
Pierskalla, C.D., Lee, M.E., Stein, T.V., Anderson, D.H. and Nickerson, R. (2004) "Understanding relationship among recreation opportunities: a meta-analysis on nine studies," *Leisure Sciences*, 26(2): 1–18.
Pollock, A. and Williams, P. (2000) "Health tourism trends: closing the gap between health care and tourism," in W.C. Gartner and D.W. Lime (eds.) *Trends in Outdoor Recreation, Leisure and Tourism*, Wallingford: CABI Publishing.
Schiffman, L.G. and Kanuk, L.L. (1987) *Consumer Behavior*, 3rd ed. Englewood Cliffs, NJ: Prentice Hall.
Sheth, J.N., Newman, B.I. and Gross, B.L. (1991) "Why we buy what we buy: a theory of consumption values," *Journal of Business Research*, 22(March): 159–70.
Shoemaker, S. (1994) "Segmenting the U.S. travel market according to benefits realized," *Journal of Travel Research*, 32(3): 8–21.
Singh, P.K. (2008) *Medical Tourism*. India: Kanishka.
Smith, P.C. and Forgione, D.A. (2007) "Global outsourcing of healthcare: a medical tourism decision model," *Journal of Information Technology Case and Application Research*, 9(3): 19–30.
Snyder, J., Crooks, V. and Turner, L. (2010) "Issue and challenges in research on the ethics of medical tourism: reflections from a conference," *Journal of Bioethical Inquiry*, 8(1): 3–6.
Woodside, A.G. and Jacobs, L.W. (1985) "Stop two in benefit segmentation: learning the benefits realized by major travel market," *Journal of Travel Research*, 24(1): 7–13.
Yoo, B.H. and Donthu, N. (2001) "Developing and validating a multidimensional consumer-based brand equity scale," *Journal of Business Research*, 52(1): 1–14.
Yoo, B.H. and Donthu, N. (2002) "Testing cross-cultural invariance of the brand equity creation process," *Journal of Product and Brand Management*, 11(6): 380–98.
Zeithaml, A.V. (1988) "Consumer perceptions of price, quality, and value: a means-end model and synthesis of evidence," *Journal of Marketing*, 52(3): 2–22.

11 Medical tourism in Asia

Thailand, Singapore, Malaysia, and India

Wong Kee Mun and Ghazali Musa

Introduction

Medical tourism appears to be a rapidly growing tourism product and market. Evans (2008) reported that the estimated worth of the worldwide medical-tourism market was about US$60 billion in 2006 and projected it to climb to US$100 billion by 2012. In an Asian context, and of direct relevance to this chapter, Singh (2008) estimated that US$4.4 billion revenue will be generated by medical tourism in Thailand, Singapore, Malaysia, and India in 2012. The expansion of medical tourism is regarded as being largely attributable to the broad globalization of health-care services (Heung *et al.* 2011), whereby regulatory boundaries between nations have diminished; therefore enabling patients to move across borders for medical treatment with greater ease.

Even though there is no agreed-upon definition of medical tourism, the phenomenon is broadly accepted as occurring when people leave their home country to another country for the purpose of paid medical care (Altes 2005; Whittaker 2008) including the stay at the destination for at least a period of post-discharge time (Whittaker 2008). Cohen (2008) stated that medical tourism occurs when both tourism and medical treatment take place at the same time. During recovery stage, patients may be spending their time recuperating at tourist resorts. The notion of medical tourism can also be observed through a traditional lens where wealthy patients from the less developed countries travel to the advanced medical centers in developed countries (Chanda 2002; Wachter 2006; Alleman *et al.* 2010). However, increasingly, medical tourism is highlighted in reverse flows of the above, whereby travelers move from the higher income developed countries to the low-cost developing countries for the purpose of medical treatment (Chanda 2002; Alleman *et al.* 2010; Vijaya, 2010; Hall 2011; Ormond 2011), coupled with potential visitation to tourist sites (Hall 2011). However, the latter purpose highlighted by Hall (2011) may not be seen as an important element in defining medical tourism by Connell (2006) and Turner (2007a).

The domain of medical tourism also covers preventive medical services such as medical check-ups and health screening (Heung *et al.* 2011). Carrera and Bridges (2006) and Lunt and Carrera (2010) pointed out that medical tourism is a subset of the larger health-tourism domain, whereby it has been transformed from a niche market into a highly competitive field within the tourism industry (Connell 2006; Heung *et al.* 2011).

Alleman *et al.* (2010) and Singh (2008) highlighted several countries around the world that have been identified as key medical-tourism destinations, including Brunei, Cuba, Colombia, Costa Rica, Hong Kong, Hungary, India, Israel, Jordan, Lithuania, Malaysia, Mexico, Philippines, Singapore, Thailand, and United Arab Emirates. Among these countries, Asia remains the key medical-tourism region (Connell 2006), particularly Thailand, India, Singapore (Connell 2006; Ernst 2006; Healy 2009; Alleman *et al.* 2010; Crooks *et al.* 2010; Lunt and Carrera 2010; Heung *et al.* 2011) and Malaysia (Lunt and Carrera 2010; Heung *et al.* 2011; Ormond 2011).

The real economic contribution of medical tourism to host countries is hard to estimate. Figures and forecasts are often contradictory, partly because of inaccurate data collection pertaining to the economic dimensions of medical tourism. Inconsistent value forecasts abound as evidenced in different research reports. India itself is estimated to contribute US$2.2 billion by 2012 (CII and Mckinsey & Company, 2002; Bookman & Bookman 2007; Singh, 2008; Yanos, 2008) while Heung *et al.* (2011) reported a staggering US$4 billion medical-tourism market in Thailand by 2012. The value from these two reports at US$6.2 billion by 2012 is well over what has been highlighted earlier by Singh (2008) as US$4.4 billion for all four countries discussed in this chapter. Therefore, the many estimated claims of economic benefits of these four countries have to be treated with caution.

In capturing the medical-tourism market, Connell (2006) recommended the importance of branding strategy (see also Chapter 9). One of the important branding exercises is perhaps hospital accreditation. As stressed by Alleman *et al.* (2010), medical services accreditation often is the determining factor used by the medical-tourism–related agencies to recommend purchase of medical services overseas to potential medical tourists. For medical tourism, the most sought after hospital accreditation is the Joint Commission International (JCI; a not-for-profit American organization that provides standards and qualifications for medical facilities. Further information can be obtained from http://www.jointcommission-international.org/). Even though Malaysia has the highest number of hospitals (35) catering for medical tourism, it has the lowest number of JCI-accredited hospitals (8). On the other hand, Singapore which has the lowest number of hospitals catering for medical tourism (20) has the highest number of JCI-accredited hospitals (18). This signifies the overall high quality and standards of medical services in almost all the hospitals in Singapore. India came second with a total of 17 JCI-accredited hospitals (out of 26), while Thailand has 14 JCI-accredited hospitals (out of 34).

As well as significant variability in the type of medical-tourism services offered by different countries and destinations there is also a corresponding range in the type of treatments that are being sought. Medical treatments being sought after by tourists include orthopedic (Alleman *et al.* 2010; Vijaya 2010; Crooks *et al.* 2011); cardiac (Chanda 2002; Alleman *et al.* 2010; Crooks *et al.* 2010; Vijaya 2010), neurology, skin diseases, endocrinology, nephrology, and urology (Chanda 2002); infertility (Alleman *et al.* 2010); liver transplant (Vijaya 2010); cosmetic/plastic surgery and dental procedures (Alleman *et al.* 2010; Crooks

Table 11.1 Motivations for medical tourism

Key motivators	*Submotivators*
Cost	1 Lower cost overseas 2 Higher cost in home country 3 Favorable exchange rates 4 Relatively affordable international air travel
Time	1 Long waiting list in home country 2 Short waiting list
Regulation	1 Treatments not approved by government (e.g. in the United States, stem-cell therapy, cancer treatment) 2 Easy accessibility to another country 3 Insurance related Not covered by insurance in home country (e.g. dental, vision, cosmetic surgery, fertility) or underinsured or no universal medical insurance available (e.g. the United States)
Medical preferences and availability	1 Expats and migrants return home for medical treatment 2 Nonavailability of certain procedures (e.g. organ transplant) in home country
Quality	1 Equal or better quality in another country 2 Medical expertise 3 Hospital hardware
Leisure tourism	1 New and exotic location in conjunction with holidays
Information availability	1 Easy access to information regarding to medical tourism destinations, knowledge and technology transfer 2 Advertising of medical facilities

et al. 2011); and certain specific treatments such as stem cell and cancer treatment (Alleman *et al.* 2010). The following section examines the motivations of medical travel to Thailand, Singapore, Malaysia, and India in more detail.

Motivations of medical travel to Thailand, Singapore, Malaysia, and India

The most commonly cited travel motivation, and perhaps the most important, is that the cost of treatment is cheaper in India, Malaysia, Singapore, and Thailand (Glinos *et al.* 2006; Milstein and Smith 2006; Healy 2009; Alleman *et al.* 2010; Crooks *et al.* 2011; Heung *et al.* 2011) as compared to the tourist-generating countries (Alleman *et al.*, 2010; Connell, 2006; MacReady, 2007; Ormond, 2011). (The key medical travel motivators are summarized in Table 11.1). Connell (2006) added that exchange rate also plays a role in determining the relative attractiveness of medical cost. For example, the Ministry of Health Malaysia (2010) has highlighted the favorable exchange of the Malaysian Ringgit as one of the reasons why medical tourists should choose Malaysia for the medical treatment.

Woodman (2007) made a direct comparison on the costs of seven major medical treatments between the United States and four prominent medical-tourism destinations in Asia: Thailand, Singapore, Malaysia, and India. Medical treatment in Asia costs six to 33 per cent less compared to what it would have cost in the United States. For example, a heart bypass procedure costs US$ 130,000 in the United States, only cost less than one-tenth in Malaysia at US$ 9,000. Similarly, a heart-valve replacement in the United States would costs about 16 times higher than in India, Thailand, and Malaysia, at US$ 160,000. Among the Asian countries, India and Malaysia appear to be the cheapest destinations for most of the major medical treatments, while Singapore is the most expensive. Nevertheless, medical treatment in Singapore is still much cheaper than it would be in the United States.

Even though the cost comparison does not include traveling cost, Connell (2006), Healy (2009), and Heung *et al.* (2011) all highlighted that the current relatively affordable cost of air travel has became one of the motivators for western medical tourists to travel to another part of the world to seek medical treatments. The introduction of the Malaysian AirAsia with low airfares has also increased the promotion of medical tourism among the four countries. For example, in its inaugural flight from Kuala Lumpur to Bangalore on May 21, 2010, 15 children who have congenital heart disease were flown together to undergo an open heart surgery at the Narayana Hrudayalaya Heart Institute in Bangalore (The Star 2010). In addition, the Indian Kingfisher Airlines introduced special medical emergency fares in an effort to benefit guests that travel together with their family members under medical emergency conditions (Kingfisher Airlines 2011). Both AirAsia and Kingfisher Airlines fly extensively within the Asian network as well as connections to the Middle East and Europe.

Countries where medical treatments are provided by the government (e.g. Canada, New Zealand, United Kingdom), often involve a long waiting list, causing its citizens to seek for speedier medical treatments in another country (Connell 2006; Healy 2009; Alleman *et al.* 2010; Ormond 2011; Woodman 2007). Thus, a shorter waiting list or immediate medical treatment (Eggertson 2006; MacReady 2007) is also one of the reasons medical tourists travel across the globe. For example, the waiting period for certain elective procedures (e.g. open-heart procedure and joint replacement) in Canada and United Kingdom can be up to a year or more while in Thailand, India, and Malaysia, these could be carried out almost immediately (Discover Medical Tourism 2008a; Meditrips India 2011).

Medical tourists may also travel overseas to seek specific medical treatments, which are not approved by their governments or are still in testing stages, such as stem-cell therapy, cancer treatment, and abortion procedures (Glinos *et al.* 2006; MacReady 2007; Woodman 2007; Alleman *et al.* 2010; Crooks *et al.* 2010; Hall 2011; Ormond 2011). Those who are not insured or underinsured or simply have no universal medical insurance available (e.g. the United States) may also need to seek medical treatments overseas in order for it to be affordable (Connell 2006; Healy 2009; Crooks *et al.* 2011; Ormond 2011). Even among those with medical insurance coverage, there are certain procedures that may not be covered by their insurance in the home country, such as dental, eye, cosmetic, and fertility procedures

(Woodman 2007). The more relaxed immigration policy in some of the Asian countries provides easy access to tourists for medical treatments which results in the flourishing of medical tourism (Healy 2009).

Expatriates and migrants may be motivated to return home for medical treatment (Lee *et al.* 2010), for cultural and social familiarity in home country (Glinos *et al.* 2006; Hall and James 2011). The nonavailability of certain medical procedures (e.g. organ transplant) in their home country, leave medical tourists with no choice but to travel abroad in search of medical solutions (Bramstedt and Xu 2007; Glinos *et al.* 2006). This is evident in the growing importance of organ transplants in India (IMTJ 2011d; Valueaddedblog 2011).

Medical tourists also appear willing to seek medical treatment overseas if they are convinced of the availability of equal if not better medical services in medical-tourism destinations compared to their home country (Glinos *et al.* 2006; Woodman 2007; Ye *et al.* 2008). The aggressive promotion of well-qualified medical practitioners and expertise (Ye *et al.* 2008) in India, Thailand, Singapore, and Malaysia, coupled with the provision of state-of-the-art medical facilities and services (Ye *et al.* 2008) are some of the motivators which attract medical tourists to seek treatment in these countries.

The concept of medical tourism would potentially not be valid without the element of leisure tourism itself (although see Chapter 1 for a further discussion of this point). Connell (2006), Turner (2007c), and Woodman (2007) have pointed out that medical tourists' decisions on the final destinations could also be motivated by their perception of the destination in terms of tourism sites. Western patients may also be looking for some new and exotic destination overseas in order to enhance their tourism experience.

Healy (2009) and Heung *et al.* (2011) noted that information technology has made information on health-tourism destination easily accessible through a click of a mouse. Kumar (2009) stated that internet is most important, followed by newspapers, the sources from which medical tourists obtain information on medical facilities and treatment offered by the Indian hospitals. Governments from all four countries that are the focus for this chapter have prepared medical-tourism web sites (e.g.: Thailand—thailandmedtourism.com; India—incredible-india.org; Singapore—singaporemedicine.com; Malaysia—myhealthcare.gov.my) on medical tourism for prospective medical tourists. Information may be obtained as a result of aggressive advertising of the medical-tourism destinations and its facilities (Ye *et al.* 2008), implemented by both the government and private medical centers. The nature of medical tourism in Thailand, Singapore, Malaysia, and India is provided in more detail below.

Medical tourism in Thailand

Medical tourism in Thailand started in the 1970s, when the demand in Western countries for cosmetic and other alternative treatments, such as sex change operations (Connell 2006), which were normally not approved by their government or were beyond the boundary of their national or private health insurance coverage began to be provided (Cohen 2008). Despite being involved early, it was not until the late 1980s to early 1990s that Thailand started to develop its medical tourism through the establishment of several private hospitals catering for both local elite and foreign patients. These hospitals are fully equipped with state-of-the-art medical facilities and techniques, luxurious hotel-appearance facilities, and highly trained medical personnel as found in the Western countries (Cohen 2008). Even though cosmetic surgery is one of the key treatments in Thailand medical tourism, the choices have expanded to a wider scope of medical treatments, including dental care (Cohen 2008).

In Thailand, economic growth and financial markets liberalization in the 1990s have strengthened the expansion of private hospitals. However, a weak internal banking and political system led the country into a severe economic crisis in the late 1990s (Lew and Hall 1999). Low purchasing power during the crisis has forced many who used to patronize private hospitals for medical treatment, to revert to public hospitals (Connell 2006; Vijaya 2010). During that period, the private hospital occupancy rates dropped by 20–30 per cent (Vijaya 2010). This phenomenon led to a combined effort from both government and private sector to lure international patients to help ensure the survival of private hospitals. The collaboration between the government and private sectors was initiated in the form of revising the government's and hospitals' policies and government-sponsored "health hub" promotional activities (Cohen 2008) to attract further foreign medical tourists.

In catering to the foreign patients' needs, private and some public hospitals provide interpreters and well-trained and certified medical personnel from overseas. Phuket Hospital, which provides treatments to 20,000 medical tourists a year, claimed to have interpreters in 15 languages (Connell 2006). The high-profile Bumrungrad International Hospital in Bangkok (Heung *et al.* 2011) is reported to have 70 interpreters and all of its staff are able to converse in English. The hospital has about 200 surgeons who have obtained certification from the United States (Connell 2006). As noted above, there are 14 hospitals in Thailand that have obtained the JCI accreditation, which is an important factor for medical-tourism–related agencies to recommend overseas health-care centers to their customers (Smith and Forgione 2007; Alleman *et al.* 2010).

Teh and Chu (2005) reported that there are about 400,000 international patients seeking medical treatment in Thailand each year. The Japanese made up the majority while patients from the United States, United Kingdom, and Middle East also contribute sizable numbers (Heung *et al.* 2011). Taffel (2004) estimated that foreign medical tourists contributed about US$1.6 billion to Thailand in 2003 while Heung *et al.* (2011) estimated that the figure could reach US$4 billion by 2012. Nevertheless, the actual forecast may be difficult to judge as the number of genuine medical tourists is rather difficult to obtain. As remarked by Cohen (2008), only the annual gross total of foreigners (that may include genuine medical tourists, expatriates, and long-term residents) who sought treatments in hospitals in Thailand was released by the governmental agencies and hospitals.

The key medical-tourism spots being highlighted by Heung *et al.* (2011) are Bangkok, Chiang Mai, Koh Samui, and Phuket. As the capital city, Bangkok tops the list, with 10 out of 14 JCI accredited hospitals (JCI 2011) being located in the city. Other medical-tourism destinations in the country are Chiang Mai, Koh Samui, and Phuket. Thailand has also sought to encourage foreign direct investment in the medical-tourism sector (Chanda 2002). Medical colleges in Thailand have seats reserved for foreign students from other developing countries, in its effort to diversity medical tourism into medical education in the areas of medicine and paramedics as well as alternative medicines and treatments.

The Tourism Authority of Thailand (TAT) launched "Thailand Medical Tourism Blog Contest" in October 2010 which attracted 219 participants from 24 countries. Among its aims were to create awareness, widen opportunities for worldwide medical tourists to access to online information on medical tourism in Thailand, and enhance confidence among foreign medical tourists on Thailand's medical tourism's quality (IMTJ 2010d). In addition, TAT also actively promotes its medical tourism online through e-marketing campaign, such as the "Healthy Beauty Holiday in Thailand" campaign in December 2010, which offered exclusive rates for several medical treatments (e.g. dental treatments, cosmetic surgery, medical check-ups). Another campaign was "You are in Good Hands" which was also carried out in the same month to promote the safety and credibility of Thailand in providing medical services, and stimulate higher arrival and longer stay among medical tourists (IMTJ 2010d). A more recent promotional effort featured the government inviting some of the major global and regional news agencies, including Fox News (USA), Xinhua (China), VNA (Vietnam), and Bernama (Malaysia), to Chiang Mai (March 2011), Phuket (April 2011), Chanthaburi (May 2011), and border provinces in the South (June 2011) for a few days tour to promote the available medical and wellness treatments (OkMedicalTourism 2011).

Medical tourism in Singapore

Singapore is frequently cited as one of the top medical-tourism destinations in Asia (Connell, 2006; Ernst, 2006; Healy, 2009; Alleman *et al.*, 2010; Crooks *et al.*, 2010; Lunt and Carrera 2010; Heung *et al.* 2011). Singapore Tourism Board (2010) itself claimed Singapore as the Asia's leading medical hub in 2009. As stated above, there are 18 hospitals and medical centers in Singapore that have obtained JCI accreditation (JCI 2011). The country is also the main direct competitor to both Malaysia and Thailand.

Singapore is targeting to attract one million patients by 2012 (Ai-Lien 2005; Connell 2006; Heung *et al.* 2011), with expected revenue between US$ 1.6 to US$ 1.8 billion (Ai-Lien 2005; Heung *et al.* 2011). It has been receiving medical tourists from different nationalities with major markets being Indonesia, Malaysia, China, the Middle East, and Japan. The majority of its European and American patients are residents who live in Asia (Connell 2006).

Singapore prefers to compete on high quality medical services instead of price (Connell 2006). Heung *et al.* (2011) stated that the country's key competitive advantages are excellence in quality, trustworthiness, safety, and international accreditation. It is well known for offering high-quality and complex medical treatments (Yap 2007; IMTJ 2010a), such as neurosurgical procedures and liver and heart transplants. Promotion is given to the application of superior technology by medical doctors who created a number of the "firsts" in Asian medical history, such as, the separation of the Nepalese twins, the first South East Asian heart and liver transplant, the first percutaneous aortic valve replacement, and the world's first operation for a rare ectopic pregnancy with a single incision exclusively through the belly button (Connell 2006; Singapore Tourism Board 2010).

Although Singapore has put much effort in promoting itself as a world-class medical-tourism destination, due to the competitive nature of medical-tourism industry in the region, Singapore is also seeking to satisfy the demand for more affordable treatments (IMTJ 2010b). The only drawback of Singapore compared with other countries discussed in this chapter is that its medical services are the most expensive. As the quality of the hospitals in Malaysia, India and Thailand are improving and of similar standards to Singapore, medical tourists may eventually choose these countries over Singapore for their medical treatment. Connell (2006) reported that Singapore has considered setting its price rates on par or slightly below Thailand.

The unique aspect of medical-tourism development in Singapore is that the industry is developed not only for the economic benefit but also to support the sustainability of expensive medical services in the country. Yap (2007) pointed out that the small population of Singapore will not be able to sustain the maintenance cost of high-quality medical facilities solely by local demand. Therefore, it is essential for the country to attract international medical tourists so that revenue gained from it can be channeled into providing health services to Singaporean citizens. The government and private sector work closely to identify demand for medical services and offer attractive prices, while maintaining sufficient profitability for the private investors.

Singapore's medical facilities are primarily privately owned. About 66 per cent of the total expenditure on health per capita in 2008 was from the private sector, a higher ratio compared to Malaysia (56 per cent) and Thailand (26 per cent) but slightly lower than India at 68 per cent (World Health Organization 2011). Parkway, Singapore's premier medical provider and the largest private medical group in Southeast Asia, runs some of the well-known hospitals in the region, such as Mount Elizabeth, Gleneagles, and East Shore hospitals. As medical tourism flourished in Asia, the group also ventured into Brunei, China, India, Indonesia, Malaysia, Sri Lanka, and United Arab Emirates (Chanda 2002; IMTJ 2010b), establishing its own hospitals or forming joint ventures with partners. Raffles Medical Group, another prominent medical provider in Singapore, also increased its overseas presence through global strategic alliances and integrated networks with medical organizations from developed countries (Chanda 2002). To further attract additional medical tourists and investors into Singapore, the government is involved in signing agreements with some Middle Eastern nations in order to offer medical services (Heung *et al.* 2011).

The Singapore government has put substantial effort into collaboration with industry actors, forming SingaporeMedicine in 2003, with the aim of promoting the country as a world-class destination in medical tourism and strengthening its image as the leading medical hub in Asia. Led by its Ministry of Health, SingaporeMedicine provides information including guides to available treatment facilities, treatment costs, and tourism activities to the international patients (SingaporeMedicine 2007). Other promotional efforts made include organizing international symposiums, conferences, and courses in the medical field, and attracting not only medical tourists, but also potential investors and international scholars in the area. Further efforts by both private and public hospitals also can be seen as well through collaboration with western hospitals such as John Hopkins University Hospital, Pennsylvania University Medical Center, Massachusetts General Hospital, and Kaiser Permanente in order to keep up to date with the latest medical trends (Health Tourism in Asia 2009). Efforts have also been made to set up an information counter at Changi airport with promotional materials and advice in order to lure international patients.

Medical tourism in Malaysia

The Malaysian government introduced the concept of medical tourism after 1998, after the wake of the Asian financial crisis (Altes 2005; Connell 2006) and realizing the need for economic diversification (Connell 2006) in order to spread its economic risks. Chee (2007) reported that the Ministry of Health had set up the National Committee for the Promotion of Medical and Health Tourism in January 1998 in an effort to develop medical tourism in Malaysia. The agency was later renamed to Malaysia Healthcare Travel Council. Although Malaysia started late in the medical-tourism sector in the region, it is catching up fast, becoming one of the top destinations (Frost & Sullivan 2010).

A total of 425,500 medical tourists visited Malaysia in 2009 and 519,000 medical tourists were expected to visit Malaysia in 2010 (IMTJ 2011b; Frost & Sullivan 2010). The impressive development of medical tourism in Malaysia is the result of excellent medical infrastructure, professional medical personnel, and backed up by strong government support and promotional activities. According to RNCOS (2011) Malaysian medical tourism is expected to grow at an average rate of 16 per cent from 2011 to 2014, and it is estimated that Malaysia will receive about 689,000 medical tourists by 2012 (IMTJ 2011b).

The Ministry of Health reported that Malaysia has achieved US$ 101.65 million from the medical-tourism sector in 2010. The revenue is expected to grow further to about US$ 116.5 million in 2011 (IMTJ 2011a). Heung *et al.* (2011) forecasted that Malaysia will achieve US$590 million of revenue by 2016. Even though the number of medical tourists is comparable to Singapore, the value generated in Malaysia is much lower. This may be explained by the relatively lower medical fees, as well as limited demand for high yield advanced medical procedures that are performed in the country. Although medical tourism's value in Malaysia is considered small compared to the key players in the region, it remains an important economic area for the Malaysian government (IMTJ 2011a).

Among the major treatments offered to foreign patients are curative medical treatments, plastic surgery, cardiac procedures, fertility treatment, general screening and wellness, and orthopedics surgery (Ministry of Health Malaysia 2010). In addition, as a multicultural society, Malaysia also offers alternative medical treatments, such as traditional Chinese medicine that may include acupuncture and Indian ayurveda treatments (The Economic Times 2011).

According to Chaynee (2003), the Malaysian strategies are in accordance with its competitive advantages. It focuses on high quality yet low price offerings in order to compete with other medical-tourism destinations. The waiting period is also short, which is an important element for many foreign patients. Malaysia also offers well-trained and highly qualified medical personnel, world-class hospitals equipped with state-of-the-art medical equipments, and excellent English proficient staff (Chaynee 2003; Heung *et al.* 2011). There are a total of eight JCI-accredited hospitals in the country (JCI 2011), located mainly in Kuala Lumpur (six) along with one each in the island city of Penang and Kuching. Although the number of JCI-accredited hospitals is small compared to Thailand, India, and Singapore, most of its private hospitals have also obtained the International Organization for Standardization (ISO) certification (Heung *et al.* 2011). Besides, medical facilities, physical attractions such as attractive beaches and resorts are among the key attractions to lure foreign patients to choose Malaysia as their medical-tourism destination (Heung *et al.* 2011).

Frost & Sullivan (2010) and UNESCAP (2007) reported that the majority of the foreign patients seeking medical treatments in Malaysia are from Indonesia, Singapore, Japan, and West Asia. Sumatrans from Indonesia are the most likely (Connell 2006; Ormond 2011) to visit the States of Malacca and Penang for medical treatments due to their close proximity and easy accessibility via ferry or airplane to Malaysia. Penang is the main medical-tourism destination in Malaysia (Ormond 2011) hosting about two-thirds of medical tourists, most of whom are Indonesians. Malaysia's strong Islamic credentials (Henderson 2003), where hospitals are serving halal food and practicing Islamic protocols, is an attractive element in attracting Middle Eastern patients (Connell 2006). Similar to Singapore, most of its European and American patients are residents in Asia (Connell 2006).

The Malaysian government has made several efforts to promote Malaysia abroad as a medical-tourism destination well as attracting local and foreign investments (Chaynee 2003; Heung *et al.* 2011). Generally, most of the private hospitals in the country are participating in the medical-tourism program organized by the government (Altes 2005). Tax incentives have been offered to investors in order to spur the medical-tourism sector (Leng 2007), and maintain competitive pricing. For example, the government is offering 100 per cent tax exemption to private hospitals that are willing to construct new hospitals or expand, modernize, and refurbish their existing ones (IMTJ 2011c). According to Yanos (2008), Malaysia is ranked first in Asia and third in the world as a top medical-tourism destination in providing attractive opportunities for both medical tourists and foreign investors.

A key issue in Malaysia in terms of the long-term sustainability of medical tourism as a product is the brain drain of its medical professionals. There is a need to lure back doctors and other medical professionals who work overseas to return by providing attractive offers as well as making Malaysia a desirable country in which to live. This move is essential in assisting the country to develop its medical-tourism sector and enhance its image as a quality health-care destination (Chong *et al.* 2005; Connell 2006). The private sector also plays an important role. For example, IMTJ (2010c) reported that in an effort to boost the medical-tourism sector, a Malaysian company is in arrangement with the well-known Johns Hopkins University in setting up a medical science teaching facility as well as a new hospital within a new medical city in Selangor State. Among other positive steps taken by private hospitals are the establishment of international customer departments, in-house travel agencies, and links with several external travel agencies and hotels for the convenience of foreign medical tourists (Ormond 2011).

Medical tourism in India

Medical tourism in India started in the mid-1990s following greater economic liberalization. This has spurred the expansion of private hospitals that are equipped with higher technological and quality medical facilities, on par to those found in the western countries (Vijaya 2010). India has been known for its successful IT industry, particularly in software sector and call centers. Moving along the expansion path, medical tourism sees itself as the next highly growing service sector in India.

Chacko (2006) and Confederation of India Industries (CII) and Mckinsey & Company (2002) estimated that about 150,000 patients would have traveled to India for medical treatment in 2004 with an annual growth rate of about 30 per cent. Bookman and Bookman (2007), CII and Mckinsey & Company (2002), Singh (2008), and Yanos (2008) further forecast that the value of medical tourism in India may reach US$2 billion by 2012.

Similar to the other countries discussed above, India also highlights the low cost of its medical services. Woodman (2007) presented an example of a bypass operation in India that would costs only about half of what a patient may need to pay in Singapore. However, Crooks *et al.* (2011) noted during the first medical tourism trade show in Toronto, Canada in November 2009, India highlighted very little about low-cost message in its promotional materials. The top three promotional messages that India stressed were credentials or accreditations, list of services, and specializations. Similarly, Heung *et al.* (2011) suggested that India's key competitive advantage in medical-tourism sector is the highly trained and qualified medical personnel.

In India, a large majority of medical doctors are attached to private hospitals. Vijaya (2010) recorded that only 10 per cent of doctors are servicing the public health sector. According to the World Health Organization (2011), the Indian government only contributed about 32 per cent to health expenditures per capita in 2008, while the remaining 68 per cent is private expenditure. Private investment in hospitals has continued to expand since 1990s and shows no sign of abating (Bhatt and Jain 2006; Mullan, 2006). Yanos (2008) also reported that India ranks fifth in most attractive medical-tourism destination globally for foreign direct investment, behind Panama, Brazil, Malaysia, and Costa Rica.

However, India's positioning in medical tourism is also unique as it offers a wide variety of alternative medical treatments such as unani, ayurveda, and homeopathic treatments. Traditional health-care centers are mushrooming in many parts of India such as the ayurvedic school in Kottakkal, Kerala (Chanda 2002).

India has 17 JCI-accredited hospitals (JCI 2011) spread across the vast geographical area of the nation. The majority of the JCI-accredited hospitals are located within the capital city of New Delhi and in Mumbai. Other cities with JCI-accredited hospitals are Bangalore, Kolkata, Chennai, Hyderabad, Kerala, Chandigarh, and Punjab areas. Perhaps among the greatest advantages of India, is the ability of staff to converse in English (Heung *et al.* 2011) and its adoption of western technology and medical protocols.

A unique aspect of India compared with the other three countries discussed in this chapter is the fact that the country is also world-renowned for medical studies. There were 229 recognized medical colleges in 2010, producing almost 34,000 medical graduates every year (Medical Council of India 2010). The number of registered medical doctors have risen from about 660,801 on average between 2000–2010 (World Health Organization 2011) to about 800,000 in 2010 (Medical Council of India 2010). The average number of registered doctors between the years 2000–2010 in India is much higher than in Thailand (18,918), Malaysia (25,102), and Singapore (8,323) combined, putting it on par with other countries such as the United States and the Russian Federation. Although, the doctor density per 10,000 population in India (6.0) is higher than Thailand (3.0), it is much lower than Malaysia (9.4) and Singapore (18.3) (World Health Organization 2011).

Realizing the promising future of the medical-tourism sector in India, the Indian government has taken numerous steps to welcome foreign direct investment. For example, Chanda (2002) reported that the government has given an approval to a German-owned company to set up a 200-bed hospital in Delhi with a high foreign equity ownership of 90 per cent. The Indian government also introduced several incentives, such as easier obtainment of long-term capital for new establishment or expansion of medical facilities, higher allowable depreciation rate for old equipment to encourage earlier replacement by new and more advanced equipment, and reduction of importation tax on life saving equipment (UNESCAP 2007). Among the leading players in the private medical sector are Apollo Hospitals, Fortis Healthcare, and Wockhardt Hospitals (Brotman 2010). As the medical tourism grows globally, Apollo group plans to set up another 32 new hospitals in India by 2012, on top of their current 30 hospital fleets and venture overseas in establishing its chain of hospitals in Nigeria, Shanghai, and Vienna (Agarwal and Bhagrath 2010).

Similar to Malaysia, India also faces the issue of medical personnel brain drain. India needs to enhance its image as a medical service provider and also attract the medical personnel themselves to work and not leave the country. Connell (2006) pointed out that private hospitals have improved and adjusted salaries offered. The annual Medical Tourism Expo is said to be able to attract an international audience and capture the attention of the Indian medical personnel who are residing overseas. In addressing medical travel issues, such as treatment and care standards, insurance coverage, and general infrastructure, the government is working closely with industry players in both medical and tourism sectors (UNESCAP 2007) in order to set up a health policy that can promote medical tourism effectively. In terms of promotion, India attended the first medical tourism trade show in Toronto, Canada in November 2009, named the "Medical Tourism Destination 2009." Brochures, flyers, and booklets were widely disseminated during the trade show (Crooks *et al.* 2011), providing substantial and relevant information on medical tourism in India to the potential tourists and investors. The Indian government also extended the market development assistance (MDA) scheme for JCI and National Accreditation Board (NABH) certified medical facilities, where financial assistance is provided for printing promotional materials, attending trade exhibitions or study tours in relations to medical tourism (Ministry of Tourism India 2011).

Challenges and opportunities of medical tourism in Thailand, Singapore, Malaysia, and India

Medical tourism is on the rise globally and the future looks promising. However, there are several issues which need serious attention from both the government and private sectors across the region. Connell (2006) indicated that while India's medical tourism booms, its population still lives with 40 per cent poverty rate and high infant and maternity mortality rates. Basic health facilities seem to be out of reach to the large majority of the population. India's government only spent about 32 per cent of total health expenditure per capita in 2008 (World Health Organization 2011) while the low-income population just could not afford to visit the private medical facilities. Vijaya (2010) criticized that India, on one hand, provides excellent world class medical facilities to international medical tourists; on the other hand, the country appears relatively oblivious to the basic medical needs of the low income population. More emphasis has been given to private sector health development at the expense of public health provision, which at the moment is far below the desirable standards. However, it is also argued that the development of medical tourism is expected to eventually improve the medical services of a nation and at the same time this improvement will eventually benefit local population.

The growth of medical tourism has caused privatization and commoditization of many medical facilities across Asia. Saniotis (2007) suggested that the privatization of many hospitals in Thailand has resulted in high medical expenses to the locals, thus making it beyond their financial capability, a situation similarly observed in India as well. The commoditization of medical facilities (Keaney 2002; Turner 2007b; Hall 2011), as has been warned by Chanda (2002), might cause an imbalance in treatment between the locals and foreign patients. The high fees charged by private hospitals may also discourage or to a certain extent prevent easy access of local residents to health services (Heung *et al.* 2011), a phenomenon that is particularly of concern in India and Thailand. This, according to Hall (2011a), Borman (2004), and Lunt and Carrera (2010), is an ethical issue for medical professionals that needs to be resolved.

In addressing the issue of privatization and commoditization of medical facilities, both government and private sectors need to seriously consider their domestic medical services policies through better working linkages between them (Chanda 2002; Vijaya 2010). India could probably learn from Singapore in addressing this issue as both the private and public sector are well connected and of similar quality. The Singapore government realizes that the foreign patient market is essential to support its domestic medical care as the domestic population is small in the country. Therefore, medical tourism is being developed as part of Singapore's social requirement toward its domestic health-care services. On the other hand, Thailand deploys high government spending on health facilities in addressing its citizen's medical requirements, with 9.9 per cent of total government expenditure being spent on health in 2008 (World Health Organization 2011).

In addition, there is also a disproportionate concentration between the development of advanced technologies and specializations in a country's medical system, where in most cases the development would be based on the interest of foreign patients rather than the locals. Vijaya (2010) commented that this is a serious issue in India, particularly in the primary care, family and community medicine.

Another adverse effect may be observed when funds from some other areas of the economy are diverted to medical tourism (Awadzi and Panda 2006). For example, the Malaysian government has been actively promoting medical tourism through tax exemption to private hospitals (IMTJ 2011c), implicating a reduction in the possible revenue generated through tax collection which is an essential element in providing sufficient public services to its citizens.

Risk is another issue which is frequently discussed by researchers. The risk faced by medical tourists may be in the forms of adverse impacts on their health instead of curing or rejuvenating. Hall (2011; Hall and James 2011) warned that medical tourism may pose biosecurity and nosocomial risks to both the patient's home country and the medical-tourism destination. These include higher rates of cross infections, spread of pandemics, transplant failures, and social issue where medical tourists seek assisted suicide. There is also risk of insufficient supply of blood in the medical destination to meet the patients' needs (Forgione and Smith 2007). Nevertheless, Alleman *et al.* (2010) and Lunt and Carrera (2010) suggested that even though such adverse implications have been reported before (e.g. Newman *et al.* 2005), the empirical evidence is still lacking in terms of quality and safety, overseas medical facilities' infection ratios, and negative events reports. Better evidence and reliable empirical data are required to better justify the issue of risk in medical tourism.

Another issue that has been widely discussed globally over the years pertaining to medical tourism is on obtaining organs for transplant procedures. Illegal organ trades have been reported in India where transplant treatment for foreign patients is widely demanded, especially kidney. According to Discover Medical Tourism (2008b), as the Indian Ocean tsunami in 2004 affected terribly the living conditions of the poor fishermen families in Chennai, they were forced to sell off their kidneys in order to sustain their lives. Poor immigrant laborers in India were also forced or being cheated to sell one of their kidneys to wealthy patients, for lack of a job opportunity (AlJazeera English 2008). Although human organ trade is banned in India, such unethical acts remain and occur at large. The Voluntary Health Association in India estimated about 2,000 kidneys were traded each year

(AlJazeera English 2008), making India one of the top five nations in human organ trade (Ben 2008). This issue is not just an unethical business transaction issue but to a greater scale, a serious humanity discomfort issue that should be dealt with if medical tourism were to continue its acceptance globally.

Government regulation is paramount as it may determine the direction of a particular nation in developing medical tourism and at the same time address the domestic medical requirements. A well-regulated medical-tourism policy will ensure the growth of the sector in the proper direction. According to Bookman and Bookman (2007), a regulated-driven medical tourism may enhance the viability of developed countries in reducing government's burden to support its top notch domestic medical care facilities (e.g. Singapore). While, developing countries may be able to gain substantial revenue to improve their health systems in accordance with the world standard, revenue gained from medical tourism could contribute to social facilities enhancement that will benefit the citizens.

As in many developing countries experience (e.g. Malaysia and India) a well-regulated medical-tourism sector with the provision of advanced and high technology work environments may be viewed as an attractive element to local talents to remain working in the country. This, together with establishing the country as an attractive place to live may be the key to reduce the international brain drain, particularly among professional medical personnel (Ramirez de Arellano 2007).

The development of medical tourism is very much dependent not only on the government but also the private sector. The aggressive and committed private sector may determine the effort level required by the government. For example, Teh and Chu (2005) mentioned that Australia, Thailand, the United States, and the United Kingdom are among the countries where the private sector plays a prominent and leading role in medical-tourism development, from analyzing possible opportunities to strategies formulation. As the government may depend on the private sector to develop medical tourism, more time and effort could be spent on the public hospitals and doctors, which are essential to meet the domestic medical care requirements. However, the excessive involvement level of the private sector in developing medical tourism may also bring some negative impact into the national health-care systems. Thus, a well-regulated health policy system is expected to be able to balance the responsibilities of both public and private sectors in developing medical tourism in the four countries.

Conclusion

Thailand, Singapore, Malaysia, and India have developed medical tourism mainly for economic reasons. Singapore uniquely however, has also developed the industry to support the sustainability of its hospitals which operate on a small population base. Much of the lure for foreign tourists to visit these countries is based on cheaper costs offered for medical treatment compared with their own countries. However, cheaper costs alone will not attract medical tourists, unless the provision of health services is at least at par with the tourist generating countries. This is perhaps a major factor inducing medical tourists to seek their medical treatment in Thailand, Singapore, Malaysia, and India with a growing number of hospitals in these countries being accredited by JCI.

The development of medical tourism in Thailand and even more so, India, has to reconciled with the quandary of whether to focus more on providing medical services to international medical tourists or on poor local residents. All these four countries have their own competitive strength. Singapore is perhaps still the premier medical tourist destination and also has the reputation of performing groundbreaking medical treatment and procedures. India is the cheapest destination which offers excellent medical facilities and services, together with the increasing popularity of contemporary medical treatment. India also produces medical doctors from its many internationally accredited medical schools. Thailand is an already established holiday destination among westerners. This augurs well for medical tourism (especially cosmetic surgery) which requires a period of recuperation which could be carried out in resorts in Thailand. Malaysia remains competitive as value for money destination, not only for medical tourists but also mainstream tourists. With greater awareness of halal tourism, Malaysia could well positioned itself as medical providers for Muslim patients, by introducing the concept of halal medical tourism.

From the detailed descriptions of the medical-tourism industry in these four countries, it is evident that all of them are, in different ways, unique in providing medical services to the global market. By continuous emphasis on providing quality health-care through accreditation and general improvement of technology as well as the quality of their medical professionals, Thailand, Singapore, Malaysia, and India may be expected to maintain or expand their significance as major international medical-tourism destinations.

References

Agarwal, K. and Bhagrath, H. (2010). *Apollo Group to Set Up 32 New Hospitals by 2012.* [Online]. Available at: http://www.themedguru.com/20100320/newsfeature/apollo-group-set-32-new-hospitals-2012-86133073.html (accessed 10 June 2011).

Ai-Lien, C. (2005) "Singapore steps up efforts to woo foreign patients," *Straits Times*, 1 September: H8.

AlJazeera English (2008) "India's illegal organ transplant," *AlJazeera English*, 1 February. [Online]. Available at: http://www.youtube.com/watch?v=ms195gMv5ww (accessed 19 June 2011).

Alleman, B.W., Luger, T., Reisinger, H.S., Martin, R., Horowitz, M.D. and Cram, P. (2010) "Medical tourism services available to residents of the United States," *Journal of General Internal Medicine*, 26(5): 492–97.

Altes, A.G. (2005) "The development of health tourism services," *Annals of Tourism Research*, 32(1): 262–66.

Awadzi, W. and Panda, D. (2006) "Medical tourism: globalization and the marketing of medical services," *Consortium Journal of Hospitality and Tourism*, 11(1): 75–81.

Ben (2008) "8 countries where human organs are harvested," *NewsPick*, 10 June. [Online]. Available at: http://news.upickreviews.com/8-countries-where-human-organs-are-harvested (accessed 19 June 2011).

Bhatt, R. and Jain, N. (2006). Financial performance of private hospitals in India: some further evidence, Indian Institute of Management Working Papers, April.

Bookman, M.Z. and Bookman, K.R. (2007) *Medical Tourism in Developing Countries*. New York: Palgrave Macmillan.

Borman, E. (2004) "Health tourism: where health care ethics and the state collide," *British Medical Journal*, 328: 60–61.

Bramstedt, K.A. and Xu, J. (2007) "Checklist: passport, plane ticket, organ transplant," *American Journal of Transplantation*, 7(7): 1698–701.

Brotman, B.A. (2010) "Medical tourism private hospitals: focus India," *Journal of Health Care Finance*, 37(1): 45–50.

Carrera, P. and Bridges, J.F.P. (2006) "Globalization and healthcare: understanding health and medical tourism," *Expert Review of Pharmacoeconomics and Outcomes Research*, 6(4): 447–54.

Chacko, P. (2006) "Medical tourism in India: issues and challenges," *MBA Review*, 4(12): 123–29, ICFAI University Press.

Chanda, R. (2002) "Trade in health services," *Bulletin of the World Health Organization*, 80(2): 158–63.

Chaynee, W. (2003) *Health Tourism to Drive Earnings*. Kuala Lumpur: Malaysian Institute of Economic Research.

Chee, H.L. (2007) Medical Tourism in Malaysia: International Movement of Healthcare Consumers and the Commodification of Healthcare, Working Paper Series No. 83, Singapore: Asia Research Institute.

Chong, W.Y., Boey, T.S., and Vathsala, N. (2005) "Promoting health tourism in Malaysia," Unpublished paper presented at the APacCHRIE conference, Kuala Lumpur.

CII and Mckinsey & Company (2002) *Healthcare in India: The Road Ahead*, New Delhi: CII & Mckinsey & Co.

Cohen, E. (2008) "Medical tourism in Thailand," *GSBejournal*, [Online]. Available at: http://gsbejournal.au.edu/1V/Journal/Medical%20Tourism%20Dr%20Cohen.pdf (accessed 5 June 2011).

Connell, J. (2006) "Medical tourism: sea, sun, sand and ... surgery," *Tourism Management*, 27: 1093–100.

Crooks, V.A., Kingsbury, P., Snyder, J. and Johnston, R. (2010) "What is known about the patient's experience of medical tourism? A scoping review," *BMC Health Services Research*, 10(266): 1–12.

Crooks, V.A., Turner, L., Snyder, J., Johnston, R. and Kingsbury, P. (2011) "Promoting medical tourism to India: messages, images, and the marketing of international patient travel," *Social Science and Medicine*, 72: 726–32.

Discover Medical Tourism (2008a) Benefits of medical tourism. [Online]. Available at: http://www.discovermedicaltourism.com/benefits/ (accessed 17 June 2011).

Discover Medical Tourism (2008b) *Transplant Surgery Abroad*. [Online]. Available at: http://www.discovermedicaltourism.com/transplant-surgery/(accessed 19 June 2011).

Eggertson, L. (2006) "Wait-list weary Canadians seek treatment abroad," *Canadian Medical Association Journal* 174(9): 1247.

Ernst, D. (2006) *Medical Tourism: Why Americans Take Medical Vacations Abroad*. San Francisco, CA: Pacific Research Institute.

Evans, R.W. (2008) "Ethnocentrism is an unacceptable rationale for health care policy: a critique of transplant tourism position statements," *American Journal of Transplantation*, 8: 1089–95.

Forgione, D.A. and Smith, P.C. (2007) "Medical tourism and its impact on the US health care system," *Journal of Health Care Finance*, 34: 27–35.

Frost & Sullivan (2010) Malaysia's medical tourism industry has healthy vitals. [Online]. Available at: http://www.frost.com/prod/servlet/press-release.pag?docid=198719183 (accessed 7 June 2011).

Glinos, I.A., Baeten, R. and Boffin N. (2006) "Cross-border contracted care in Belgium hospitals," in M. Rossenmöller, M. McKee and R. Baeten (eds) *Patient mobility in the European Union: learning from experience*. Copenhagen: European Observatory on Health Systems and Policies.

Hall, C.M. (2011) "Health and medical tourism: a kill or cure for global public health?," *Tourism Review*, 66(1/2): 4–15.

Hall, C.M. and James, M. (2011) "Medical tourism: emerging biosecurity and nosocomial issues," *Tourism Review*, 66(1/2): 118–26.

Health Tourism in Asia (2009) Medical tourism in Singapore. [Online]. Available at: http://www.healthtourisminasia.com/singapore.htm (accessed 5 June 2011).

Healy, C. (2009) "Surgical tourism and the globalization of healthcare," *Irish Journal of Medical Sciences*, 178: 125–27.

Henderson, J.C. (2003) "Managing tourism and Islam in Peninsular Malaysia," *Tourism Management*, 24: 447–56.

Heung, V.C.S., Kucukusta, D. and Song, H. (2011) "Medical tourism development in Hong Kong: an assessment of the barriers," *Tourism Management*, 32: 995–1005.

International Medical Travel Journal (IMTJ) (2010a) "SINGAPORE: latest medical tourism statistics from Singapore," *International Medical Travel Journal: News*, 27 October. [Online. Available at: http://www.imtj.com/news/?EntryId82=255529 (accessed 6 June 2011).

International Medical Travel Journal (IMTJ) (2010b, August 26). SINGAPORE: Singapore sees rise in medical tourism. *International Medical Travel Journal: News*. [Online]. Available at: http://www.imtj.com/news/?EntryId82=246031 (accessed 6 June 2011).

International Medical Travel Journal (IMTJ) (2010c, October 8). MALAYSIA: relaxation of rules on advertising may help medical tourism to Malaysia. *International Medical Travel Journal: News*. [Online]. Available at: http://www.imtj.com/news/?EntryId82=252541 (accessed 7 June 2011).

International Medical Travel Journal (IMTJ) (2010d, December 9). THAILAND: Thailand medical tourism back on track. *International Medical Travel Journal: News*. [Online]. Available at: http://www.imtj.com/news/?EntryId82=261705 (accessed 16 June 2011).

International Medical Travel Journal (IMTJ) (2011a, March 11). MALAYSIA: Malaysia expands health tourism and plans laws on fertility treatment. *International Medical Travel Journal: News*. [Online]. Available at: http://www.imtj.com/news/?EntryId82=278529 (accessed 7 June 2011).

International Medical Travel Journal (IMTJ) (2011b, April 1). MALAYSIA: cost effective treatment boosting the growth of Malaysia medical tourism. *International Medical Travel Journal: News*. [Online]. Available at: http://www.imtj.com/news/?EntryId82=282387 (accessed 7 June 2011).

International Medical Travel Journal (IMTJ) (2011c, May 19). MALAYSIA: tax exemption for private hospitals to boost medical tourism in Malaysia. *International Medical Travel Journal:News*,19May.[Online].Availableat:http://www.imtj.com/news/?EntryId82=289724 (accessed 7 June 2011).

International Medical Travel Journal (IMTJ) (2011d) "INDIA, SRI LANKA: developments in Indian health tourism," *International Medical Travel Journal: News*, 4 January. [Online]. Available at: http://www.imtj.com/news/?EntryId82=265279 (accessed 20 June 2011).

Joint Commission International (JCI) (2011) *Joint Commission International (JCI) Accredited Organizations*. [Online]. Available at: http://www.jointcommissioninternational.org/JCI-Accredited-Organizations/ (accessed 7 June 2011).

Keaney, M. (2002) "Unhealthy accumulation: the globalization of health care privatization," *Review of Social Economy*, 60(3): 331–56.

Kingfisher Airlines (2011). Kingfisher Airlines introduces medical emergency fares under its care fares portfolio, Press Release 7 February. [Online]. Available at: http://www.flykingfisher.com/media-center/press-releases/kingfisher-airlines-introduces-medical-emergency-fares-under-its-care-fares-portfolio.aspx (accessed 17 June 2011).

Kumar, S. (2009) "Designing promotional strategies for medical tourism in India: a case study of an ophthalmic hospital in NCR," *Health and Population: Perspectives and Issues*, 32(2): 86–95.

Lee, J.Y., Kearns, R.A. and Friesen, W. (2010) "Seeking affective health care: Korean immigrants' use of homeland medical services," *Health and Place*, 16(1): 108–15.

Leng, C.H. (2007) Medical tourism in Malaysia: international movement of healthcare consumers and the commodification of healthcare. Asia Research Institute Working Paper Series, 83. [Online]. Available at: http://www.ari.nus.edu.sg/docs/wps/wps07_083.pdf (accessed 5 June 2011).

Lew, A.A. and Hall, C.M. (1999) "The impacts of the Asian crisis on tourism," *Current Issues in Tourism*, 2(4): 277–78.

Lunt, N. and Carrera, P. (2010) "Medical tourism: assessing the evidence on treatment abroad," *Maturitas*, 66: 27–32.

MacReady, N. (2007) "Developing countries court medical tourists," *Lancet*, 369(9576): 1849–50.

Medical Council of India (2010) *Annual Report 2009-2010*. [Online]. Available at: http://www.mciindia.org/AboutMCI/AnnualReports.aspx (accessed 10 June 2011).

Meditrips India (2011) *Advantage India*. [Online]. Available at: http://www.meditripsindia.com/advantage_india.html (accessed 17 June 2011).

Milstein, A. and Smith, M. (2006) "America's new refugees—seeking affordable surgery offshore," *The New England Journal of Medicine*, 355: 1637–40.

Ministry of Health Malaysia (2010) Healthcare industry: one of the fastest growing sectors in Malaysia. [Online]. Available at: http://www.myhealthcare.gov.my/en/index.asp?page=overview&;subpage=about_medical_tourism (accessed 10 June 2011).

Ministry of Tourism India (2011) *Medical tourism*. [Online]. Available at: http://www.tourism.gov.in/TourismDivision/AboutContent.aspx?Name=TourismInfrastructureDevelopment&CID=18&INO=12 (accessed 17 June 2011).

Mullan, F. (2006) "Doctors for the world: Indian physician emigration," *Health Affairs*, 25(2): 380–93.

Newman, M.I., Camberson, A.E. and Ascherman, J. (2005) "*Mycobacteria abscessus* outbreak in US patients linked to offshore surgicenter," *Annals of Plastic Surgery*, 55(1): 107–10.

OkMedicalTourism (2011) *Thai government's drive to boost medical tourism revenues to 100 billion baht (US$3.3bn) by year 2015*. [Online]. Available at: http://www.okmedicaltourism.com/2011/04/30/thai-government%E2%80%99s-drive-to-boost-medical-tourism-revenues-to-100-billion-baht-us3-3bn-by-year-2015/ (accessed 17 June 2011).

Ormond, M. (2011) "Medical tourism, medical exile: responding to the cross-border pursuit of healthcare in Malaysia," in C. Minca and T. Oakes (eds) *Real Tourism: Representation, Practice and the "Material" in Contemporary Travel*, London: Routledge.

Ramirez de Arellano, A. (2007) "Patients without borders: the emergence of medical tourism," *International Journal of Health Services*, 37: 193–98.

RNCOS (2011). Strong government support to drive medical tourism industry in Malaysia. Press Release, 9 June. [Online]. Available at: http://www.rncos.com/Press_Releases/Strong-Government-Support-to-Drive-Medical-Tourism-Industry-in-Malaysia.htm (accessed 10 June 2011).

Saniotis, A. (2007) "Changing ethics in medical practice: a Thai perspective," *Indian Journal Medical Ethics*, 3: 24–25.

SingaporeMedicine (2007). Accolades and accreditations. [Online]. Available at: http://www.singaporemedicine.com/healthcaredest/accolades_acred.asp (accessed 5 June 2011).

Singapore Tourism Board (2010) *Discovering Your Singapore: Singapore Tourism Board Annual Report 2009/2010*. [Online]. Available at: http://www1.yoursingapore.com/annualreport/PDF/STB_AR_2009_2010.pdf (accessed 5 June 2011).

Singh, P.K. (2008) *Medical Tourism*. India: Kanishka.

Smith, P.C. and Forgione, D.A. (2007) "Global outsourcing of healthcare: a medical tourism model," *Journal of Information Technology Case and Application Research*, 9(3): 19–30.

Taffel, J. (2004) "Fixed up in a foreign land," *Sydney Morning Herald*, 9 December: 4–5.

Teh, I. and Chu, C. (2005) "Supplementing growth with medical tourism," *Asia Pacific Biotech News*, 9(8): 306–11.

The Economic Times (2011) "Ayurveda a popular alternative medicine in Malaysia," *The Economic Times*, 4 January. [Online]. Available at: http://articles.economictimes.indiatimes.com/2011-01-04/news/28424512_1_alternative-medicine-traditional-medicine-siddha-medicine (accessed 10 June 2011).

The Star (2010) "AirAsia touches hearts in first flight to Bangalore," *The Star*, 21 May. [Online]. Available at: http://thestar.com.my/news/story.asp?file=/2010/5/21/nation/6305060&;sec=nation (accessed 17 June 2011).

Turner, L. (2007a) "From Durham to Delhi: medical tourism and the global economy," in J.C. Cohen-Khler and M.B. Seaton (eds.) *Comparative Program on Health and Society Lupina Foundation Working Papers Series 2006–2007*, Toronto: Munk Centre for International Studies, University of Toronto.

Turner, L. (2007b) "Canadian medicare and the global health care bazaar," *Policy Options, September*: 73–77.

Turner, L. (2007c) "First world health care at third world prices; globalization, bioethics and medical tourism," *BioSocieties*, 2: 303–25.

UNESCAP (2007) "Patients without borders: an overview of the medical travel industry in Asia, its challenges and opportunities." Paper presented at UNESCAP EGM, Bangkok, Thailand. [Online]. Available at: http://www.unescap.org/esid/hds/lastestadd/medicaltbkgdpaper%5Bfin%5D021007.pdf (accessed 5 June 2011).

Valueaddedblog (2011) "India fast becoming international destination for kidney transplants due to affordability & skill: expert," *Valueaddedblog*, 11 February. [Online]. Available at: http://valueaddedblog.wordpress.com/2011/02/11/india-fast-becoming-international-destination-for-kidney-transplants-due-to-affordability-skill-expert/ (accessed 20 June 2011).

Vijaya, R.M. (2010) "Medical tourism: revenue generation or international transfer of healthcare problems?," *Journal of Economic Issues*, 44(1): 53–69.

Wachter, R.M. (2006) "The 'dis-location' of U.S. medicine—the implications of medical outsourcing," *The New England Journal of Medicine*, 16 February.

Whittaker, A. (2008) "Pleasure and pain: medical travel in Asia," *Global Public Health*, 3(3): 271–90.

Woodman, J. (2007) *Patients Beyond Borders, Singapore Edition*. North Carolina: Healthy Travel Media.

World Health Organization (2011). *World Health Statistics 2011: 118-134*. [Online]. Available at: http://www.who.int/whosis/whostat/EN_WHS2011_Full.pdf (accessed 27 November 2011)

Yanos, M. (2008) Top 5 medical tourism destinations. *Nuwireinvestor*, 31 March. [Online]. Available at: http://www.nuwireinvestor.com/articles/top-5-medical-tourism-destinations-51502.aspx (accessed 5 June 2011).

Yap, J. (2007) *Singapore: Medical Travel and Consumer Driven Health Care*. [Online]. Available at: http://www.aarpinternational.org/resourcelibrary/resourcelibrary_show.htm?doc_id=545751 (accessed 5 June 2011).

Ye, B.H., Yuen, P.P., Qiu, H.Z. and Zhang, V.H. (2008) "Motivation of medical tourists: an exploratory case study of Hong Kong medical tourists," Paper presented at APTA annual conference, Bangkok, Thailand.

12 Claiming 'cultural competence'

The promotion of multi-ethnic Malaysia as a medical tourism destination

Meghann Ormond

Introduction

In recent decades, significant attention by the Malaysian government has been given to the overseas promotion of Malaysia's internal ethnic, linguistic and religious diversity in order to strategically weave the country into lucrative and productive cross-border networks and alliances via cosmopolitan claims to belongings that seem to transcend those of the nation-state (Bunnell 2002). This pursuit of transnational capital and geopolitical recognition has engendered a re-scripting of national identity along newly valorised multi-cultural lines, concealing ethnic tension with its emphasis on 'unity in diversity' (Najib 2009). This chapter argues that Malaysia's burgeoning medical tourism industry is profoundly entrenched in this task, engaging in 'strategic cosmopolitanism' (Mitchell 2003, 2007) to court select patient-consumers from around the globe by tapping into a range of belongings shared by Malaysians themselves. Touted right alongside promises of significant economic savings, 'world-class' medical facilities and cutting-edge technology and procedures is Malaysia's 'cultural expertise' in catering to the diverse lifestyles of international patient-consumers (e.g., linguistic needs, religious practices and dietary requirements). With health care increasingly commodified, such non-medical, culturally orientated patient-centred care factors are held within the industry to play an expedient role in destinations' ability to capture the 'right' markets.

In the following pages, I explore how claims to natural 'cultural competence' and expertise get mobilised in the promotion of Malaysia as a medical tourism destination and what sorts of power relations this is thought to expedite. I begin by placing medical tourism within the context of discourses and practices of multi-culturalism by looking at its growing relationship with the 'cultural competence' movement in health care. In the second part, I engage with the interpellation of the 'strategic cosmopolitan Malaysian' reconfigured by state discourse on cultural diversity that shifted in light of political and economic recognition of the value of Malaysia's ethnic, linguistic and religious pluralism in a globalising world. The third part traces this conceptualisation and mobilisation of domestic cultural diversity as international cultural competence and resemblance by looking at how Malaysia is presented as a 'home away from home' for select foreign patient-consumers whose receipt of 'culturally competent' care in Malaysia confers prestige upon, reflects and reinforces a range of cultural, social, economic and political attributes imagined to be able to successfully link Malaysia into diverse global networks.

Culture and cultural competence

Concern with 'cultural competence' in health care entered mainstream training and practice in the 1980s to address the needs of an increasingly diverse population in the United States experiencing poor health outcomes. Various approaches have since been taken up largely in countries with ethnic, linguistic and religious minority groups deemed to be marginalised in relation to the dominant formal healthcare systems in place. As such, cultural competence in health care has been closely linked to multi-cultural policy that recognises diversity as legitimate and identifies and responds to the varied 'needs' perceived to stem from that diversity. Betancourt *et al.* (2002: v) define it as 'the ability of systems to provide care to patients with diverse values, beliefs and behaviors, including tailoring delivery to meet patients' social, cultural, and linguistic needs … [such that it serves as] a vehicle to increase access to quality care for all patient populations'. Some critics of this expression of multi-culturalism, however, suggest that 'culturally competent' practices may work to discriminate against people further by 'inadvertently reinforc[ing] racial and ethnic biases and stereotypes' (Gregg and Saha 2006: 543) that conflate race, ethnicity and biology with 'culture' (Shaw 2005: 292). 'Culture', they suggest, is in fact 'frequently defined in a rather uncomplicated fashion – as a fixed, knowable entity that guides individuals' behavior in linear ways', reifying it as bounded, homogenous and static – such that practitioners risk 'seeing stable cultural norms or predictable culturally based behaviors where none exist' (Gregg and Saha 2006: 543). The narrow definitions of 'culture' as the birthplace, language and ethnicity of 'the Other' that are frequently employed, therefore, preclude practices of 'cultural humility' that acknowledge the simultaneous multiplicity of cultural belongings conditioned by gender, sexual preference, age, ability, socio-economic status and so on (Tervalon and Murray-García 1998).

While ample critical literature exists on 'cultural competence' in health care within high-income countries home to significant migrant and minority populations, few studies have so far examined the significance of 'cultural competence' within the scope of medical tourism, where patient-consumers cross borders oftentimes into lower-income countries in the pursuit of private medical care. Tellingly, what has been written often attends to decisions by some economically comfortable migrants to return to their countries of origin for what they find to be more 'culturally appropriate' health care. For example, in their study of Korean immigrants' preferred use of 'homeland medical services', Lee *et al.* (2010: 110) suggest that familiarity with the structures and hierarchies of their 'native' national health systems, expectations of medical authority and patient handling, proximity of family and friends and the lack of linguistic obstacles serve to both comfort and empower these transnational patient-consumers, returning a sense of control over their health and bodies. Whittaker (2009), in her work on reproductive tourism, meanwhile, examines the decision by some Thai migrant women married to Westerners to return to Thailand for in vitro fertilisation (IVF). Her respondents underscore the importance of receiving care 'at home', though the urban clinics they patronise are located far from their families' villages. 'Home' here instead translates into ease in communication and familiarity with specifically national healthcare practices. In both cases, returning 'home' becomes a 're-assertion of place' (Whittaker 2009: 320) that, by selecting a healthcare system appropriate 'to culture and the social construction of health and illness' (Elliot and Gillie 1998: 337), redresses a sense of 'placelessness' experienced through migration.

With much literature on 'cultural competence' in health care embedded in domestic multi-cultural politics, attempting to explore 'cultural competence' in medical tourism complicates the tendency to focus on social rights and healthcare equity within the national domain by expanding the scope to transnational inter-cultural relationships mediated largely within a highly globalised for-profit healthcare sector. Significantly, Betancourt *et al.*'s (2002) definition of 'cultural competence' in health care cited above also recognises it 'as a business strategy to attract new patients and market share', something which has oft been over-looked in more conventional treatment of the issue. The desire to reduce 'cultural distance' between prospective patient-consumers and healthcare providers, however, constitutes a *fundamental* preoccupation within the global medical tourism industry. Providers are largely concentrated in lower-income countries and the 'gold-mine' medical tourist markets, hailing from upper-income countries, are yet to be fully convinced of the benefits when faced with what one prominent medical travel guidebook refers to as 'the added pressure of having to tolerate cultural diversity' (Woodman 2008: 48–49) abroad when patient-consumers are at their most physically and emotionally vulnerable. Consequently, numerous industry conference sessions are dedicated to, for example, 'Attracting and catering to Islamic patients and special-needs international patients' and 'How to attract Americans to your hospital' (Medical Travel World Congress 2008), while promotional materials industry-wide frequently highlight private facilities' and even entire countries' ability to offer 'culturally appropriate care' and linguistic proficiency in order to attract prospective medical tourists (Ormond 2011). Furthermore, in light of the Joint Commission International (JCI) accreditation scheme's recent focus on the significance of cultural competence in patient-centred care, trade-orientated publications like *Medical Tourism Magazine* are beginning to identify with greater intensity the need for cultural and linguistic competency training and guidelines to be established throughout the industry. Medical tourism does not need to start from scratch. It can and should take advantage of a now-established field and 'translate and integrate' some of the procedures that have proved successful in caring for local patients from diverse backgrounds (Salimbene 2010).

Salimbene (2010) here refers to cross-cultural training programmes that have been widely adopted by medical schools and clinics in the United States to foster sensitivity to the diverse cultural and religious beliefs that shape understandings of the body, health care and end-of-life practices, decision making and the handling of difficult news about one's health status. Yet Jagyasi (2010) finds that training in cultural competence has so far been limited to cultural diversity within one geography because most of the patients were coming from one geography with different cultures and beliefs. However, medical tourism has turned the situation upside down and now patients come from an entirely different geography, which has created a significant need for bilateral cultural understanding.

Jagyasi's (2010) observation counters Salimbene's (2010) suggestion that existing Western-based cultural competence training and practices simply be adopted into medical tourism contexts by recognising that medical tourism discourses, practices and directionalities are producing complex ways of performing 'cultural diversity' in these 'new' geographies of health care.

Strategic cosmopolitanism

A Southeast Asian country with Malays comprising around 60 per cent of the population and the remainder Chinese (25 per cent), Indians (8 per cent) and indigenous peoples (7 per cent), Malaysia's strength in the global economy discursively pivots increasingly on its cultural diversity, underscored by Prime Minister Najib Razak's (2009) assertion that 'What makes Malaysia unique is the diversity of our peoples... [T]his unity in diversity... has always been our strength and remains our best hope for the future'. Yet this has not always been as self-evident as he suggests. Intra-ethnic tensions resulted in positive discrimination policies symbolised by the 1970 New Economic Policy (NEP) that favoured the *bumiputera* ('sons of the soil'), and more specifically the Malay, over other ethnic groups in the strategic arenas of business, employment, education and property ownership so as to redistribute wealth within the country. By the 1990s, however, the Malaysian state began to locate value in the country's diversity with its increasing involvement in the global market, reframing ethnic division as multi-cultural wealth. Policy discourse shifted from protecting the *Bangsa Melayu* ('Malay nation') specifically to 'establish[ing] a united, progressive and prosperous *Bangsa Malaysia*' ('Malaysian nation') more broadly [Economic Planning Unit (EPU) 2000]. This 'multicultural "rescripting" of the nation or national identity' (Bunnell 2002: 106) sought to redraw the ethnicised biopolitical contours that have so profoundly shaped the direction and the subjects of national development in Malaysia. No longer only focused on making the *bumiputera* competitive within their own country, the objective was now for all Malaysians, regardless of ethnicity, to contribute towards the government's aspirations for Malaysia to reach 'developed' country status by the year 2020 – 'a new type of nationalist project for a new international age' (Hilley 2001: 131). This was reinforced more recently with the withdrawal of the 30 per cent *bumiputera* equity requirement in 2009 for investment in a range of areas that included tourism, health and social services.

In spite of this progressive opening-up along neoliberal lines, however, the *significance* of ethnic, linguistic and religiously based difference has not dissolved. Instead, these political changes have served to legitimise, cultivate and capitalise on the cultural diversity within the state to attract investment (Mitchell 1996). It is reinforced and re-articulated, recalling Yúdice's (2003: 23) observation that the 'representation of and claims to cultural difference are expedient insofar as they multiply commodities and empower community'. In her work on 'flexible citizenship' practices which traces the 'complicated accommodations, alliances and creative tensions between the nation-state and mobile capital', Ong (1999: 16–19) observes that the nation-state remains key in determining the terms of 'the new modes of subject-making and the new kinds of valorised subjectivity' relevant to successfully attracting transnational capital. The Malaysian state's strategy, therefore, can be read as seeking to turn its population's diverse ethnic, linguistic and religious backgrounds into a platform from where to selectively foster lucrative and socio-politically advantageous transnational linkages.

Mitchell (2003, 2007) distinguishes between multi-culturalism and what she terms 'strategic cosmopolitanism'. Discourses of *multi-culturalism* have been employed by the state to construct a 'multicultural self' that is conditioned to 'work with and through difference, and... to believe in the positive advantages of diversity in constructing and unifying the nation' (Mitchell 2003: 388). In this post-national moment, meanwhile, Mitchell goes on to posit a shift in the scale of citizenship, from the state's previous focus on fostering citizen-subjects to the cultivation of self-regulating subjects whose belongings are increasingly multiple and, though articulated by its rationalities, reach beyond the national domain. These subjects are trained to engage in *strategic cosmopolitanism*, with the neo-liberal state involved in the cross-border promotion of its subjects' expertise, derived in no small way from their diverse cultural backgrounds, in order to more effectively disseminate the state's ideals and desires at home and abroad (Mitchell 2007: 709). This cosmopolitanism can thus be interpreted not in the sense of an elite, rootless liberal universality, but rather as '[a] repertoire of imaginaries and practices' that 'involves symbolically or physically crossing defined boundaries and claiming a degree of cultural versatility' (Jeffrey and McFarlane 2008: 420).

While Mitchell's model suggests a more or less unidirectional shift from a nation-building multi-cultural policy orientation to one of 'strategic cosmopolitanism', the Malaysian context challenges such linearity. Since the introduction of the more inclusive concept of the 'Malaysian nation', multi-culturalism *has* served as a key political instrument used within the scope of the 'new type of nationalist project for a new international age' (Hilley 2001: 131). Yet the broader context for this shift is significant, introduced in parallel with neoliberal policy that substantially redefined the relationship between the state and its citizenry in multiple basic socio-economic domains such that the drive to increase profit through harnessing transnational flows inspired the re-scripting of diversity discourse domestically. This shift endowed the state with control over its subjects through the recognition, categorisation and regulation of such difference on the basis of a narrative of national coherence through tolerance of the Other. As a result, the Malaysian state increasingly anchors its international legitimacy in its 'expertise' in mediating between a range of cultures and social realities domestically, by acting as 'a unifying ground' (Yúdice 2003: 89) in which difference, hybridity and transnationalism are recognised and valued so as to establish cultural affinities useful for tapping new markets.

Following on decades of policies favouring Malays, the official recognition and inclusion of subjectivities previously marginalised within the nation-state as fundamental to sustaining the country's economy in a globalised context is a marked departure from the protectionism of yore. This neoliberally inspired inclusiveness contrasts with the status of non-Malays prior to the discursive turn casting internal diversity in the positive light of 'multiculturalism'. Strategically embracing 'unity in diversity', the Malaysian state reaps benefit by allying its newly 'empowered' population – now vital to positioning Malaysia as a key partner to Asia's emerging superpowers and important global diasporas (e.g., ethnic Chinese in Indonesia and Singapore) – with international markets (Bunnell 2002). Similarly, through equating being Malay with being Muslim and, therefore, part of the *'umma'* (global faith community), the state seeks to de-emphasise its substantial Malay population's ethnic identity and instead capitalise on religious belonging in order to attract investment and improve trade with other predominantly Muslim countries, particularly the wealthy Gulf states (Ong 1999).

The strategic cosmopolitan use of domestic diversity is particularly clear with the 'Malaysia, Truly Asia' campaign. Faced with declining tourism figures in the late 1990s, a nation-branding exercise was deemed necessary to set Malaysia apart from other Asian destinations and remedy its 'lack of "distinctiveness"' (Prakash 2007: 3), with some identifying Malaysia's mixture of peoples as a barrier to developing a marketable tourism identity. Turning this very diversity into a selling point, the Malaysian government decided 'to promote Malaysia as a melting pot of three major Asian cultures (Malay, Chinese and Indian)… convey[ing] the idea of unity in diversity' (Prakash 2007: 4). The campaign's promotional material displayed prominently within and outside of the country portrays 'a bevy of local beauties' representing Malay, Chinese, Indian and indigenous ethnic groups '"selling" its multiculturalism and cultural diversity [by] representing all the major civilisations in Asia as its tourism image' (Amran 2004: 2). Malaysia was rapidly recast as a mini-Asia, home to '[t]he wonders of Asia in one exciting destination' (Tourism Malaysia 2009).

Malaysia's diversity, brought about through centuries of trade, migration and colonial rule, is sustained today by the infrastructure and administrative models set up during colonial times and incorporated post-Independence. As such, Malaysia is cast as a privileged territory – Yúdice's (2003) 'unifying ground' – in which East and West harmoniously unite under the guiding expert hand of uniquely cosmopolitan Malaysians – fluent in 'Asian values', setting out the contours of a progressive Islamic modernity and confidently managing postcolonial linkages that have permitted Malaysians to acquire valuable expertise in and regarding the West. In harnessing Malaysia's very own cultural hybridity or 'in-betweenness' (Bhabha 1994), state discourse navigates the post-Cold War 'civilisational' political context, working the East/West dialectic to its benefit (Ong 1999). If 'discourses of location can be used to naturalise boundaries and margins under the guise of celebration, nostalgia or inappropriate assumptions of sameness' (Kaplan 2007: 187), then what we see with Malaysia is a complex rhetorical use of 'sameness' not based upon a supposed internal homogeneity but rather drawing upon assumptions of ethnic, linguistic and religious affinities that extend beyond Malaysia's borders, permitting the state to engage in a range of transnational networks made possible by its subjects' diversity.

Cultural resemblance in Malaysian medical tourism

Medical tourism destinations are dependent upon successfully recognising and responding to the diverse 'needs' and expectations of foreign patient-consumers. Critically, however, these 'needs' risk being reified as the cultural idiosyncrasies of the 'Westerners', 'Middle Easterners', 'East Asians' and so on that they serve. Responding to the 'needs' of patient-consumers from 'desirable' markets through claims to 'culturally appropriate' care expertise has the potential to renegotiate and re-value existing cultural dynamics within the destinations themselves. Increasingly, this is done on the basis of promoting care expertise through claims to cultural similarity or 'resemblance' (see Shaw 2005, 2010) with prospective patient-consumers. Such practices effectively serve to 'mobilise notions of specificity, difference and recognition that both depend on and construct racialised ethnic identities' (Shaw 2010: 524) in order to create differentiation in the medical tourism market. This section, therefore, offers a reading of how Malaysia's strategy of '"visualisation" for global audiences' has been mobilised in the medical tourism industry, re-scripting the country's domestic diversity as a cornerstone in both its attractiveness to mobile capital and geopolitical relevance (Bunnell 2002).

Malaysia has long been a popular tourism destination thanks in part to its image as a tolerant, safe and moderate majority Muslim country that accommodates the lifestyles of Muslims and non-Muslims alike – conveyed as a 'home away from home' (Palany 2004) for many international visitors. With tourism the second largest contributor to the country's gross domestic product (GDP) and the most productive service sector (Henderson 2009: 141), the suggestion by then Tourism Minister Azalina Othman that 'all of us [Malaysians] need to be aware that Malaysia is a tourist country – a "tourist star" – and it is the equal responsibility of ALL Malaysians to see that our tourism products and facilities are well maintained' (Kok 2009) enjoins Malaysians to act as ambassadors of a commoditised Malaysia, deftly leaving '[m]any of the social and cultural issues embedded in the [national] branding campaign unexamined' (Ooi 2004: 107).

How is the similarity represented in the notion of 'home away from home' that gets constructed by the medical tourism industry? The Malaysian state plays a key role in selectively filtering who enters and contributes to fomenting its image. It has been involved in facilitating the industry's development since first identifying medical tourism as a strategic pillar for national economic growth following the Asian Financial Crisis, partnering with the private sector for its cultivation and promotion (Chee 2008). Through the efforts of three ministries (Health, Tourism, and International Trade and Industry), the Association of Private Hospitals of Malaysia and 35 private hospitals selected by the government to represent the 'Malaysia Healthcare' brand, prospective medical tourists receive the official message via media coverage and trade fairs and missions about what sets Malaysia apart from other destinations.

Echoing the 'Malaysia, Truly Asia' campaign's 'human rainbow' imagery (Yúdice 2003: 177), the government's medical tourism websites [e.g. Ministry of Health Malaysia (MOH) 2009; Tourism Malaysia 2009] urge, 'It must be Malaysia!', against backdrops of 'world-class' facilities endowed with state-of-the-art technology, bucolic natural landscapes and an array of concerned yet spirited highly qualified multi-ethnic medical staff 'with internationally recognised qualifications' who are unified by their common concern for ensuring the best for international visitors. A 'safe and politically stable country', readers are told, Malaysia is home to a 'tolerant multicultural and multiracial society' that 'accommodates patients of different cultures and religions' and ensures ease in communication with its multi-lingual staff (Tourism Malaysia 2007; MOH, 2009). This emphasis highlights the industry's focus on the centrality of cultural credentials in ensuring international patient-consumers' satisfaction with their overall therapeutic experience.

Following the identification of medical tourism as an engine for economic growth, the National Committee for the Promotion of Health Tourism in Malaysia (NCPHT) was set up to promote Malaysia as a 'centre of medical excellence' (Chua 2002), bringing together institutional players in the domains of medical care and tourism to formulate a plan of action to promote and develop the industry. The NCPHT selected target countries from which to attract foreign patient-consumers and classified them into four market segments (MOH 2002; Chee 2007). The first segment comprises the Association of Southeast Asian Nations (ASEAN) countries with emerging middle classes (e.g. Indonesia, Cambodia and Vietnam), collectively perceived as lacking sufficient access to quality medical care. The second focuses on the Middle Eastern middle class, hailing mainly from the Gulf states, seeking care outside of their home region. The third includes countries where medical care is sufficiently expensive to make patient-consumers look abroad to save money (e.g. United States, Singapore and Japan). The final group comprises countries with socialised healthcare systems in which waiting times for procedures are deemed common (e.g. United Kingdom and Canada).

Underlying the choice of these segments was the drive to portray Malaysia as a 'value for money' destination, appealing to a transnational bourgeoisie instead of the up-market patients already targeted by one of Malaysia's strongest regional competitors: Singapore. To be distinct from other pocketbook-friendly destinations like Thailand and India, Malaysia's internal diversity and its 'cultural credentials' were touted as a marketing strength with which to attract broader segments of the global market via specific appeals to cultural similarities with Middle Easterners, Westerners and other Asians. Yet there are significant differences between the NCPHT's targets and the markets that actually exist. In reality, these markets are very small, with Middle Easterners resenting an insignificant 0.4 per cent of all foreign patient-consumers treated and 'Westerners' barely comprised 5 per cent (of which Americans, a 'gold-mine' clientele to which many global destinations aspire, accounted for only 1.22 per cent) in 2007 [Association of Private Hospitals of Malaysia (APHM) 2008]. Rather, the vast majority of foreign patient-consumers are from Malaysia's immediate neighbours. Below, I take a brief look at cultural competence claims mobilised in Malaysia to capture these different market segments and their relevance to the state project of 'strategic cosmopolitanism'.

Westerners

As noted earlier, medical tourism destinations are touted for their linguistic, cultural and economic proximity or 'resemblance' (Shaw 2010) to desirable foreign patient-consumers. With the contours of the country's current healthcare system and infrastructure laid out under British occupation, today many Malaysian medical professionals continue to receive at least part of their medical training in Anglophone countries, which is perceived to give Malaysian hospitals a strong competitive advantage in the international medical tourism market. Many medical travel facilitators that feature Malaysia as a destination use this to situate the country as a destination in which medical tourists from high-income countries can feel at home. *Patients Beyond Borders,* a medical travel guidebook, for example, proclaims that 'Western culture is ingrained throughout the country', with English being 'universally and comfortably spoken' (Woodman 2008: 283). Med Retreat (2010), meanwhile, waxes that

> Multi-ethnic, multi-cultural, and multi-lingual, Malaysia is an excellent choice for meeting the healthcare needs of international medical tourism patients… Being a former British Colony, English is spoken everywhere… Many of the private hospitals in Malaysia are also applying for JCI Accreditation in order to attract more international patients. Our partner hospitals in Malaysia are either already JCI accredited, or are in their final stages, are American managed, or are sponsored by some of the largest American companies.

While there is a nod to the colourful and exotic, with imagery of 'traditional' costume and constant assertions of the country's vibrant diversity, at the same time significant effort is made to underscore that Malaysian medical professionals were trained and abide by standards and codes established elsewhere, upsetting the notion that practice and belief in biomedical science and technology are somehow universal, a 'culture of no culture' (Traweek 1988, Taylor 2003: 161). The prospective medical tourist is reassured that Malaysia is sufficiently integrated into the right kinds of global networks to guarantee an excellent 'world-class' (read 'sufficiently "first-world"') medical experience.

Middle Easterners

Middle- and upper-class Middle Easterners have long travelled abroad, chiefly to Western countries (e.g. United States, United Kingdom and Germany), for medical care (Kangas 2002). Yet, demand changed significantly after 9/11. To illustrate this, in 2001 some 44 per cent of medical tourists from one Middle Eastern country went to the United States to receive medical care yet, by 2003, this figure dropped to a mere 8 per cent, attributed to the difficulty encountered by these prospective patients and their companions in obtaining visas to enter the United States (Ehrbeck *et al.* 2008:

8). It took six years for these numbers to return to their pre-9/11 levels. During this in-between period, many destinations involved in the rapidly expanding medical tourism industry sought to tap this market. A 2003 Malaysian Institute of Economic Research report suggested that Malaysia 'bank on its Islamic credentials to attract medical patients from the Middle East' since, in addition to the abundance of tasty *halal* food and the likelihood of prayers to be recited before surgery, 'also working towards Malaysia's advantage is the current geopolitical situation' (Wong 2003) that vilifies and discriminates against Muslims, and Arab-Muslims in particular. In return, Middle Eastern interest boosted claims about the quality of care in Malaysia: 'While patients used to go to the US and the UK for medical treatment previously, these are not favoured choices anymore and Malaysia, with its international-class medical facilities and as a Muslim majority nation, is the perfect alternative' (*TTG Asia* 2004). The ability to attract Middle Eastern patient-consumers through the provision of 'Muslim-friendly' care holds significant symbolic currency in the context of the Malaysian state's broader efforts to assert an image of a model modern Muslim country, remaining at the heart of promotional efforts today (Bernama 2009).

Southeast Asians

Medical tourism has striking regional relevance for Malaysia. Official figures for 2007 indicate that at least 89 per cent of the foreign patients at Malaysian private medical facilities hailed from Asia, with 80 per cent coming from its immediate neighbours (APHM 2008). The significant number of patient-consumers from surrounding countries can be attributed to the region's substantial range of socio-economic realities and healthcare systems, which leads middle-class nationals of poorer countries with difficult access to quality medical care like Indonesia in particular to seek Malaysia out. In recognition of the significance of these regional healthcare-motivated cross-border flows, today most of the 35 private hospitals endorsed by the Health Ministry for medical tourism focus their promotional efforts (e.g., trade fairs, brochures, local recruiters, talking-engagement 'road-shows' with doctors) largely on ASEAN countries, with hospitals in Malaysia's 'heavyweight' medical travel destinations of Penang and Malacca focusing particularly on the nearby Indonesian island of Sumatra (Ormond 2011). They attract Indonesian patient-consumers by catering to their 'needs' with recruiters operating in Indonesian cities and special hospital reception desks staffed with Bahasa Indonesia speakers. Promoters are quick to emphasise not only the geographical but also the ethnic, religious and linguistic proximity generated through centuries of trade and migration between Malaysians and their Indonesian neighbours in sibling-like terms. As one anonymous tourism official notes,

> We have a similar language, which is mutually intelligible – only complicated by differences in pronunciation… They're mostly Muslims. Weather-wise, it's normal – hot there, hot here. Rain there, rain here. Food-wise, it's still the same taste. They are familiar with us and we are familiar with them… How do we get them [Indonesian patient-consumers]? It comes down to the comfort that comes from similarity.

Efforts made to position Malaysia as a prime destination within the ASEAN region therefore draw upon 'shared' Southeast Asian characteristics and have far-reaching impacts on the way in which Malaysia is positioned within Asia, ASEAN and among its neighbours, as 'a centre of medical excellence in the region' (Tourism Malaysia 2007).

Conclusion

This chapter has sought to complement and complicate commonly held notions about who moves where and why in medical tourism by calling attention to strategic efforts in medical tourism destinations to draw more – yet select – international patient-consumers. Such efforts are not based solely upon the economic or time-sensitive factors to which their successes are often attributed but also, and perhaps increasingly, upon the promise of recognising and meeting the diverse culturally specific 'needs' of foreign patient-consumers. In light of the lack of scholarly treatment linking medical tourism with the growth of calls and practices within the industry for greater 'cultural competence' in order to reduce the 'cultural distance' between patient-consumers and healthcare providers, I have tried to use this space to think through how the extension of 'culturally competent' health care to non-nationals interpellates a spectrum of reconfigured and newly valorised citizen-subjects in order to tap potentially lucrative patient-consumer markets by investing in and naturalising similarities with them. Reaching beyond borders to attract foreign patient-consumers, medical tourism promotion is premised upon destinations' ability to effectively demonstrate their openness to the use of their healthcare system by non-nationals. Increasingly, the display of this openness calls upon a 'repertoire' of claims to 'cultural versatility' (Jeffrey and McFarlane 2008) as much as the international standardisation of medical practice.

This requisite versatility has been naturalised and discursively couched in the expertise of a postcolonial, multi-cultural Malaysia. With its re-scripting of the value of internal linguistic, religious and ethnic differences in order to be more attractive to mobile capital, the state creatively casts itself as a prime facilitator for its subjects' diversity, serving as the 'unifying ground' (Yúdice 2003) upon which 'unity in diversity' (Najib Razak 2009) is made possible. The country, we are told, has ample 'natural' experience in catering to the needs of a broad range of international patient-consumers because those diverse 'needs' and considerate responses to them are shared and practiced by Malaysians themselves. Malaysians understand the importance of having access to *halal* food. They already converse in a variety of languages and dialects. Their doctors have gained experience in prestigious universities and medical facilities from around the globe. Their similarities with their international clientele derive from the diversity found, and made possible, within Malaysia. This 'strategic' brand of cosmopolitanism breaks with universalising conceptions of cosmopolitanism that favour the cultivation of a deterritorialised 'global citizenship' which transcends cultural difference. Rather, it thrives by reifying and commoditising particular expressions of cultural difference – capitalising on the production of related goods and services rendered more valuable through the niche differences they appear to represent and satisfy.

References

Amran H. (2004) 'Policy and planning of the tourism industry in Malaysia'. In *Policy and Planning of Tourism Product Development in Asian Countries, Conference proceedings, The Sixth Asian Development Research Forum (ADRF) General Meeting*, 7–8 June, Bangkok.

Association of Private Hospitals of Malaysia (APHM) (2008) *Medical tourism statistics for 2002–2007*, e-mail correspondence, 9 April.

Bernama (2009) 'Saudi Arabia: A good option for Malaysian business', *Bernama*, 17 March. Online. Available at: http://www.bernama.com.my/bernama/v3/news_lite.php?id=396766 [accessed 30 June 2009].

Betancourt, J.R., Green, A.R. and Carrillo, J.E. (2002) 'Cultural competence in health care: Emerging frameworks and practical approaches', *Field report, The Commonwealth Fund*. Online. Available at: http://www.azdhs.gov/bhs/cchc.pdf [accessed 15 May 2011].

Bhabha, H.K. (1994) *The Location of Culture*, London: Routledge.

Bunnell, T. (2002) '(Re)positioning Malaysia: High-tech networks and the multicultural rescripting of national identity', *Political Geography*, 21: 105–124.

Chee H.L. (2007) 'Medical tourism in Malaysia: International movement of healthcare consumers and the commodification of healthcare', *Asia Research Institute Working Paper Series*, 83, January.

Chee H.L. (2008) 'Ownership, control and contention: Challenges for the future of healthcare in Malaysia', *Social Science and Medicine*, 66: 2145–2156.

Chua J.M. (2002) Speech by YB Dato' Chua Jui Meng, Ministry of Health Malaysia. In *Fourth Meeting of the National Committee for the Promotion of Health Tourism in Malaysia*, Ministry of Health, Kuala Lumpur, 11 April. Available at: http://www.cornerstone-msc.net/aphm_portal/index.cfm?menuid=26 [accessed 15 April 2009].

Economic Planning Unit (EPU) (2000) 'Eighth Malaysia Plan (2001–2005)', Putrajaya: Prime Minister's Department. Available at: http://www.epu.gov.my/rm9/html/english.htm [accessed 15 April 2009].

Ehrbeck, T. Guevara, C. and Mango, P.D. (2008) 'Mapping the market for medical travel', *The McKinsey Quarterly*, May. Available at: http://www.medretreat.com/templates/UserFiles/Documents/McKinsey%20Report%20Medical%20Travel.pdf [accessed 16 February 2009].

Elliot, S.J. and Gillie, J. (1998) 'Moving experiences: A qualitative analysis of health and migration', *Health and Place*, 4(4): 327–339.

Gregg, J. and Saha, S. (2006) 'Losing culture on the way to competence: The use and misuse of culture in medical education', *Academic Medicine*, 81(6): 542–547.

Henderson, J.C. (2009) 'Tourism policy and cultural heritage in multi-ethnic societies: a view of Malaysia', *International Journal of Tourism Policy*, 2(1/2): 138–144.

Hilley, J. (2001) *Malaysia: Mahathirism, hegemony and the new opposition*, London: Zed Books.

Jagyasi, P. (2010) 'Understanding culture in medical tourism', *Dr Prem.com/Blog*, 2 July. Online. Available at: https://drprem.wordpress.com/2010/07/02/understanding-culture-in-medical-tourism-by-dr-prem-jagyasi-medical-tourism-magazine/ [accessed 15 June 2011].

Jeffrey, C. and McFarlane, C. (2008) 'Performing cosmopolitanism', *Environment and Planning D: Society and Space*, 26: 420–427.

Kangas, B. (2002) 'Therapeutic itineraries in a global world: Yemenis and their search for biomedical treatment abroad', *Medical Anthropology*, 21: 35–78.

Kaplan, C. (2007) *Questions of travel: Postmodern discourses of displacement*, Durham, NC: Duke University Press.

Kok, C. (2009) 'Finding the right strategies', The Star, 21 February. Online. Available at: http://biz.thestar.com.my/news/story.asp?file=/2009/2/21/business/3275918&;sec=business [accessed 23 February 2009].

Lee, J.Y.N., Kearns, R. and Friesen, W. (2010) 'Seeking affective health care: Korean immigrants' use of homeland medical services', *Health and Place*, 16(1): 108–115.

Medical Travel World Congress (2008) Proceedings. In *Medical Travel World Congress*, Kuala Lumpur, 25–28 February.

MedRetreat (2010) Malaysia, *MedRetreat*. Online. Available at: http://www.medretreat.com/destinations/malaysia.html [accessed 12 July 2010].

Mitchell, K. (1996) 'In whose interest? Transnational capital and the production of multiculturalism in Canada', in R. Wilson and W. Dissanayake (eds) *Global/Local: Cultural Production in Transnational Imagery*, Durham: Duke University Press.

Mitchell, K. (2003) 'Educating the national citizen in neoliberal times: from the multicultural self to the strategic cosmopolitan', *Transactions of the Institute of British Geographers*, 28: 387–403.

Ministry of Health Malaysia (MOH) (2002) Malaysia's health 2002: Technical report of the Director-General of Health, Kuala Lumpur: Ministry of Health Malaysia.

Ministry of Health Malaysia (MOH) (2009) Reasons to choose Malaysia as a health tourism destination, *Malaysia Healthcare*. Online. Available at: http://www.myhealthcare.gov.my/index.asp?page=why_malaysia&;subpage=reason_to_choose [accessed 15 August 2009].

Mitchell, K. (2007) 'Geographies of identity: the intimate cosmopolitan', *Progress in Human Geography*, 31(5): 706–720.

Najib, Razak (2009) Overview of 1Malaysia, 1Malaysia. Online. Available at: http://www.1malaysia.com.my/index.php?option=com_content&;view=article&id=358&Itemid=93&lang=en [accessed 30 June 2009].

Ong, A. (1999) *Flexible citizenship: The cultural logics of transnationality*, Durham/London: Duke University Press.

Ooi C.S. (2004) 'Poetics and politics of destination branding: Denmark', *Scandinavian Journal of Hospitality and Tourism*, 4(2): 107–128.

Ormond, M. (2011) 'Medical tourism, medical exile: Responding to the cross-border pursuit of healthcare in Malaysia', in C. Minca and T. Oakes (eds), *Real Tourism: Practice, Care and Politics in Contemporary Travel*, London: Routledge.

Palany, H.M. (2004) 'A strategic approach to health tourism', *Asian Hospital and Healthcare Management*, 1 July. Online. Available at: http://www.asianhhm.com/healthcare_management/health_tourism_malaysia.htm [accessed 2 February 2007].

Prakash, S. (2007) 'Tourism Malaysia. Creating "Brand Malaysia"', *ICFAI Centre for Management Research*, ICMR Case Collection, MKTG178.

Salimbene, S. (2010) 'Cultural and linguistic competency – A forgotten issue', *Medical Tourism Magazine*, 2 March. Online. Available at: http://www.healthtourismmagazine.com/article-detail.php?issue=issue-5&;article=cultural [accessed 15 June 2011].

Shaw, S.J. (2005) 'The politics of recognition in culturally appropriate care', *Medical Anthropology Quarterly*, 19(3): 290–309.

Shaw, S.J. (2010) 'The logic of identity and resemblance in culturally appropriate health care', *Health*, 14(5): 523–544.

Taylor, J.S. (2003) 'The story catches you and you fall down: Tragedy, ethnography and "cultural competence"', *Medical Anthropology Quarterly*, 17(2): 159–181.

Tervalon, M. and Murray-García, J. (1998) 'Cultural humility versus cultural competence: A critical distinction in defining physician training outcomes in multicultural education', *Journal of Health Care for the Poor and Underserved*, 9(2): 117–125.

Tourism Malaysia (2007) 'Health tourism in Malaysia', Press release, November. Available at: http://www.tourismmalaysia.gov.my/corporate/mediacentre.asp?news_id=127&;page=news_desk&subpage=archive [accessed 2 July 2009].

Tourism Malaysia (2009) 'Spa'. Online. Available at: http://www.tourism.gov.my/en/activities/default.asp?activity_id=2 [accessed 20 July 2010].

Traweek, S. (1988) *Beamtimes and Lifetimes: The World of High Energy Physicists*. Cambridge, MA: Harvard University Press.

TTG Asia (2004) 'Striking medical jackpot', *TTG Asia*, 9–15 January. Online. Available at: http://www.ttgasia.com/index.php?option=com_contentandtask=viewandid=2265 [accessed 5 June 2007].

Whittaker, A. (2009) 'Global technologies and transnational reproduction in Thailand', *Asian Studies Review*, 33(3): 319–332.

Wong C. (2003) 'Health tourism can boost coffers', *The New Straits Times*, 19 April. Online. Available at: http://www.highbeam.com/doc/1P1-82787688.html [accessed 25 February 2009].

Woodman, J. (2008) *Patients beyond Borders*, 2nd edition, Chapel Hill, NC: Healthy Travel Media.

Yúdice, G. (2003) *The Expediency of Culture: Uses of Culture in the Global Era*, Durham, NC: Duke University Press.

Part V

Conclusion

The contested spaces of medical tourism

13 The contested futures and spaces of medical tourism

C. Michael Hall

The chapters in this volume demonstrate a number of approaches and foci in examining medical tourism. For many edited volumes such a variety of papers, even if they have several common themes, can be regarded as a negative. However, in the case of the present volume the different approaches and perspectives on medical tourism actually provide a very accurate account of the diverse and often conflicting agendas and interests that exist within medical tourism.

In their review of both the then extant academic literature as well as a series of media reports Mainil *et al.* (2011) identified four different discourses in medical tourism: a medical discourse, market discourse, ethical discourse and a patient discourse. The characteristics of the medical discourse includes high-end solutions; awareness of superior medical services; patient care; decision-making power; medical quality and management quality and standards; and the utilisation of medical technology. The market discourse was noted by a focus on business and its values (what Mainil *et al.* (2011) referred to as 'essence'), a problematic relationship with ethical issues; the interrelationships between international trade, medicine and a globalising economy; business values; and the patient as consumer. Ethical discourse(s) was framed by questions with respect to medical standards as well as patient-centred ethics; the relationship between medical tourism and global health and public health, including individual versus collective rights; the relationship between public and private health provision; the medical and health rights of local populations; and the ethics and responsibilities of medical staff. In the final discourse, that of patient discourse, Mainil *et al.* (2011) noted that there was a move over time from a submissive patient perspective to that of a patient as user/decision maker. Other aspects included health literacy of patients; communication, and health choices, including that of destinations; and the overall position of the patient in commercial and medical systems.

To the four discourses identified by Mainil *et al.* (2011) a fifth can be added, that of the governance and regulation of medical tourism. Although the topic cuts across the other discourses, and particularly ethical issues given that policy and regulation reflect the values, including ethical values, of decision makers, it is a substantive focus for debate and discussion in its own right (Bagheri 2010; Perfetto and Dholakia 2010; Shalev 2010; Storrow 2010; Cook *et al.* 2011; Martínez Álvarez *et al.* 2011; Meghani 2011; Turner 2011; Whittaker 2011). A key issue for medical

Table 13.1 Discourses of medical tourism and their relationship to the chapters in this book

Discourse	*Chapter*
Medical discourse	Lunt *et al.*, Ch. 2; Cook *et al.*, Ch. 4
Market discourse	Gan, Ch. 3; Kotikova and Schwartzhoffova, Ch. 7; Lam *et al.*, Ch. 8; Boga and Weiermair, Ch. 9; Kim *et al.*, Ch. 10; Wong and Musa, Ch. 11
Ethical discourse	Lunt *et al.*, Ch. 2; Cook *et al.*, Ch. 4; Pforr and Locher, Ch. 5; Smith *et al.*, Ch. 6; Ormond, Ch. 12
Patient discourse	Lunt *et al.*, Ch. 2; Boga and Weiermair, Ch. 9; Ormond, Ch. 12
Governance and regulatory discourse	Lunt *et al.*, Ch. 2; Cook *et al.*, Ch. 4; Pforr and Locher, Ch. 5; Smith *et al.*, Ch. 6; Wong and Musa, Ch. 11

tourism from ethical, patient, and business perspectives is that there is no effective global regulation of the medical industry (Lunt and Carrera 2010, 2011). Indeed, medical tourism, but especially more controversial forms such as transplant tourism, stem-cell tourism, and xenotourism present a range of profound challenges to increasingly ill-equipped healthcare systems which have been fundamentally reshaped by neoliberal policies and post-welfare state citizenship regimes that have led to new forms of health governance and regulation premised on the extension of market relationships (see Chapter 4). However, the challenge is not just an economic issue of greater efficiency and effectiveness in medical systems per unit cost, it is also fundamentally one of ethics, values, and principles as decisions as to how health systems are organised and what is included or excluded is fundamentally a political and philosophical decision. Table 13.1 indicates how the various chapters in this book relate to the four discourses.

Yet, as Hall (2011a) notes, the regulation of medical tourism faces the same issues as the regulation of other goods and services, even if they carry potential health risks, in that the primary regulatory structures are economic, and the World Trade Organization (WTO) regime plays a vital role in this, rather than risk or health oriented (Hall 2011b). Nevertheless, it is also important to remember that rights of access are granted by the state, even if some of those rights may have been passed on to other bodies such as the WTO. Even though globalisation is an important factor for the growth of international tourism the state's role in regulation, let alone development of the field, remains critical. The state continues to play a significant role as an arbiter of citizenship and hence as a mediator of entry and exit (Coles and Hall 2011). Arguably, this role has been reinforced around the world since the events of 9/11. Enhanced security measures and new visa regimes are all measures demanded by state governments not just as responses to the perceived and actual threats of terrorism but also to notable health hazards such as the swine flu pandemic of 2009 (Hall 2010). The state-based view of international relations and trade continues to be the basis for understanding most individual movements across territorial borders. At its simplest, without a passport or identity card, travel is not sanctioned. There is no 'right' to engage in international travel (Hall 2005). Indeed, under international covenants, such as the

Universal Declaration of Human Rights, the rights to enter another country do not exist. Even the advisory Universal Declaration of Human Rights only postulates a right of exit and entry to one's own country and freedom of mobility within a citizen's own country. Therefore, the nature of the passport or identity card determines what other permissions are necessary (such as visas, entry permits, fees) for entry or departure, or not as the case may be. As such, the complex geographies of regulation and rights of entry play significant roles in determining global patterns of medical travel and tourism (Coles and Hall 2011).

Arguably, the most significant piece of international law with respect to cross-border mobility for tourists is the General Agreement on Trade in Services (GATS) (Coles and Hall 2011; see also Chapter 2). In this the movement of natural persons constitutes one of the modes of supply for services including mode 4, which covers travel for business services and consumption abroad, and mode 2 which covers travel for leisure, educational and health consumption (Hall and Coles 2008). Interestingly, Kordvani (2006) argues that the real barrier to the movement of persons is not created by states exercising their right to regulate cross-border mobility but rather by the administration of that right in an unreasonable, subjective and discriminatory manner which is inconsistent with article VI(1) (Domestic Regulation) of the GATS.

Given the lack of specific international law providing access to other countries, the rights of travellers outside their normal jurisdiction have been mainly conferred in the area of consumer rights; in other words, as 'consumer citizens' they have rights that accompany their responsibilities as visitors (Coles and Hall 2011). Sometimes these pertain to their statutory rights and hence to the levels of service delivery they (like other consumers) may expect from tour operators, travel agents or medical travel brokers and organisers, accommodation providers and hospitality businesses (depending on how they arrange and organise their trips), as well as the medical service providers themselves. Such a situation of consumer citizenship is a logical outcome of processes of neoliberal governance whereby people are encouraged to see themselves as individualised and active subjects responsible for enhancing their own well-being (Larner 2000). And, although, as Lunt *et al.* noted in Chapter 2, the twin identities of citizen and consumer distinguish Europeans from their American counterparts where medical tourists are more accurately described as active consumers rather than citizens exercising rights to treatment, there remains a clear shift in European health policy towards a more market oriented and public-private programme (see also Chapters 5 on Germany and 6 on Hungary).

As Cook *et al.* put it in Chapter 4, 'Caught up in all of these global/local medical controversies is, of course, the individual health consumer who has to make sense of it all, and increasingly has to take responsibility for the management of their own health regime'. This conception of an 'active' or 'big society' can arguably also be linked to the growth of the wellness movement, including wellness and health tourism, whereby a particular politics of self is presented in which we are all encouraged to '"work on ourselves" in a range of domains including the "counter cultural movements" outside the purview of traditional conceptions of the political' (Larner 2000: 13).

Given the global spread of neoliberal health paradigms, it is therefore not surprising that the globalisation of medicine, including with respect to medical tourism, throws up as Cook *et al.* note in Chapter 4, 'all kinds of problems for patients who are only really enmeshed in nation-state safety nets, many of which are close to atrophied.' As they observed, the neoliberal paradigm struggles to deal effectively with problems, such as those found in international medical tourism, which exhibit the following characteristics:

- If a medical problem has a large technical component, it becomes almost impossible for individuals to make informed choices;
- Unless it takes the form of a pandemic, when a health problem has global implications there are often no effective global regulatory mechanisms to manage it (indeed, it can be argued that even if it is a pandemic it can be difficult to regulate and intervene to prevent further spread) (see Hall 2011b);
- The paradigm of self-responsible patients only encourages individuals to seek desired treatments that could be 'irregulated';
- How do we manage health consumers who have engaged in 'risky' consumption practices when returning to a country that has a moratorium, ban or stringent regulations on the procedure? (after Cook *et al.*, Chapter 4).

The neoliberal project is therefore marked by a set of contradictions that raise considerable questions as to the long-term viability of large scale medical tourism, for while mobility and access are integral to the medical tourism business model they paradoxically pose significant issues of control and regulation, especially with respect to biosecurity (see also Chapters 2 and 4 over concerns of the implications of medical tourism for population health). This is primarily because a standard means of reducing health risk that relate to human mobility is to restrict or slow access or, at the most extreme, to quarantine or deny access altogether (Hall and James 2011), with a consequent impact on the tourism industry which, of course, depends on cross-border mobility (Hall 2010).

However, tourism is not only affected by pandemics and epidemics but also contributes to their spread (Tatem *et al.* 2006; Feng *et al.* 2008; Tatem 2009; Hall and James 2011b). In the case of the rapid worldwide spread of the coronavirus that causes SARS it was clear 'that as for other infectious diseases, evolution and spread is facilitated by the mobility of the society either through air travel or the densely populated urban areas especially in Asia' (Raptopoulou-Gigi 2003: 81). In order to combat the spread of disease and viruses many countries and regions have introduced biosecurity strategies to enhance their economic and resource security. Biosecurity refers to the protection of a country, region or location's economic, environmental and/or human health from harmful organisms, including pests and disease (Hall 2005; Hall *et al.* 2010). As Hooker (2008: 127) notes, 'Amid an effectively global, interconnected, and highly networked economy, health scares reassert the validity of borders: prosperity is equated with security, which decodes to border control for health'.

As per the discussion above the capacity to manage international regimes is limited and fraught with difficulties (Hall 2011b). The leading international legal instrument with respect to health is the International Health Regulations (IHR) (2005) that is binding on 194 member countries, including all Member States of the World Health Organization (WHO). The scope of the IHR (2005) is not limited to any specific disease or manner of transmission, but instead disease is defined as an 'illness or medical condition, irrespective of origin or source, that presents or could present significant harm to humans' (WHO 2008: 7). The most recent version of the IHR was developed 'in consideration of the growth in international travel and trade, and the emergence or re-emergence of international disease threats and other public health risks' (WHO 2008: 1), and represents a 'paradigm shift' in considering global public health in that there is a move from control at borders to containment of health threats at source; from a specific list of diseases to all public health threats; and from preset measures to adapted response (WHO 2007). As a result it should not be surprising that there are significant differences in national response to international disease threat (Coker and Mounier-Jack 2006; Ortu *et al.* 2008; Oshitani *et al.* 2008; Mensua *et al.* 2009; Hanvoravongchai *et al.* 2010). For example, Martin *et al.* (2010) found substantial differences across Europe in the extent to which national pandemic policy and plans have been integrated with public health legislation and regulation. They found that European countries differ in the range and the nature of intervention measures authorised by law, the extent to which borders could be closed to movement of persons and goods during a pandemic, and the degree of access to health care of non-resident persons (Martin *et al.* 2010). As Hall and James (2011: 119) suggested

> The development of the most recent version of the International Health Regulations 'to prevent, protect against, control and provide a public health response to the international spread of disease in ways that are commensurate with and restricted to public health risks, and which avoid unnecessary interference with international traffic and trade' (Article 2 of the IHR (2005) in WHO 2008: 10), provides an extremely interesting counterpoint to the growth of international medical tourism.

Health risk is inherent to human mobility (Wilson 1995, 2010; Hall 2005, 2006). However, medical tourism is intrinsically different with respect to increasing biosecurity risk because individuals who engage in medical tourism are deliberately travelling to a medical environment and engaging in medical practices that expose them to pathogens and microbiologic fauna and flora that are qualitatively different from those found in their home environment. Indeed, one of the lessons of SARS and recent pandemics is that healthcare institutions have emerged as a major potential source of infection (Fahey 2007; Waterer 2011). Hall and James (2011) therefore suggest that medical tourism therefore increases the risk of nosocomial infections, also referred to as 'hospital' or 'healthcare acquired infections' (Leahy 2008; Reed 2008; Allegranzi *et al.* 2011; see also Chapter 2). At any time, over 1.4 million people worldwide suffer from infectious complications acquired in hospital (WHO 2002) with the elderly (>65) being particularly vulnerable (Strausbaugh 2001). Also of significance is that it is generally recognised that nosocomial infections and other complications are under-reported (Dettenkofer *et al.* 2003; Uçkay *et al.* 2008; Greig and Lee 2009). As Hall and James (2011) suggested, although medical tourists represent only a small percentage of ill post-travel patients (0.1 per cent of Field *et al*'s (2010) population of 6957 ill returned travellers), if that percentage were to be extrapolated as a percentage of the global international travel market, the resulting figure would be double the estimated four million people who travel internationally each year for medical treatment (Wilson 2010).

Hall and James (2011) provide numerous examples of tourism related nosocomial infections including

- the role of travel in the spread of noroviruses (gastric flu) (Koopmans 2009);
- multi-resistant infections in repatriated tourists after a natural disaster (Uçkay *et al.* 2008);
- mycobacterial infections following cosmetic surgery (Centers for Disease Control 1998, 2004);
- complications following arthroplasty (joint replacement) (Cheung and Wilson 2007) and aesthetic surgery (Jeevan *et al.* 2011);
- hepatitis B as a result of unhygienic hospital conditions (Löscher *et al.* 1999);
- hepatitis C virus infections as a result of holiday haemodialysis (Bhattacharya *et al.* 2009; Patel *et al.* 2010).

Balaban and Marano's (2010) review of studies of commercial organ transplantation, primarily in China and India, although limited, suggests a higher incidence of post-operative tissue rejection and severe infectious complications among transplant tourists compared to other transplant patients. Similarly, substantial concerns have been raised about the risks associated with xenotransplantation and 'stem-cell tourism' (Nelson 2008; Kimball and Hodges 2010; Cook *et al.* 2011; also see Chapter 4) although perhaps the most high-profile recent case is that of NDM-1.

The NDM-1 case

Muir and Weinbren (2010) reported the case of a dialysis patient who had visited and dialysed in India 18 months previously and who had acquired a highly resistant *Escherichia coli*. The organism was found to be a New Delhi metallo-β-lactamase (NDM-1) producer, acquisition of which is strongly associated with medical contact with Pakistan or India. This enzyme confers resistance to all known antibiotics except polymyxins and, sometimes, tigecycline. Spread of resistance is thought to occur by plasmid-mediated transfer. This case raised a number of important issues, particularly concerning renal dialysis patients who dialyse in countries where carbapenemase-producing bacteria are common (India, Pakistan, United States, Israel, Greece, Turkey) while on holiday or during return visits to family. According to Muir and Weinbren (2010: 240) 'these patients may use, or be admitted to, a number of healthcare facilities within a short period of time. All these factors could facilitate rapid spread of NDM-1 with potentially serious consequences'. In addition to concerns over the spread of antibiotic resistant bacteria such cases also incur substantial costs with respect to the need for deep cleaning of potentially affected areas as well as patient screening and room controls (see Chapter 2). The potential dangers of outsourcing medical procedures offshore as part of attempts to improve health service economy and efficiency were indicated in Kumarasamy *et al.*'s (2010: 6) observation, 'It is disturbing, in context, to read calls in the popular press for UK patients to opt for corrective surgery in India with the aim of saving the NHS money. As our data show, such a proposal might ultimately cost the NHS substantially more than the short-term saving and we would strongly advise against such proposals. The potential for wider international spread of producers and for NDM-1-encoding plasmids to become endemic worldwide, are clear and frightening'.

However, the NDM-1 case also created much controversy because of its affects on perceptions of Indian medical services. Even though the review of NDM-1 by Kumarasamy *et al.* (2010) concluded, 'Several of the UK source patients had undergone elective, including cosmetic, surgery while visiting India or Pakistan. India also provides cosmetic surgery for other Europeans and Americans, and blaNDM-1 will likely spread worldwide,' the association of NDM-1 with New Delhi (because the Swedish patient of Indian origin who had travelled to New Delhi and picked up the infection in which the drug-resistant strain was first identified (Yong *et al.*, 2009) was widely criticised in India by media and public officials (Pandey 2010). The Kumarasamy *et al.* (2010) study was described by the officials of the Indian health industry as 'malicious propaganda', and as a 'conspiracy' by members of the Indian parliament who also associated it with the activities of multi-national pharmaceutical companies (Pandey, 2010). The irony perhaps being that the lead author of the study was based in India while a number of papers on the topic have also had authors based in India (e.g. Krishna 2010; Nataraj 2010). Nevertheless, Indian Ministry of Health officials were reported as saying, 'We strongly refute the naming of this enzyme as New Delhi metallo beta lactamase… We also refute that hospitals in India are not safe for treatment, including medical tourism,' while MP SS Ahluwalia of the opposition Bharatiya Janata Party stated 'When India is emerging as a medical tourism destination, this type of news is unfortunate and may be a sinister design of multi-national companies' (Pandey, 2010). Perhaps also reflecting the marketisation not only of the medical discourse but also the increasing influence if not dominance of the business discourse of medical tourism in the setting of some countries' health trade policies. Yet in such a situation when an individual chooses to travel to another country for medical treatment and returns to his or her home only to endanger public health and affect the provision of medical care to others who should pay the cost of such actions?

Conclusion

The market-oriented approach to health by which access to medical support is not a right but something to be consumed has undoubtedly been a major factor together with the internationalisation of tourism mobility and medical services and technologies in the growth of medical tourism. At the heart of the growth in medical tourism also lies the unmet need of patients due to long-waiting lists, high cost of treatment at home, unavailability of particular treatments and a wish for privacy (Lunt and Carrera 2011: 58). Medical tourism is therefore perhaps more a reflection of the policy debates and economic difficulties that exist in the health and medical services of the tourist generating countries as it is in the attractiveness of the medical tourism destination.

Despite enthusiasm by some supranational agencies for the promotion in International medical and health tourism (Economic and Social Commission for Asia and the Pacific, 2009) there are, as this and several other chapters in the book have indicated, major concerns with respect to the potential personal and public health costs of medical tourism. This is particularly the case with issues of quality and long-term health costs to the home country as well as the contribution of medical tourism to the dispersal of biosecurity risks such as disease and drug resistant bacteria (Koh 2008; Hall and James 2011). Undoubtedly the risks attached to medical tourism both for individuals as well as the spread of disease and resistant bacteria are a significant area for future research (Noël 2007; Balaban and Marano 2010; Crooks *et al.* 2010; Fernando *et al.* 2010; Moellering 2010; Talbot *et al.*, 2010; Cantón and Lumb 2011; Sydnor and Perl, 2011). Such research should include not only medical studies but also assessments of travel behaviour, motivation, level of consumer information and the appropriateness of the regulatory framework for medical related travel (Martin *et al.* 2010; Hall 2011a; Hall and James 2011; see Chapter 2). Yet to do this effectively requires greater interdisciplinary or post-disciplinary research by which, given the lack of mutual understanding and knowledge of each other's field, there is increasing engagement between the medical profession and tourism researchers. For example, there needs to be greater recognition of the implications of different trip stages for the psychology of decision making, regulation, commercial practice and long-term effects of engagement in medical tourism (Table 13.2) (after Hall 2005).

Arguably there also needs to be a more substantive ethical and policy debate on medical tourism. In the case of the latter there often appears the prospect that some governments are happy for medical tourism to occur if it reduces their own costs. However, such a stance often means they have not recognised the potential long-term costs of medical tourism to public health systems and population health (Hall and James 2011; see Chapter 2). With respect to ethics, Mainil *et al.* (2011) suggest that ethical debate on medical tourism is to be noted in the medical literature but is not so prominent in tourism studies. However, they also go on to note that ethical discourses have themselves changes and have evolved into an upgraded market discourse on medical tourism. 'Medical tourism, as a sector which represents financial streams and economical drivers in addition to the provision of health care to international patients, is also subject to the non-discursive reality of market principles and the presence of national, international and local markets' (Mainil *et al.* 2011: 33). The neoliberal project therefore not only affects how medical services are provided and the role of medical tourism within them but also the way in which such provision is thought about.

Table 13.2 Stages of medical tourism and their implications

Stage of medical tourism	*Location in tourism system*	*Primary legal and regulatory responsibility for the medical tourist and related issues*	*Key element of consumer psychology*	*Key elements in commercial supply of medical tourism services*	*Medical care issues*
1 Decision to travel	Generating region	Home country of tourist. If paid for by health insurer or public health agency then legal responsibilities may lay with the organisation rather than the individual	Travel decision making and anticipation; state of health	Advertising, marketing and the provision of information to potential consumers and encouragement to purchase	Medical condition of traveller. Appropriate counselling prior to travel and the provision of informed consent
2 Travel to destination	In transit	Depends on legislation of carrier's and/or transit country and agreements with the country of the tourist. Carrier's legal and commercial requirements for passengers with medical conditions. Coverage of travel insurance with respect to medical issues	Travel to the destination	Appropriate travel advice	Appropriateness and nature of travel given medical condition
3 Activities at destination	Destination	Depends on legislation of destination country on rights of international visitors, their citizenship and agreements with the country of the tourist. Commercial responsibility of the medical responsibility to consumer may only exist while located in service provider's facilities. Coverage of travel insurance with respect to medical issues	Experiences at the destination	Supply of quality medical and tourism services at destination	Medical treatment and care and provision of recovery support services. Identification of post-treatment actions and responsibilities at destination after leaving provider's care
4 Travel from destination	In transit	Depends on legislation of carrier's and/or transit country and agreements with the country of the tourist. Carrier's legal and commercial requirements for passengers with medical conditions. Coverage of travel insurance with respect to medical issues	Travel from the destination	Appropriate travel advice and medical support if required	Appropriateness and nature of travel post-treatment. Issue of responsibility for treatment complications
5 Recollection of the trip and destination upon return to permanent residence	Generating region	Home country of tourist. Depending on legislation of country of treatment and agreements between destination and home country there may be an ongoing legal relationship between the individual and the destination country	Recollection of the trip and destination experiences and influence on future health, medical and tourism decision making	Medical and commercial follow-up and encouragement to utilise service again and gain positive word-of-mouth	Post-treatment care. Who is responsible for complications and treatment related illness post travel? Who is responsible for any public health implications?

The growth of medical tourism is grounded in a neoliberal vision of self-regulated international trade in health services and the failure of some governments to respond to increasing demands for public health services from their own population. Yet the way medical tourism has evolved is not a 'natural outcome'. It is the result of deliberate decisions by governments as to their spending, economic, welfare and taxation priorities. Medical tourism is also developing in a manner that raises substantial questions about equity to medical and healthcare access as well as the long-term implications of medical tourism which, yet again, may see the public pay for private sector opportunism by having to cover for 'market inefficiencies'. However, no health system or clinical governance methodology is perfect. In seeking to assess the costs and benefits of medical tourism it is therefore imperative that they are assessed not only at the level of the individual traveller and the business imperatives of the destination medical facility but also in terms of global and national public health and the medical facilities in the country of origin of the medical tourist. It is hoped that this books goes some small way in promoting this discussion.

References

Allegranzi, B., Nejad, S.B., Combescure, C., Graafmans, W., Attar, H., Donaldson, L. and Didier, D. (2011) 'Burden of endemic health-care-associated infection in developing countries: systematic review and meta-analysis', *The Lancet*, 377(9761): 228–41.

Bagheri, A. (2010) 'Global health regulations should distinguish between medical tourism and transplant tourism', *Global Social Policy*, 10(3): 295–7.

Balaban, V. and Marano, C. (2010) 'Medical tourism research: A systematic review', *International Journal of Infectious Diseases*, 14 (Supp. 1) (14th International Congress on Infectious Diseases (ICID) Abstracts): e135.

Bhattacharya, S., Price, N., Boxall, E., Adu, D., Lipkin, G., Smith, S. and Osman, H. (2009) 'Holiday haemodialysis and imported hepatitis C virus infection: A series of sixteen cases in two large haemodialysis units', *Journal of Clinical Virology*, 4(4): 296–9.

Cantón, R. and Lumb, J. (2011) 'Emerging resistance in Gram-negative pathogens and implications for clinical practice', *Future Microbiology*, 6: 19–22.

Centers for Disease Control (1998) 'Rapidly growing mycobacterial infection following liposuction and liposculpture – Caracas, Venezuela, 1996–1998', *Morbidity and Mortality Weekly Report*, 47(49): 1065–7.

Centers for Disease Control (2004) 'Brief report: Nontuberculous mycobacterial infections after cosmetic surgery – Santo Domingo, Dominican Republic, 2003–2004', *Morbidity and Mortality Weekly Report*, 53(23): 509.

Cheung, I.K. and Wilson, A. (2007) 'Arthroplasty tourism', *Medical Journal of Australia*, 187(11-12): 666–7.

Coker, R. and Mounier-Jack, S. (2006) 'Pandemic influenza preparedness in the Asia–Pacific region', *The Lancet*, 368(9538): 886–9.

Coles, T. and Hall, C.M. (2011) 'Rights and regulation of travel and tourism mobility', Journal of Policy Research in Tourism, *Leisure and Events*, 3(3): 209–23.

Cook, P.S., Kendall, G., Michael, M. and Brown, N. (2011) 'The textures of globalization: Biopolitics and the closure of xenotourism', *New Genetics and Society*, 30(1): 101–14

Crooks, V.A., Kingsbury, P., Snyder, J. and Johnston, R. (2010) 'What is known about the patient's experience of medical tourism? A scoping review', *BMC Health Services Research*, 10(266), doi: 10.1186/1472-6963-10-266.

Dettenkofer, M., Wilson, C., Ebner, W., Norgauer, J., Rüden, H. and Daschner, F.D. (2003) 'Surveillance of nosocomial infections in dermatology patients in a German university hospital', *British Journal of Dermatology*, 149(3): 620–3.

Economic and Social Commission for Asia and the Pacific (ESCAP) (2009) *Medical Travel in Asia and the Pacific. Challenges and Opportunities*, Bangkok: United Nations Economic and Social Commission for Asia and the Pacific.

Fahey, B.J. (2007) 'Behavioral and cultural aspects of transmission and infection', in F.R. Lashley and J.D. Durham (eds) *Emerging Infectious Diseases: Trends and Issues*, 2nd ed., New York: Springer.

Feng, J., Huang, J. and Nicoll, A. (2008) 'Foresight China II: Identification and detection of infectious diseases', in D. Zheng, H. Chen, H., Rolka and B. Lober (eds) *Biosurveillance and Biosecurity. International workshop, BioSecure 2008*, Raleigh, NC, USA, December 2, 2008, Proceedings, Berlin: Springer-Verlag.

Fernando, G.A.T.P., Collignon, P.J. and Bell, J.M. (2010) 'A risk for returned travellers: The 'post-antibiotic era'', *Medical Journal of Australia*, 193(1): 59.

Field, V., Gautret, P., Schlagenhauf, P., Burchard, G-D., Caumes, E., Jensenius, M., Castelli, F., Gkrania-Klotsas, E., Weld, L., Lopez-Velez, R., de Vries, P., von Sonnenburg, F., Loutan, L. and Parola, P. for the EuroTravNet network (2010) 'Travel and migration associated infectious diseases morbidity in Europe, 2008', *BMC Infectious Diseases*, 10, doi:10.1186/1471-2334-10-330.

Greig, J.D. and Lee, M.B. (2009) 'Enteric outbreaks in long-term care facilities and recommendations for prevention: a review', *Epidemiology and Infection*, 137: 145–55.

Hall, C.M. (2005) *Tourism: Rethinking the social science of mobility*, Harlow: Prentice Hall.

Hall, C.M. (2006) 'Tourism, disease and global environmental change: The fourth transition', in S. Gössling and C.M. Hall (eds.) *Tourism and Global Environmental Change: Ecological, economic, social and political interrelationships*, London: Routledge.

Hall, C.M. (2010) 'Crisis events in tourism: Subjects of crisis in tourism', *Current Issues in Tourism*, 13(5): 401–7.

Hall, C.M. (2011a) Health and medical tourism: Kill or cure for global public health? *Tourism Review*, 66(1/2): 4–15.

Hall, C.M. (2011b) 'Biosecurity, tourism and mobility: Institutional arrangements for managing tourism related biological invasions', Journal of Policy Research in Tourism, *Leisure and Events*, 3(3): 256–80.

Hall, C.M. and Coles, T.E. (2008) 'Introduction: tourism and international business – tourism as international business', in T.E. Coles and C.M. Hall (eds) *International Business and Tourism: Global issues, contemporary interactions*. London: Routledge.

Hall, C.M. and James, M. (2011) 'Medical tourism: Emerging biosecurity and nosocomial issues', *Tourism Review*, 66(1/2): 118–26.

Hall, C.M., James, M. and Wilson, S. (2010) 'Biodiversity, biosecurity, and cruising in the Arctic and sub-Arctic', *Journal of Heritage Tourism*, 5(4): 351–64.

Hanvoravongchai, P., Adisasmito, W., Ngoc Chau, P., Conseil, A., de Sa, J., Krumkamp, R., Mounier-Jack, S., Phommasack, B., Putthasri, W., Shih, C-S., Touch, S. and Coker, R. for the AsiaFluCap project (2010) 'Pandemic influenza preparedness and health systems challenges in Asia: results from rapid analyses in 6 Asian countries', *BMC Public Health*, 10, doi:10.1186/1471-2458-10-322.

Hooker, C. (2008), "SARS as a 'health scare'", in Ali, S.H. and Keil, R. (Eds.), *Networked Disease: Emerging Infections in the Global City*, Wiley-Blackwell, Chichester, pp. 123–37.

Jeevan, R., Birch, J. and Armstrong, A.P. (2011) 'Travelling abroad for aesthetic surgery: Informing healthcare practitioners and providers while improving patient safety', *Journal of Plastic Reconstructive and Aesthetic Surgery*, 64(2): 143–7.

Kimball, A.M. and Hodges, J. (2010) *'Risky trade and emerging infections'*, in *Institute of Medicine, Infectious Disease Movement in a Borderless World*, Washington, DC: The National Academies Press.

Koh, T.S. (2008) 'Gram-negative resistance in Singapore: A historical perspective', *Annals Academy of Medicine Singapore*, 37(10): 847–54.

Koopmans, M. (2009) 'Noroviruses in healthcare settings: A challenging problem', *Journal of Hospital Infection*, 73(4): 331–7.

Kordvani, A. (2006) 'Hospitality, politics of mobility, and the movement of service suppliers under the GATS', *Melbourne Journal of International Law*, 7: 74–103.

Krishna, B.V.S. (2010) 'New Delhi metallo-beta-lactamases: A wake-up call for microbiologists', *Indian Journal of Medical Microbiology*, 28(3): 265–6.

Kumarasamy, K.K., Toleman, M.A., Walsh, T.R., Bagaria, J., Butt, F., Balakrishnan, R., Chaudhary, U., Doumith, M., Giske, G.C., Irfan, S., Krishnan, P., Kumar, A.V., Maharjan, S., Mushtaq, S., Noorie, T., Paterson, D.L., Pearson, A., Perry, C., Pike, R., Rao, B., Ray, U., Sarma, J.B., Sharma, M., Sheridan, E., Thirunarayan, M.A., Turton, J., Upadhyay, S., Warner, M., Welfare, W., Livermore, D.M. and Woodford, N. (2010) 'Emergence of a new antibiotic resistance mechanism in India, Pakistan, and the UK: a molecular, biological, and epidemiological study', *Lancet Infectious Diseases*, 10(9): 597–602.

Larner, W. (2000) 'Neo-liberalism: Policy, ideology, governmentality', *Studies in Political Economy*, 63: 5–25.

Leahy, A.L. (2008) 'Medical tourism: The impact of travel to foreign countries for healthcare', *Surgeon*, 6(5): 260–1.

Lunt, N. and Carrera, P. (2010) 'Medical tourism: Assessing the evidence on treatment abroad', *Maturitas*, 66(1): 27–32.

Lunt, N. and Carrera, P. (2011) 'Systematic review of web sites for prospective medical tourists', *The Tourism Review*, 66(1/2): 57–67.

Löscher, T., Keystone, J.S. and Steffen, R. (1999) 'Vaccination of travelers against hepatitis A and B', *Journal of Travel Medicine*, 6(2): 107–14.

Mainil, T., Platenkamp, V. and Meulemans, H. (2011) 'The discourse of medical tourism in the media', *Tourism Review*, 66(1/2): 31–44.

Martin, R., Conseil, A., Longstaff, A., Kodo, J., Siegert, J., Duguet, A-M., Lobato de Faria, P., Haringhuizen, G., Espin, J. and Coker, R. (2010) 'Pandemic influenza control in Europe and the constraints resulting from incoherent public health laws', *BMC Public Health*, 10, doi:10.1186/1471-2458-10-532.

Martínez Álvarez, M., Chanda, R., Smith, R.D. (2011) 'The potential for bi-lateral agreements in medical tourism: A qualitative study of stakeholder perspectives from the UK and India', *Globalization and Health*, 7, article number 11, doi: 10.1186/1744-8603-7-11.

Meghani, Z. (2011) 'A robust, particularist ethical assessment of medical tourism', *Developing World Bioethics*, 11(1): 16–29.

Mensua, A., Mounier-Jack, S. and Coker, R. (2009) 'Pandemic influenza preparedness in Latin America: analysis of national strategic plans', *Health Policy and Planning*, 24(4): 253–60.

Moellering Jr., R.C. (2010) 'NDM-1-A cause for worldwide concern', *New England Journal of Medicine*, 363(25): 2377–9.

Muir, A. and Weinbren, M.J. (2010) 'New Delhi metallo-β-lactamase: a cautionary tale', *Journal of Hospital Infection*, 75(3): 239–40.

Nataraj, G. (2010) 'Editorial: New Delhi metallo beta-lactamase: What is in a name?' *Journal of Postgraduate Medicine*, 56(4): 251–2.

Nelson, B. (2008) 'Stem cell researchers face down stem cell tourism', *Nature Reports Stem Cells*, Published online: 5 June 2008, doi:10.1038/stemcells.2008.89.

Noël, J. (2007) 'Current concerns in transplantation', *Bulletin of the World Health Organization*, 85(12): 905.

Ortu, G., Mounier-Jack, S. and Coker, R.J. (2008) 'Pandemic influenza preparedness in Africa is a profound challenge for an already distressed region: analysis of national preparedness plans', *Health Policy and Planning*, 23(3): 161–9.

Oshitani H., Kamigaki T. and Suzuki A. (2008) 'Major issues and challenges of influenza pandemic preparedness in developing countries', *Emerging Infectious Diseases*, 14(6): 875–80.

Pandey, G. (2010) 'India rejects UK scientists' 'superbug' claim', *BBC News South Asia*, 12 August. Online. Available at: http://www.bbc.co.uk/news/world-south-asia-10954890 (accessed 1 February 2011).

Patel, P.R. Thompson, N.D., Kallen, A.J. and Arduino, M.J. (2010) 'Epidemiology, surveillance, and prevention of hepatitis C virus infections in hemodialysis patients', *American Journal of Kidney Diseases*, 56(2): 371–8.

Perfetto, R. and Dholakia, N. (2010) 'Exploring the cultural contradictions of medical tourism', *Consumption Markets and Culture*, 13(4): 399–417.

Raptopoulou-Gigi, M. (2003) 'Severe acute respiratory syndrome (SARS): A new emerging disease in the 21st century', *Hippokratia*, 7(2): 81–3.

Reed, C.M. (2008) 'Medical tourism', *Medical Clinics of North America*, 92(6): 1433–46.

Shalev, C. (2010) 'Stem cell tourism-A challenge for trans-national governance', *American Journal of Bioethics*, 10(5): 40–2.

Storrow, R. (2010) 'The pluralism problem in cross-border reproductive care', *Human Reproduction*, 25(12): 2939–43.

Strausbaugh, L.J. (2001) 'Emerging health care-associated infections in the geriatric population', *Emerging Infectious Diseases*, 7(2): 268–71.

Sydnor, E.R.M. and Perl, T.M. (2011) 'Hospital epidemiology and infection control in acute-care settings', *Clinical Microbiology Reviews*, 24(1): 141–73.

Talbot, E.A., Chen, L.H., Sanford, C., McCarthy, A. and Leder, K. (2010) 'Travel medicine research priorities: Establishing an evidence base', *Journal of Travel Medicine*, 17(6): 410–5.

Tatem, A.J. (2009) 'The worldwide airline network and the dispersal of exotic species: 2007-2010', *Ecography*, 32: 94–102.

Tatem, A.J., Hay, S.I. and Rogers, D.J. (2006) 'Global traffic and disease vector dispersal', *Proceedings of the National Academy of Sciences*, 103(16): 6242–7.

Turner, L.G. (2011) 'Quality in health care and globalization of health services: Accreditation and regulatory oversight of medical tourism companies', *International Journal for Quality in Health Care*, 23(1): 1–7.

Uçkay, I., Sax, H., Harbarth, S., Bernard, L. and Pittet. D. (2008) 'Multi-resistant infections in repatriated patients after natural disasters: lessons learned from the 2004 tsunami for hospital infection control', *Journal of Hospital Infection*, 68(1): 1–8.

Waterer, G. (2011) 'Controlling epidemic viral infection', *Current Opinion in Infectious Diseases*, 24(2): 130–6.

Whittaker, A. (2011) 'Cross-border assisted reproduction care in Asia: Implications for access, equity and regulations', *Reproductive Health Matters*, 19(37): 107–16.

Wilson, M.E. (1995) 'Travel and the emergence of infectious diseases', *Journal of Emerging Infectious Diseases*, 1(2): 39–46.

Wilson, M.E. (2010) 'Global travel and emerging infections', in *Institute of Medicine, Infectious Disease Movement in a Borderless World*, Washington, DC: The National Academies Press.

World Health Organization (WHO) (2002) *Prevention of Hospital-Acquired Infections: A Practical Guide*, 2nd ed., WHO/CDS/CSR/EPH/2002.12, Geneva: Department of Communicable Disease, Surveillance and Response, WHO.

World Health Organization (WHO) (2007) *International Health Regulations (2005) Areas of Work for Implementation*, June 2007, WHO/CDS/EPR/IHR/2007.1,Geneva: WHO.

World Health Organization (WHO) (2008) *International Health Regulations (2005)*, 2nd ed., Geneva: WHO.

Yong, D., Toleman, M.A., Giske, C.G., Cho, H.S., Sundman, K., Lee, K. and Walsh, T.R. (2009) 'Characterization of a new metallo-betalactamase gene, blaNDM-1, and a novel erythromycin esterase gene carried on a unique genetic structure in Klebsiella pneumoniae sequence type 14 from India', *Antimicrobial Agents and Chemotherapy*, 53(12): 5046–54.

Index